CELIBACY & SOUL

Celibacy & Soul

EXPLORING THE DEPTHS OF CHASTITY

Susan J. Pollard

Celibacy & Soul
Exploring the Depths of Chastity
Copyright © 2015 by Susan J. Pollard
First Edition
ISBN 978-1-77169-013-3 Paperback
ISBN 978-1-77169-018-8 eBook

Published simultaneously in Canada, the United Kingdom, and the United States of America by Fisher King Press. For information on obtaining permission for use of material from this work, submit a written request to:

permissions@fisherkingpress.com

Fisher King Press
www.fisherkingpress.com
+1-831-238-7799

Many thanks to all who have directly or indirectly provided permission to quote their works. Every effort has been made to trace all copyright holders; however, if any have been overlooked, the author will be pleased to make the necessary arrangements at the first opportunity. See pages 217 - 218 for a list of contributing individuals and organizations.

Book design by Literary Aficionado
www.literaryaficionado.com

Front cover image *Meditation* © is from an original painting by Mary Southard CSJ.
www.southardart.org

DEDICATION

To all those living in to and out of the depths of chastity

CONTENTS

LIST OF FIGURES

9. Heimkehr des Verlorenen Sohnes (The Homecoming of the Prodigal Son) - 5Ga.102. c. 1668, painting by Rembrandt van Rijn, Museum of St. Petersburg. ARAS Online Archive. New York: The Archive for Research in Archetypal Symbolism: available from www.aras.org: 5/1/14.

10. Creation of Adam (and Eve) - 5Ga.070. c. 1500, ceiling fresco by Michelangelo Buonarroti, Sistine Chapel, Rome. ARAS Online Archive. New York: The Archive for Research in Archetypal Symbolism: available from www.aras.org: 5/1/14.

11. The Trinity - 5Fa.009. c. 1411, icon, by Andrei Rublev, Cathedral of the Trinity of St. Sergius, Tretiakov Gallery, Moscow. ARAS Online Archive. New York: The Archive for Research in Archetypal Symbolism: available from www.aras.org: 5/1/14.

12. Madonna del Parto (Madonna of the Birth) - AA379419. c. 1410/20-92, fresco by Piero della Francesca, Cemetery Chapel, Monterchi, Italy. Photo Credit: Gianni Dagli Orti/The Art Archive at Art Resource, NY.

13. Christ and St. Menas - 5Ba.004. c. 500, Coptic icon by unknown artist, Louvre, Paris. ARAS Online Archive. New York: The Archive for Research in Archetypal Symbolism: available from www.aras.org: 5/1/14.

PRELUDE

This book is particularly for women and men religious who have chosen to live into celibate chastity. I am also aware that there are other people who actually live celibate love, and though not vowed to this way of life, they know the way of celibate love is their path. This book is also for you because everyone has a beauty of singularity whether single or partnered.

Some people live their singularity more starkly. You may find yourself celibate not by choice and you may hope it is a temporary stage. Maybe life interrupted your plans with the death of a loved one, the loss of a relationship, the situation of illness, the trauma of abuse, or you simply didn't settle down with the desired partner and you want to find meaning in your life as a celibate person. *Celibacy and Soul: Exploring the Depths of Chastity* could also be useful for colleagues in the helping professions. As a Jungian analyst and clinical psychologist, I am aware that my work as a therapist asks a celibate kind of loving that can be catalyst for change in both clients and in practitioners.

You will hear many voices through this work. That word *voice* is loaded, especially since realizing that the Hebrew word for *throat* means *soul—one's inner perceptive depth that yearns for life.* In particular, you will hear the voices of those who share their experience of living celibate chastity in the Catholic tradition and who are reasonably content with their choice and calling. On my blog, you can read the questionnaire to which these fifteen women and twelve men, who were contacted through co-researchers, replied. You also find there some exercises to follow your reading.

These Respondents who are sisters, nuns, monks, brothers and priests are aged from their late 20s into their 70s. They live in a physically celibate way and not in a sexual partnership for religious reasons. From their responses you can sometimes detect that they come from countries including Australia, Africa, England, Italy, Switzerland and the United States of America. You hear my voice as I bring together their insights and other commentaries that come from big dreams called *myths*. I include a few dream snippets that I have been given permission to share, and passages from literature, theology and psychology. Hopefully this interplay will happen seamlessly and with a touch of beauty. For in psyche's awakening, beauty is essential.

Why such a compilation? It has firm psychological and spiritual grounding. The insights come from different fields and layers of people's experience. We can know rationally and have information, have a hunch about matters, and we can have a feeling for things that touch the heart and gut. I want all those different ways of knowing and understanding to find a place in this exploration. Clients, good friends and colleagues, as well as my experience of chaste love as a Sister of St. Joseph of the Sacred Heart, teach and pose new questions about this vocation and way of being human. Some I can address in this book and some remain beyond my finding adequate words. As another friend reminded me to tell you, what you read is coming out of *all of who I am, as I am*.

The call to live consecrated celibacy is not a decision that one simply makes. In that sense, it is rather like marriage. Consenting to the way of celibate love is about a sense of rightness for the individual. In the words of one respondent,

> *I sense it is my call and see myself fundamentally happy as a celibate.* (David)

Why would people make such a choice? Why choose a life that is without the intimacy of a marriage partnership? Does it mean that, although someone professes no active sexual partnership, their emotional development is immature? Listen to this woman's reflections and her passion and vitality:

> *I am sure that in the experience of my life it is love that makes celibacy not just possible but inevitable...I remember the beginnings. I recall I felt God's love and responded with love. I was in my mid-twenties at the time and had been in love before. This was more intense and non-resistible and, despite the exigencies of life, it has remained that way and deepened.* (Ruth)

When it comes to the heart of celibate love, or loving with no strings attached, I acknowledge it has to do with the mystery of love that transcends understanding as these words intimate:

> *I am in a state of yearning, a dynamic of going further. For me, celibacy has something to do with life…for going into the Unknown.* (Judith)

Judith goes on to explain that celibacy chosen for religious reasons does not want to cut off sexuality. Rather its energy infuses all of one's being and relationships. Although difficult to articulate, it makes sense that the impulse to unconditional love expressed as celibate love comes from a deep layer in the psyche that Swiss psychiatrist, Carl Gustav Jung, called the *collective unconscious*. From this stratum, Jung proposed that the archetype of the Self moves psyche: one's soul, mind and spirit. I am conscious of what Jung called this spark of the Greater Self who is the Other within every person and the One "who lives in me, behind blind eyes."[1]

In whatever way individuals envisage their call in life, I see it as becoming who one could be by attending to an inner essence. As I write what I know of the transformative potential of celibate love, I find myself in a space of "betwixt and between." An earlier transitional time was my entering the Sisters of St. Joseph, a Religious Congregation of Women Religious founded in Australia for the education of children of poor people and now worldwide with diverse ministries. Recalling that beginning stage of religious life, I can identify steps in transition. From a secular perspective, analytic training also involved making transitions—from candidate to practitioner. On that latter journey that began in my forties, it was a relief to find greater emphasis on the individual's finding her way through psychoanalytic requirements.

Fortunately, in most Religious Congregations, times have changed and those entering and considering religious life are met with approaches that consider more the needs of individuals rather than a rigid group approach where everyone is expected to fit a mould. My generation of

---

1   Fernando Pessoa, *Poems of Fernando Pessoa*, 137; C.G. Jung, "Psychology and Religion," CW 11.

women and men religious did come through a more regimented initiation as you may have found in your education or career.

Speaking of transitional times in life, ethnologists suggest that participants go through four distinct stages. They include a period of separation from the group and a liminal time of feeling lost and yet on the way. When the third stage of completing the journey arrives, a culmination point may come with persons giving back to the community something of value.

The strands I am gathering stretch back a long way. My reason for writing is to pass on some of what I have gleaned about a subject that is not high on the popularity list: yet one that is fascinating, demanding, inspiring and always just beyond reach. It seems that now is the right time, with controversies about celibacy and issues of sexual abuse in the church, to try to bring to light another side of celibate love that needs to be told. I know this work will have limitations and leave questions—and that is fine.

With simple flair, Marge Denis, Canadian facilitator, once commented that questions are valuable because they point back to the "Quest-I (am)-On." So the Quest in which we are engaged will unearth more searching just as it did for the poor fool and disturbed woman in the Grail legend.[2] While not accusing celibate women and men of foolishness and derangement, one could wonder if there are traces of these symptoms in making such a radical choice.

You can make up your mind as you listen to people who are at home with their choice to live this way. You might ask: why focus on those who are relatively at peace with their commitment to celibate love? There are many stories of those who are disenchanted and, while not denying their voices, in this work I have chosen to hone in on the perspective of those who find some meaning and contentment.

I am curious about what contributes to the aesthetic of celibate chastity, that is, the beauty of this way. What motivates some people not only to accept but to consciously consent to and embrace this vocation for life? Can they become more vital and compassionate human beings? I know that in the past the accent tended to a more rigid purity instead of seeing celibate chastity as the loving gift of oneself to God and liv-

---

2 Wolfram von Eschenbach, *Parzifal.*

ing with moderation and elegance.[3] I am also aware that understanding needs to take account of the anaesthetic of celibate chastity as well as the aesthetic. By *anaesthetic*, I mean *a deadening* physical and psychological condition, which is a risk for those who vow religious chastity or find themselves celibate.

People can and sometimes do choose religious celibacy to avoid suffering. When this motivates the individual's choice, the anaesthetic of celibate chastity cripples the person's emotional life. As artists and philosophers have observed, the price of disowning one's life is inevitably a dulling of consciousness, of imagination and of one's humanity. The price of perversion is tragic because everyone loses.

From the standpoint then of the aesthetic and anaesthetic of celibate love, the question emerges. Is celibate chastity really worthwhile or am I fooling myself? This is really the question of the Grail reworded to ask "Whom does celibate love serve?" While knowing whom it should serve, I want to explore the question of whether celibate love, and in particular celibate chastity, can lead women and men to an inner creativity which precludes rather than denigrates a total union with another.[4]

I have recently discovered that *aesthetic* describes *one who perceives*, to which Kant added, "a sensuous perception."[5] That clarification gives me a key for which I also thank Angelus Silesius, poet and mystic, who wrote: "a rose needs no why; she blooms, because she blooms."[6] So the litmus test could be: do women and men who are celibate, sexual and spiritual individuals—who profess to live the archetype of celibate love—have a beauty and fragrance about them that tells a story of love?

---

3 J.A. Simpson & E.S.C. Weiner, *The Oxford English Dictionary*, 57.

4 Walter Abbott, *The Documents of Vatican* 2, 71; John Paul II, *Vita Consecrata*, http://www.vatican.va/roman_curia/congregations/ccscrlife/documents/hf_jp-ii_exh_25031996_vita-consecrata_en.html. Retrieved June 6, 2014.

5 Della Thompson, *The Concise Oxford Dictionary of Current English*, 21; John Feehan, *The Singing Heart of the World*, 175.

6 Angelus Silesius, unknown source.

Figure 1: Our Lady of Guadalupe, by unknown artist. Source:
ARAS Online Archive. Reprinted with permission.

THE DARK VIRGIN AND THE LABYRINTH

In preparation for this writing journey, a priest friend gave me a picture of *The Dark Virgin*, Our Lady of Tepeyac, whose image faces me now as I write. In Jungian terms, I see her as an archetypal expression of the positive shadow, accompanying and encouraging me to write on the transformative potential of celibate love. By positive shadow I mean she is portraying that which I have yet to translate into my own life and perhaps never will. Across countries and cultures, there are different images of the Black Virgin. In this image, she appears as a young pregnant girl who is remarkably self-contained.

Her story, which you might consider legend, goes back to Mexico of the 16th century. Juan Diego was a nondescript Indian returning home when a woman dressed as an Aztec princess appeared. She told him to go and ask the Bishop to build a shrine in that remote place for her Son. While Diego tried to ignore this strange woman, she persisted. On the second occasion of their meeting, the woman instructed Diego to take to the Bishop a Castilian rose which she provided. He did as directed and when Diego opened his cloak to take out the rose, the Bishop saw not only a rose unfamiliar to that country, but an image of Mary of Guadalupe etched on the man's cloak. Devotion to Our Lady of Guadalupe grew and spread and this pilgrimage became known and loved particularly in South America.

Why include such an anecdote? Jungian Analyst and mentor, Dr. Sonja Marjasch, used to recommend telling a story instead of giving an explanation. I have taken her advice and added this snippet about a young indigenous woman, who in Catholic tradition, is referred to as "the Rose of Sharon" from Solomon's great love poem "the *Song of*

Songs."[7] The rose intimates passion, instinct and healing. It has a habit of turning up, as do other archetypal images or universal patterns, when opposites like the human and divine intersect.

There are other reasons that I am pleased to place myself in the company of this Rose of Guadalupe. As I look at this image, my eyes return to a tiny cross woven into Mary's dress. It reminds of the meeting of opposites through her Crucified Son. Synchronistically, another gift I was given for the journey is a cross of Murano glass with a golden figure just visible at the centre. The multi-coloured cross calls to mind the gift givers. They are two friends who though not vowed to celibate love, bring this kind of unqualified love and respect to the homeless men and women among whom they work.

Making associations to journeys, soul companions and the meeting of opposites take me to Dante Alighieri's epic poem, *Divina Comedia.*[8] When Dante and Beatrice finally reach the end of their pilgrimage, they come face to face with the red and white rose which Beatrice identifies as Mary. Those of you familiar with C.G. Jung's writing on spiritual transformation might recognise *sub rosa* as an alchemical (or old chemical) term for a movement in the personality towards wholeness. For that interior and beautiful opus, I am aware that the necessary transforming fire is the Spirit of love…and what does it require of us? Jung suggests:

> …the opus consists of three parts: insight, endurance and action…[9]

Could I invite you to come to this book as you would go on pilgrimage—with anticipation, with fresh eyes and with open heart? I am grateful to those who have shared their comments and stories. They offer a thread, a narrative clew (an old English name for a ball of yarn). This metaphorical ball can unwind as we walk through a kind of labyrinth that may feel sometimes confusing. May I assure you, labyrinths have a centre, and the path that leads in to that mid-point takes one back to the entrance.

---

7 *Song of Songs*, 2:1, in *The New Jerusalem Bible*.
8 Dante Alighieri, *The Divine Comedy*, Vols. 1, 2 & 3.
9 C.G. Jung, "Letter to Olga Frobe-Kapteyn," in *Letters*, Vol.1, 375.

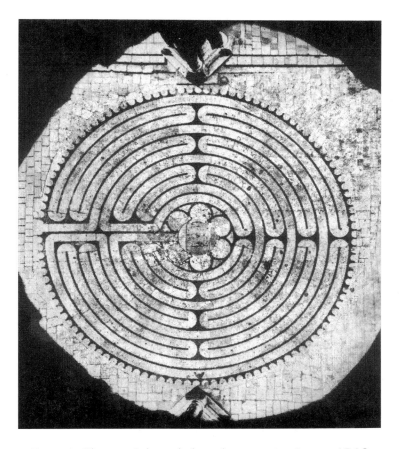

Figure 2: Christian Labyrinth, by unknown artist. Source: ARAS
Online Archive. Reprinted with permission.

As an old image of pilgrimage, the labyrinth is an encouraging symbol.
Later I will describe the myth of the labyrinth and invite you to use it as
a way of understanding celibate love. At this stage, enough to note that
at the centre of the Christian or Chartres labyrinth is the five-petalled
Rose of Sharon, with its reminder of love and eternity. I am intimating that this journey takes psyche, or the soul, into the unknown, past
death, into eternity and into love.

CHAPTER ONE

THE FIRST MOVEMENT: PSYCHE'S AWAKENING

As I look at significant words, one of the delightful discoveries is uncovering their early roots and meanings. *Psyche* is the Greek word for *butterfly* and also translates as *soul*. Those working in the psychological field are intended to be at the service of the soul who, like the butterfly, must pass through a number of transformations until, entirely remade, the winged creature emerges from its cocooned space. That is not all. What is left with the soul's final transformation is silk. This image provokes a question: what silk will remain when my life ends? I do not have a partner, nor children of my own and no material wealth to bequeath. That trace of silk has to be of another kind that is real even if not so easy to see or touch.

The ancients enjoyed storytelling and they quote many episodes concerning Psyche where she is personified as the Soul. Some of these stories I include because they simply open our heart. Frequently, soul or psyche was pictured in a place of vulnerability, resilience and in the grace of life unfolding. In literature and in Jungian psychology, the soul was described with her Latin name of the *anima*. She was portrayed as a feminine inspirer accompanying the artist and poet on their creative endeavours. I was fascinated when a friend wished me the attention of the Muses as well as the breath of the Spirit on my writing endeavour.[10]

Psyche also needs Spirit. An Orphic tale speaks of Eros as vitality and the Spirit of love that is the origin of heaven and earth.[11] Staying with

---

10   C.G. Jung, "Alchemical Studies," CW 13 ¶ 435.
11   Marija Gimbutas, *The Goddesses and Gods of Old Europe*, 102.

this mythopoetic tradition, the *breath of Spirit* translates into the Jewish as *Ruah*. At the beginning of creation, Genesis tells of the divine Spirit sweeping over the waters. She is Sophia, God of wisdom, Shekinah of God at play. The presence of the creative Spirit is in the gentle breeze. At Pentecost, the Spirit also comes with a transforming gust of wind and tongues of fire to those gathered.[12] One priest described *spirituality* as *the Spirit in reality*. Another Respondent saw the presence of the Spirit embodied in tell-tale touches that she describes as:

> *creative, passionate, caring, forgiving, healing, giving, receiving, listening and being!* (Janice)

In this way, Spirit gives birth to Eros and recreates. I find it relevant that, rather than speaking of Eros, John of the Cross refers to "desire" as "the force of love."[13] This distinction uncovers more about the spiritual and psychological meaning of love that Jung conveyed in this remark, "people think that Eros is sex, but not at all, Eros is relatedness."[14] This relatedness urges individuals to go into the unknown with the "love (that) bears all things and endures all things."[15] I hear that sense of Eros in Patrick's description of what celibacy means to him now:

> *...it is a radical way of loving...A deep and rich way of loving both intimate and affectionate without genital intercourse...A constant call to intimate relationship with God and an extraordinary gift that continues to draw me into the stillness and silence of a mysterious inner ocean of love.*

In Greek myth, Psyche or the Soul is pictured as a beautiful woman who goes into the unknown: into that *inner ocean*. Awakening can come with an unexpected shock. When have you had an experience that changed you irrevocably? I felt a reawakening when over 20 years ago I began my doctoral research on this subject in Zurich. This exploration took me into new vistas, which a dream from that time foreshadowed.

---

12 Acts 2:4 in *The New Jerusalem Bible*.
13 Andres Rafael Luevano, *Endless Transforming Love*, 11.
14 C.G. Jung, *Dream Analysis: Notes of Seminars Given in 1928-1930*, 172.
15 1 Corinthians. 13:7 in *The New Jerusalem Bible*; C.G. Jung, *Memories, Dreams, Reflections*, 387.

I dreamt that *I was walking with an unknown companion across a field of white flowers and looking for a path, which could be just over the rise.* It may seem a little strange to include dreams. Yet I find them helpful as we journey into this realm where the unconscious is recognised as intimately affecting the conscious life. Following a call to vowed religious life that includes celibacy is like responding to a dream. It can bear traces of the Persephone-Demeter story that can take hold and jolt one out of or into life.

Can the Christian understanding of soul shed some additional light? My question takes me to an expression coined by St. Paul where he describes Christians as earthen vessels holding a treasure. The treasure to which the apostle was referring was their life in Christ.[16] Living one's life with this realization of Christ's presence can make all the difference. For medieval mystic Meister Eckhart it was "the break through."[17] In the 20th century, Edith Stein, who was a contemplative nun of Jewish background, referred to this attitude as a growing consciousness of being a bearer of grace.[18]

A tension exists between the gift of grace and the vulnerability of psyche. Jung took a view of creative tension. He envisaged that at the heart of life is a self-regulating complex, a diamond point that functions like an inner animating sense.[19] The graciousness of the Self, of the God dimension, does not depend on a person's being worthy or psychologically all together. Speaking with that awareness, an older woman religious who suffered with endogenous depression could say in spite of her agitation, *I know God loves me and nothing can ever stop that love.* Like a vessel, her psyche could feel overwhelmed by the unknown and yet relate to and be growing in and through the paradox because of the expansive love of God.

There can be times when the realization of grace is whisked away. Many of the Respondents remarked that in the early days of their commitment, they had been unaware of just what chastity, or their vow of foregoing sexual intercourse, entailed. Awakenings often come later and

16   2 Corinthians. 4:7 in *The New Jerusalem Bible*.
17   C.G. Jung, "Psychological Types," CW 6, ¶ 425.
18   Edith Stein, *The Hidden Life*, 38.
19   C.G. Jung, "Symbols of Transformation," CW 5, ¶ 344.

are true of many life decisions. As someone remarked, his initial choice was about following a spiritual call into religious life and *celibacy just went with the territory*. Vows do not safeguard anyone from falling in love or from feeling and falling into any of the darker emotions. When that occurs, vowed or not, I can feel a deep conflict with previous commitments and need strong and true friends to stand with me through emotional upheaval and maturation.

This awareness deepens as I work with clients who are at crossroads. It can be beneficial for them to go back to their earliest memory of vocation, be it to celibate chastity, to marriage or to another partnership as they reaffirm an earlier choice or come to another decision. Jung described a conscious sense of call and response as essential for a vibrant life. That experience might be almost indefinable as Jung explains:

> What…induces persons to go their own way and to rise out
> of unconscious identity with the mass…Not necessity…Not
> moral decision…Vocation…a daemon whispering to them of
> new and wonderful paths.[20]

A sense of vocation could come early or later in life and may also change in expression as a person or as life changes. Awareness of being drawn to consecrated celibacy might go back to an early and simple knowing as a child. A defining experience might come in which the soul hears the call of the Greater Self. The latter is theological language for the mystical marriage which I hear in Jane's response:

> *Yes I have had significant religious experiences in which I have
> tasted the presence, the love and invitation of God. I have come
> to know myself as God's beloved.*

While beauty awakens psyche to the Spirit, the sense of vocation deepens through pruning experiences of grief and loss. Suffering gets the soul moving. It can change one's sense of being a victim of fate to a consciousness of having a destiny. The shift that comes from deep

---

20   C.G. Jung, "The Development of Personality," CW 17, ¶¶ 299-300.

within and beyond the Self has diverse ways of breaking through to consciousness.

Psyche's Development

Growth has to do with identity and something new emerging from the unconscious and wanting expression. Psyche needs to brave challenge and to change. If we avoid certain life tasks, we often encounter them later in another form. On my meeting with some clients, Jung's favourite comment sometimes comes to mind and can be paraphrased: "What difficulty in life are you avoiding?" The question points to a complex, a knot or stuckness that people need to recognise and address.

C.S. Lewis gives an analogy of psyche's hard won development in, *Till We have Faces.*[21] Taking the perspective of the older sister, Lewis retells the journey of the soul with the Greek myth of "Psyche and Eros." Psyche is portrayed as a captivating woman who stirs the animosity of Aphrodite, the goddess of beauty. As life teaches, disturbing emotions like jealousy frequently precipitate action. The problem is not having normal troublesome emotions but working with them—growing in wisdom through conflict.[22]

Psyche's beauty, which aroused the envy of family as well as of gods, eventually led the young woman to be taken prisoner and abandoned on a hilltop. It was Aphrodite's plan for Psyche to be the victim of wounding but her son pricks himself with love's arrow. Like the West Wind of Botticelli's painting, Eros takes Psyche to his domain with the warning never to look at him or he would leave her.

In the dark of night and to the delight of them both, Eros comes to Psyche's bed. (You are possibly hearing echoes of John of the Cross' Canticle of the Soul and the *Song of Songs* which similarly allegorize God's love for the Soul). Yet the human heart is restless. While Psyche is enraptured, she also misses her sisters and convinces Eros to let them visit. Strife ensues. The envious sisters convince the naïve woman to kill Eros before he murders her. As Psyche stands ready to stab her sleeping

21   C.S. Lewis, *Till We Have Faces.*
22   Greek Myth and Characters, http://www.greekmythology.com. Retrieved June 7, 2014.

lover, the lamp reveals his beauty. At that moment, a drop of oil falls on Eros's shoulder and wakes him. As forewarned, Eros flies off and a distraught Psyche realises her folly.

The next phase of Psyche's journey is triggered. Psyche holds some hope as love wants to be rediscovered. Psyche must meet four seemingly impossible tasks. They include sifting and sorting grain, gathering wool, collecting water and then going to the underworld to bring back Aphrodite's box of fragrance. In some ways, I feel as if I am facing similar trials. I am encouraged by the knowledge that, while Psyche has to go through these ordeals, she gets help from some down-to-earth sources and finally, despite or maybe because of her curiosity, Eros finds her!

I think this myth of an arduous journey in hope of transformation can apply to celibacy and to celibate love. It points to a mystery beyond the journeying image to accentuate that what we are now is instinctively emerging.

Psychosocial Stages of Life

Psychological development has other motifs besides the journey theme. Gail Sheehy updated her description of *Passages* with *New Passages* for post-modern woman and man.[23] Today we favour more scientifically evidence-based explanations of psychic development. The field of neuroscience is contributing insights on the mind's functions and on the brain's ability to fire and be re-wired. These findings are realigning principles for how the inner and outer universes work. Yet all are still metaphors for describing psyche's maturation.

In Western culture, we are familiar with the psychosocial stages of human development that Erik Erikson describes.[24] In what are cycles rather than stages, Erikson envisaged that generativity is released in and around individuals who meet their responsibilities in life and in their relationships. As I understand generativity, it includes, but is more than creativity or productivity. Akin to sexuality, generativity maximises our capacity to receive and to give life.

---

23   Gail Sheehy, *New Passages*.
24   Erik Erikson, *Childhood and Society*.

Erikson was aware of the alternative of stagnation and resentment that could happen to those who avoid life's conflicts, stay adolescent and then target others.[25] That negativity, which indicates another kind of psychological pain, can be written over the faces of men and women. Atmosphere and environment facilitate or block psyche's development. On a collective level where debate is quashed, as sometimes happens with controversial issues in church circles, psyche is thwarted and persons who do not fit are excluded.

In *Quest for the Living God*, Elizabeth Johnson raises new perspectives on contentious issues and has received censure from some church authorities.[26] Similarly, the recent investigation of women religious in the United States by Vatican authorities is a controlling intervention that does not impress, encourage dialogue or deepen trust among adult Christians.

I acknowledge that putting the topics of celibacy and spirituality, which are two essential aspects of life for a nun, monk, priest, Catholic sister or brother, into the public arena has caused me some hesitation. There is reluctance to expose soul to a wider and critical gaze. In a negative sense, it is also mixed with a hesitancy and wavering courage to put myself on the line: I mean a diffidence to own my controversial and undervalued profession to religious chastity that is magnified by current attitudes to celibacy, sexuality and spirituality. I am faced with that question quoted earlier from Jung's repertoire, "What difficulty in life are you avoiding?"

It prompts me to reconsider what depth psychology calls individuation or the process of becoming oneself. Jung pictures individuation as a person's maturing through two distinct stages which he calls the first and second half of life. I will refer to that framework occasionally. It sounds as if (and is a little like "in the beginning," or as developmental psychology would say "from the moment of birth") the individuation process begins even without our consciousness. Psyche's growth happens not in isolation but in a definite cultural context that shapes us. Para-

25 Erik Erikson, *Childhood and Society*, 266-268.
26 Elizabeth Johnson, *Quest for the Living God*.

doxically this maturation is both stable and dynamic and its purpose is completion of the personality.

Myths like "Psyche and Eros" give an idea of how maturation occurs. What wakes individual psyches? What breaks through to the soul? Love and suffering penetrate unconsciousness. Everyone, vowed or not vowed, needs the affective element of love or passion to come alive. In that rousing, life takes on more colour, vitality and substance.

In the first stage of life, the development of the ego grows alongside the shadow of our unwanted and neglected aspects. As children we learn not to throw a tantrum to get our way but to find more acceptable means of having our needs met. Alongside the ego and the shadow, the persona grows. The latter is how we like to appear to the world. It is necessary to have a sense of achievement and recognition, which our various roles bring. Then psyche can take both risky and laborious steps. Some women and men who entered religious life in their teens may experience problems with a suspended adolescence. They either consciously face such delays or remain emotionally retarded, as this man bravely acknowledges and shares:

> *I was too young to even consider celibate life. I guess I just grew into it and accepted my life accordingly.* (Thomas)

No matter who we are, there is a daily struggle with the shadow of our disowned aspects that fuels individuation. Ego needs to move through various stages of psycho-sexual development. The myths about life and death trace a pattern for individuating or maturing. In these collective tales, we learn that the heroic ego must go into the labyrinth or venture out on the Grail quest. They show that one must persevere when the going is hard, be courageous even when terrified, and trust intuition when all else fails. From those big stories, we find encouragement and reassurance that the journey is worthwhile. This humanizing process is like becoming truly celibate: it requires time, patience and trust.[27]

The second stage of life, of individuation, prompts a keener awareness of the soul, the need of Spirit and of life's passing. Inescapably it prods the meaning of one's life and death. Some events in life, like

---

27 C.G. Jung, "The Structure and Dynamics of the Psyche," CW 8, ¶ 688.

inevitable ageing can throw us into a midlife crisis where we face our inability to depend solely on ourselves. They bring us to an edge where psychic rebirth or renewal is possible. I am edging past that middle age and stage that Dante captures at the beginning of his "Divine Comedy."

I agree with the poet's description of the disorientation, isolation and emotional confusion that befall many people at turning points. The uncanny stirring that occurs around significant times prompted my taking a sabbatical from my professional life in educational administration. In 1989 I literally set off in search of meaning and in search of myself. An outer journey became an image for inner exploration that seemed like "a journey without maps."[28] Gradually I would come to see it as *a circumambulation*—taking me to the desert of the Kalahari, to the high Alps of Switzerland and to those depths of the psyche that we all share.[29]

A Holding Environment: The Space of Intimacy

However you describe the stages and passages of life—with post-modern or pre-modern metaphors—the importance of a holding environment is clear. British psychologist, Donald Winnicott, developed this concept.[30] He knew the importance of a safe space because of his clinical work with traumatised children during World War II. Essentially, psyche requires a stable environment to emerge.

In almost theological terms, Winnicott talks about the Self progressively taking shape in and through our lives. He describes a process of in-dwelling. Slowly, the little child's true Self personalizes and actualizes in her body as she is first held in mother's womb and then held in the safe embrace of caregivers. No wonder that touch is important right through our lives.

In the language of human development, I can hear echoes of the myth of Sophia where God's Spirit comes to earth, "the female figure of cosmic power."[31] Through her mothering, a pristine Spirit grows stronger in the infant. A psychoanalyst whose voice you will hear often in this

---

28 Graham Greene, *Journey Without Maps*.
29 C.G. Jung, "Psychology and Alchemy," CW 12, ¶ 38.
30 D.W. Winnicott, *The Maturational Processes and the Facilitating Environment*.
31 Elizabeth A. Johnson, *Quest for the Living God*, 21.

work is mentor and friend, Dr. Ian Baker. Ian left some metaphorical pieces of silk with trainees like me, and that wisdom survives his death. Pertinent here is his description of the soul, or psyche, as being shy by nature and taking time and needing a place of trust in which to thrive.

Jung proposed that the parental figures also give to psyche that first image of what it is to be a woman or man. When significant others mirror encouragement and loving acceptance of us, a solid grounding in celibate love or loving with no strings attached is given. In that reliable circle, psyche comes to know a for-giving love. Can someone who has not had a good enough parenting be capable of understanding unconditional love? No one comes through childhood psychologically unscathed and here is the hope that Jungian psychology offers.

Analytical Psychology takes a constructive view that, in spite of one's history, there is the central activator of the Self, "imago Dei."[32] A Jungian perspective sees this essence at work in the psyche through the individuation process that is life. In a self-regulating manner, the whole personality grows. It does matter what kind of childhood we experience. Even with a miserable start, Jung's clinical experience points to the energy of the Self, prompting us towards better psychological and emotional health.

While early damage to the child may cause a chronic unhinging of the personality, a more wholesome environment can support psyche's capacity to love. That milieu includes healthy relationships, positive attachment figures and creative opportunities. Kent Hoffman is a contemporary psychotherapist whose perspective complements Jung's outlook. His developmental psychology that is encapsulated in the next quote, gives heart to many clients and clinicians:

Whether I believe it or not, I am tenderly and lovingly held.[33]

On one of my usual morning walks, I found on my path a feather with shades of bluey pink to lapus lazuli to sea green. Its beauty remind-

---

32   C.G. Jung, "The Archetypes and the Collective Unconscious," CW 9, ¶ 5; Genesis 9:6 in *The New Jerusalem Bible*; John Paul 11, *Veritatis Splendor*, 90.

33   Kent Hoffman, http://www.thirsthome.org/ - resources. Retrieved January 6, 2012.

ed me of a sculpture that caught my attention outside an Ursuline Convent in Quebec. The bronze is dedicated to women religious everywhere. It is simply called "Feather on the Hand" and shows the hand of God with one feather lightly resting on the palm. In her response, Frances expresses that fundamental holding:

> *Hands have always been important to me—to be carved on the palm of God's hand is very significant; to rest in God's hands gives me rest, protection, security, love—they are my nest, always warm and comforting.*

With such assurance, psyche's capacity for intimacy grows. The Latin *intimo* means *inmost*. Intimacy does not necessarily mean being sexually active. One young client said to me, "I can do sex but intimacy scares me." Intimacy suggests an openness to trust and to love and a capacity for forgiving. It is a sense of God's containing her that makes the chaste celibate, unavailable to marriage and yet capable of loving. As in married chastity, celibacy is "ultimately (a relationship)...of loving fidelity."[34] I hear these elements, coupled with beauty, in Frank's description of celibacy:

> *A beautiful celibate life would be coming to know oneself as a lover. First of all a lover of God is a life of faith and hope. A lover of God is not as obviously tangible as being a lover with another of God...A celibate becomes a lover. That's the first—one needs to become a whole self... There is no one other than God in this first opening of myself. So I am lover that way. The important matter is an openness of my whole self. That is how I would say it.*

As Frank clarifies, fidelity is a chastity that partners give to each other in an outer or an inner marriage of conscious loving commitment. Whether one is a vowed celibate or in a partnership, one's integrity—like all virtue—deepens slowly through the highs and lows of life. We cannot create life alone. One's being is shown up and shaped in self-giving relationships. It explains why one director of novices would remark, "You know, fidelity isn't an easy thing!" We knew that she was talking about something in our relating that we had to work at over time rath-

---

34   Pierre Teilhard de Chardin, "The Evolution of Chastity," in *Toward the Future*, 65.

er than about prohibitions on sexual behaviour: something to do with fidelity and with integrity "because I would be less myself if I did not."[35]

---

35 Joan Chittister, *The Fire in These Ashes*, 88.

CHAPTER TWO

OPENING THE BOX ON TABOO SUBJECTS

Body, Sexuality, Particular Friendships, Spirituality

In the story of Psyche's search for Eros, she is required to accomplish certain tasks. The most difficult is to find Aphrodite's fragrance box, which is located somewhere in the nether world. With help from friends, Psyche succeeds. She is, however, curious and does the forbidden. Psyche opens the box…just as we are doing now on a few sensitive subjects.

Taboos of silence concerning the body have led to shame and guilt about sexuality and to a warped spirituality. What sexuality and spirituality have in common is passion. Rather than killing Eros, it is essential to relate with others in ways that keep passion alive. Fear of this primal energy has sometimes hindered healthy friendships for some in religious life and priesthood. As Tim, a Religious Order priest, noted:

> *Passion is a key ingredient of pastoral effectiveness, and passion is I believe well-directed sublimated libido…More libido means more evident need for discipline but potentially higher delight in ministry that flows from graced passion.*

In some novitiates and seminaries, warnings were given about growing too attached to particular or passionate friends; such warnings hindered the mature growth of some celibate religious. Fear did a disservice to friendship as it engendered worry about closeness and intimacy. In conversation, one priest remarked that what he heard was to avoid friendship. Only later and with difficulty did he learn to accept friends and address difficulties with loneliness and lonesomeness. Anxiety had blocked his confronting those actual issues. These are subjects to which I will return later in what I term the "unfillable space."

Thank God for the particular friends that I have had and still have in my life—and for the mistakes that I and they have made. They are women and men who I know will care about me when I am at my best and at my worst. I don't need to prove anything. I am valued for who and what I am. They are not silent about what I need to hear. What's more, we laugh a lot together: this I find is an absolute necessity for wellness.

I am aware that affection can fan into misdirected passion and that common sense is important. Many of the Respondents recognised that close friendships are gifts that deserve fostering in normal and inclusive ways. Conversations with close friends to clarify boundaries, and, where needed, a conversation with a mentor or supervisor can help in growing into this capacity.

Am I attached to particular friends and are they to me? Yes: with a secure attachment that allows others into the circle. Do I possess them or do they me? No: yet I know that I have a particular place in their affections as they have in mine. Jesuit theologian, Karl Rahner, captures that sense when he speaks of those whom we love, and especially those who have died, as carrying a special part of us into eternity.[36] Little by little, we are taken into that greatest unknown by those whom we love and who have completed the journey. I am reminded of the lyrics in the theme song from the film *Titanic*: "My heart will go on and on." They hint at the transcendence of loving and the gift of sexuality.

Sexuality is energy and encompasses all of who I am physically, intellectually, socially, emotionally and morally. It is a vital instinct that writer, Nadine Gordimer, describes as "reaching out to otherness."[37] This energy, arising keenly at adolescence, is an important aspect of who I am as a human being. Contrary to general understandings, sexuality is more than my biological or psychological identity as female or male and more than genital behaviour. This energy of being, receiving and giving

---

36 Karl Rahner, *Encounters with Silence*, 53-55.
37 Nadine Gordimer, "Writing and Being." http://www.nobelprize.org/nobel_prizes/literature/laureates/1991/gordimer-prose-e.html. Retrieved June 14, 2013.

life, is the gift of life. I hope I am conveying the comprehensive picture that Evelyn and James Whitehead give of one's sexuality.[38]

Like all instinctual energy, sexuality is charged with feeling and can trigger depleting emotions of lust, anger, anxiety and greed. Fear can cause us to stifle disturbing emotions because of parental, church, educational and other social conditioning. The shadow then grows as such energies are unconsciously repressed rather than feelings acknowledged and, then if there is need, healthily suppressed.

The failure to parent oneself often shows in the body. Neglect is the worst kind of abuse. Caring for the body involves healthy eating, sleeping, exercise, opportunities for relating and relaxation to increase metabolic rate and enable life energies to find a constructive rather than destructive channel. Contempt and shame about normal bodily functions and guilt about affective needs distort persons' thinking and feeling about themselves. Instead of allowing that any consuming obsession for the material world can exclude a spiritual dimension, the body and sexuality have been too frequently demonised and burdened with sin and shame! The next Respondent describes sexuality well. Frank clarifies that even without genital expression, human sexuality means showing care and concern:

> *The irruption of God into human life has given us the freedom to humanize sexuality by participation or abstention. It's a freeing message. Note too, that many who freely engage in sexual activity are not "normal"... We each have to find freedom in our sexuality and some of us are called to find it as celibates.*

As with the body, there is a need to recover a positive attitude to sexuality. Collective attitudes have sometimes tended to view anything to do with the body as sinful, weak and too dangerous to even name. That kind of thinking also infects and distorts attitudes to celibacy. Frances, one of the more senior women Respondents, illustrates a restrictive atmosphere through which she had to grow:

> *...I remember once the novice director asking if I knew about the facts of life—I said yes. As far as I knew it was only about*

---

38   J. & E. Whitehead, *A Sense of Sexuality*, 45.

my monthly period. I knew it happened every month—I didn't
know why…in spite of that beginning, I feel I'm a reasonably
normal person.

Sexuality needs to be seen in an historical framework. Some Eastern and Western philosophies that predate and influence Christianity
hold a negative attitude to the body that is projected on to an inferior
feminine. The Hebrew Scripture forbade Jewish men to go to the Greek
gymnasium because participants had to be naked. Women did not have
the freedom to go to participate and, considered as inferior men, they
did not even rate a mention. Gnostic ideas considered Spirit to be noble
and the material world as evil. In his letters, St. Paul warns about the
dangers of the flesh. The history of psychology describes Freud's sexual
theory exposing a bizarrely repressive society which Patrick's comment
supports:

Celibacy touches more the affections (the heart) rather than the
genitals (sex).

The sex revolution of the 1960s and 70s in many Western countries
ruptured the silence that had hung around sexuality. Previously, sexuality and issues like sexual misconduct and orientation were swept under
the carpet. The community marginalized gay men and women. Homosexuality barely made mention of the possibility of women's gay orientation. Like other complexes, attitudes to sexuality come from society,
culture, church and family, and these attitudes, including homophobia,
can change over time. For example, early editions of the Diagnostic
Statistical Manual of Mental Disorders, published by the American
Psychiatric Association, considered homosexuality as sexual deviation.
The diagnosis was revised to sexual orientation disturbance. Then in
the DSM-IV edition the diagnosis was removed altogether from mental
disorders.[39]

Another example of changing opinion is seen in regard to masturbation. It has moved from serious sin, a threat to sanity, to more tolerance.
The collective shadow (like the personal shadow) holds valuable aspects
and also charged aspects that need periodic examining to find healthier

---

39   Diagnostic and Statistical Manual of Mental Disorders (DSM-IV).

expression. Naiveté is not a virtue. Jackie gives a candid account of how maturing as a celibate woman came through facing her vulnerability with ordinary and also overwhelming sexual desires:

> *When I was younger, handling sexual feelings was difficult and I often felt guilty about sexual feelings. I experienced great longings to be held and caressed. In my mid 30s and early 40s the difficulties were about sex and relationships; later, in my 40s and 50s it was about having no children. I have felt attracted to some men and one such relationship developed.*

Owning our dilemmas and mistakes can give more freedom to become who we profess to be. It means facing questions such as: "How can I address natural energies without going overboard and using others in a relationship?" and "Why are celibate people reluctant to share knowledge of what helps and what hinders healthy sexuality?" I am suggesting a kinder and more wholesome initiation into womanhood and manhood that respects persons' physical, emotional and affective needs. Opening an intimate area in one's life for conversation with trustworthy others may feel primitive at first. That awkwardness lifts as one takes small steps and grows in confidence, as did the previous Respondent.

In Jackie's sharing of an erotic pattern that caught her unawares, we see how the instinctual energy of sexuality changes according to a person's age and health. This vitality bubbles along as an effervescence, which is essential for the survival of humankind. It includes sexual orientation, masculine and feminine traits and relatedness to heterosexual and homosexual aspects of identity. Part of this natural beauty is that women and men show differences in their functioning and perception of reality. Complementarity can happen when respect for gender difference is not only given room but invited.

For example, scientists tell us that men have 10-20 times more testosterone than women while women have more oxytocin or the cuddle hormone that is essential for bonding.[40] Feelings of love come from a very early part of the brain called the cerebral cortex, and euphoria can overcome rationality. Love does change everything. Couples in love

---

40   A. & B. Pease, *Why Men Want Sex and Women Need Love*, 15-16.

show an increased level of dopamine or the happiness hormone and love can also cause mayhem. The latter can cause confusion in both women and men because of fear of rejection and a negative self-image. That insecurity may fog one's sense of sexual attractiveness and performance. As these elements are integrated or in inner turmoil, self-regard and the capacity to relate with others are affected. As Jane remarks:

> *All people have to find their way to rich, full, human loving. It is no use being celibate but a cold fish.*

Sexuality lived as a celibate person does not mean that earthiness, physical comfort, sensual pleasure, intimate and loving relationships are to be relinquished, whatever the popular expectation. For example, *chaste celibacy* is defined in the Oxford dictionary as *consciously abstaining from marriage because of an obligation or a principle.*[41] This is a curt description which is accurate, remiss, and colourless.

To get closer to the reality of this complicated and compelling word I want to go to its opposite. There is no such word as *un-celibacy* although there are different ways of being not celibate. I consider it is not celibate to be an asexual being and deny one's femininity or masculinity. Nor is it celibate to avoid showing tenderness instead of befriending others. It is not celibate to allow oneself to become hard, malcontent or a "lemon." I want to highlight that although celibate women and men choose not to engage in an active sexual partnership, their emotional development does not have to be immature or cut off. Rather, as Jane and Brendan affirm, celibacy becomes integral to their identity and their relating with others:

> *...how I am, whose I am, how I am to love.* (Jane)

> *...it has given me freedom to become my deeper self and made me present to others.* (Brendan)

As with sexuality, spirituality also belongs to our human nature and is not the exclusive domain of religiously inclined people. I propose that spirituality motivates and stands behind the choice of healthy celibate

---

41   Della Thompson, *The Concise Oxford Dictionary of Current English*, 124.

chastity. Dictionary exploration clarifies that spirituality incorporates beliefs that put a person in touch with a principle of meaning, which animates and enlivens the body. Going a step further, the Greek word for *spiritual, pneuma,* which translates as *spirit or breath,* suggests that spirituality, like sexuality, is about life and vibrancy. Patrick describes a force field that links sexuality with spirituality. Both point to the sacred and to the importance of relationship that includes masculine and feminine:

> *For me the sexual drive is strong or high. It seems to me that the sexual drive is the same relational dynamic at work in my relationship with God who for me is both Father/Mother, Source of all being, Eternal Word, Jesus and Holy Spirit of Love. This God-given sexual drive like gravity attracts me and draws me into relationship.*

From a Jungian perspective, spirituality is a dynamic impulse that comes from both within and beyond the personality. In addition to the sex instinct, the power instinct and other complexes that knit us together or get us stuck, Jung identified the religious instinct. I think of this innate quality extending beyond ego and as my Spirit reaching out to the Holy Spirit: to what Rudolf calls the *Numinosum,* the *Holy.*[42] Faith in the unknown is very different from a mindless faith. Jung proposed that neurosis was healed to the extent that individuals came to own their religious instinct that they encountered through ordinary life situations.

A friend conveyed this broader understanding of spirituality and the religious instinct when she urged me to go on my inner and outer journeys as on pilgrimage. It altered my thinking and seeing. This attitude implies a trust in the Self to which many mystics call attention: a receptivity and readiness to be open in one's life circumstances to "the breakthrough."[43] It is the aesthetic of perception that Christ often put before His disciples: "Are you still without perception?"[44] Putting the

---

42 Rudolf Otto, *The Idea of the Holy,* 6.
43 C.G. Jung, "Psychological Types," CW 6, ¶¶ 425-429.
44 Mark 8:21 in *The New Jerusalem Bible.*

analogy another way, the ego-driven personality needs to be open to an unexpected experience of the Self, one of "waiting upon God."[45]

As a man of his time, Jesus Christ embodied this attitude in a revolutionary way speaking "of God as his own Father and so (making) Himself and all humanity God's equal."[46] Many have contributed to a Christian spirituality by letting God's image be more visible in their lives. For example, in the 6th century, St. Gregory the Great suggested a contemplative way that he called "resting in God."[47] For deepening and staying with this attitude, the medieval anchoress and beguine, Julian of Norwich, envisaged all reality as revealing God's love.[48] An accent on the ubiquity of contemplative knowing comes out of this woman's reflections and her sharing with others:

> *Experience has always been the compelling thing for me but much*
> *more recently, I have thought about this way of living according*
> *to felt experience more rigorously. I am convinced that the love of*
> *God that some would label 'mystical' is commonplace among peo-*
> *ple whom I have known and loved and listened to deeply.* (Ruth)

In her writings, St. Teresa of Jesus (1515-1582) calls such awareness and communication with God the prayer of simplicity. St. Teresa found that a stage of quiet preceded that of mystical union, which she described as spiritual betrothal and the inner marriage. According to her contemporary, St. John of the Cross, inner transformation came from contemplation that he described as an in-flowing "…which fires the soul in the Spirit of love."[49]

An anonymous 19th century Russian pilgrim found that spirituality was growing in union with God through the prayer of the heart. His experience of intimacy and transformation came through the faithful recitation of the Jesus prayer that he learned in the *Philokalia*. That title translates as the *Love of Divine Beauty* and contains reflections on the

---

45   Anthony Storr, *Solitude*, 196.
46   John 5:18 & Philippians 2:7 in *The New Jerusalem Bible*.
47   Thomas Keating, *Open Mind, Open Heart*, 20.
48   Evelyn Underhill, *The Mystic Way*, 175.
49   Andres Rafael Luevano, *Endless Transforming Love*, 77.

mystery of God by the desert mystics.[50] Prayer is simply breathing in and out of the Gospel invocation, "Lord Jesus Christ, Son of God, have mercy on me." In this way, the crippled pilgrim found a strength that suffused and affected all of his life. Four Respondents referred to this type of prayer as significant. Tim remarked:

> *I am learning to pray in Christ through breathing in and out in the Spirit.*

Devout Buddhists know this mindfulness as the practice of the heart sutra. It is what the monk Thich Nhat Hanh describes as the touch of the Holy Spirit through breathing in and out of love and understanding for oneself and others.[51] One of the Respondents referred to this monk's writing as helpful for her living. I hear the same restorative movement in a quietening practice that Carmelite nun, Edith Stein, described as "looking up and into the face of the Eternal."[52] For Thomas Merton, Trappist monk and writer, spirituality is a growth into purity of heart that he described as "integrity."[53]

In all of these descriptions, spirituality appears very close—a gazing at and a desire to respond to life. These perspectives contain a sense of quiet joy and mystery that stirs the heart and the imagination. Through these complexes of spirituality and celibate love, I hear a "telos" or a prompting towards a conversion of heart that William James sees as a natural unfolding.[54] In psychological language, Jung proposes that individuation is a similar intentional process. And the purpose? Whatever the descriptive term, it seems that individuals, as many Respondents affirm, desire life and will submit to a process in which their whole being—body, mind, soul, spirit—participates and is renewed.

50   Helen Bacovcin, *The Way of a Pilgrim*, 120; John Paul 11. *Vita Consecrata*. http://www.vatican.va/roman_curia/congregations/ccscrlife/documents/hf_jp-ii_exh_25031996_vita-consecrata_en.html. Retrieved June 6, 2014.

51   Thich Nhat Hanh, *Living Buddha, Living Christ*, xvi.

52   E. Stein, *The Hidden Life*, 3.

53   Thomas Merton, *The Wisdom of the Desert*, 9.

54   William James, *The Varieties of Religious Experience*, 228.

The Place of Dreams

What is the place of dreams in becoming a spiritual and sexual self? Whether one is celibate or partnered or partnered and celibate, listening to the unconscious breaking through dreams can be a guide too easily forgotten. Ruth picks up this thread and refers to German theologian, Dorothee Soelle.[55]

> *This respected Protestant theologian...suggests that there are various ways to God...Dorothee looks at cultures that value mystical experience in everyday life and points out modern Western cultures are not strong on this. She reflects on cultures where a mother would say to a little child, "What did you dream last night?"* (Ruth)

For making us conscious of the unconscious, Sigmund Freud, pioneering Austrian psychologist and contemporary of Carl Jung, contributed a seminal work on *The Interpretation of Dreams.*[56] While Freud's psychoanalytical work may have fallen into disrepute in some circles, he brought a realization of the power of the unconscious that constantly tries to get its message through to us in dreams, mishaps and foibles.

Carl Jung developed Sigmund Freud's psychological ideas and observations. Beyond the personal unconscious, Jung hypothesized another level. He proposed that from the collective unconscious, archetypes arise and their affective images get us moving. Jung's self-observations, client work and research convinced him of these layers of psyche through which he perceived the guiding archetype of the Self: the "imago Dei." ("image of God")[57]

During sleep, our level of consciousness is lowered. The voice of the unconscious is able to speak her language through the strange imagery of our dreams. They may have a peaceful or weird aspect and even be frightening nightmares that literally try to wake us up to something requiring attention. In writing *Celibacy and Soul: Exploring the Depths*

---

55   Dorothee Soelle, *The Silent Cry: Mysticism and Resistance*, 11.
56   S. Freud, *Interpretation of Dreams.*
57   C.G. Jung, "The Archetypes of the Collective Unconscious," CW 9, I, ¶ 5; Colossians 1:15 & Genesis 9:6 in *The New Jerusalem Bible.*

of Chastity, I am grateful for dreams. They indicate different possibilities that I have not yet considered. I also want to thank those clients who have given me permission to quote their dreams along with some relevant background of the dreamer. (Incidentally, anyone I quote is no longer actually working in analysis with me).

In therapeutic work, I witness how dreams lead to the heart of issues that people need to address. In the next vignette, the dreamer, whom I call Adrienne, was sexually abused as a child. She is a capable woman who holds leadership roles in her Religious Congregation. Through her dreams we were able to revisit experiences that left her feeling *scarred and her legs cut from beneath her*. One of the healing images in her later dreams was when a child aspect of her-self showed up at the door with suitcase in hand and wanting to stay. The symbol of the child, her self, was alive and returning.

It is fascinating that in myth and in literature, the psychological state of virginity is often pictured as a child leading one to an inner home. In dreams too, renewal is recognised as the divine appearing as a child. This childlike redeeming quality reconnects the searcher to something original. In cosmic terms, that virginal quality is expressed as the dawn of a new day. I smile to myself remembering Ian Baker's counsel: he would say something that may sound a little kitsch but indicates a fresh start: "Today is the first day of the rest of my life." In Scripture, Christ describes that attitude as an inner transformation that happens in us through baptism. This second birth takes the individual beyond appearances to faithfully searching out the will of God.

In this "being born for a second time," Christ discriminates between what is considered of usual worldly importance and what is an attitude and a way of living that incorporate a spiritual life.[58] The requirement to enter into this life which is God's kingdom means welcoming the child, as did Adrienne. Having symbolically accepted the child, Adrienne went on to explore questions like her view of body and sexual intercourse, her own psychosexual development and complex feelings around sexual abuse by a loved relative which also meant her reviewing her choice of vowed celibacy. Coming to a new consciousness depends on inspiration

---

58 John 3:1-10 in *The New Jerusalem Bible*.

as well as courage. As with any visit or gift, persons are free to welcome and be open to the wisdom of the dream that then takes them deeper into life's journey.

Recovering Myth Consciousness

Like Dante, to whom Freud alludes at the beginning of *The Interpretation of Dreams,* we can find ourselves at times confused and lost "in a dark wood."[59] At those junctures, we need to rediscover myth, or what Jung calls an awareness of the divine life within and around us.[60] As the collective stories reiterate, the forest is the place that can provoke a needed change in attitude that takes us further into the meaning of our lives.

Midlife crises are acute examples of these transition points. People might leave a marriage, take time out from their religious vocation, change ministries, throw in their jobs, have an affair, experience health problems, or have an accident. Something dramatic occurs to halt people in their tracks and to re-assess where they are going in life. For finding a way through the difficult places of celibacy, I want to give an example of another kind of dream. Not a personal dream, not recounting a client's dream, but turning to one of the big human dreams as myth is sometimes described. I am sure that theologian, Dorothee Soelle would agree that myth, as she observed about the personal dream, has fallen out of modern consciousness and we need intentionally to recover its wisdom. In this book, you will come across a number of myths. In a transitional time in Israel, when the Hellenistic preceded the Roman occupation, Greek philosophy came into and greatly informed Jewish and subsequently Christian perspectives. In this way, Greek myths have filtered through to many cultures.

One such influential story is the Labyrinth that weaves through *Celibacy and Soul: Exploring the Depths of Chastity.* I chose the image of the Chartres labyrinth to go on the brochure of my analytical practice because it depicts what I understand as happening in the psychological process. Analysis, like celibate love, is a journey of initiation, and the old wisdom story offers a template for finding one's way.

---

59 Dante Alighieri, "Inferno," Canto 2:3, *The Divine Comedy*, Vol.1.
60 C.G. Jung, *Memories, Dreams, Reflections*, 373.

In the myth of the Cretan labyrinth, which is an earlier archetypal expression of the Chartres labyrinth, Ariadne is the daughter of King Minos. *Ariadne* is another name for *soul or psyche*. Her Cretan name which translates as "Utterly Pure" points to her virginal nature. Another of her titles is "Mistress of the Labyrinth."[61] It is not surprising that Ariadne knows and holds the clew that offers a means of escape from the Minotaur, which lies in wait at the centre of the labyrinth.

What is the point for celibacy and soul? Metaphorically, Ariadne, alias Psyche and otherwise named the Soul, holds a thread which sheds light. Some expressions like, "I've lost the thread," point out what it means to lose the gist of something. On such occasions, we need Ariadne to step forward. Her red thread is symbolic of feminine intuition and consciousness that are critical in the face of personal and world issues like famine and nuclear disaster, war, the plight of refugees and collapsing economies. What could motivate us to take up the thread collectively and look at such concerns?

Passion motivates psyche. In the myth, Ariadne falls in love with Theseus who has come to Crete to confront what has been killing his people. The clew is the simple and crucial gift that Ariadne gives to the heroic ego when he ventures into the labyrinth to face the monster. Ariadne tells Theseus to unwind the clew and, on his return, to allow the thread to guide him back. The heroic aspect, having listened to love, goes into the unknown where he slays the raging bull-man that is imprisoned at the centre. Following the thread out of the labyrinth, Theseus is able to take Ariadne by ship to Naxos. Something strange happens on that island and the heroic aspect forgets and abandons Ariadne. Finding and forgetting all seem part of the human drama and the hazard of passionate love. Yet in the wings, Dionysus, the god of love, is waiting for Ariadne to make her, his own.

While there are no actual minotaurs on this journey into understanding the potential of celibate chastity, facing up to anxieties and challenges is part of every human life whether people are celibate or not. The motifs of this myth that include courage, betrayal, perseverance, forgetfulness, abandonment, attraction, love and hope are constants in

---

61 A. Ronnberg & Kathleen Martin, *The Book of Symbols*, 714-715.

the human story. For everyone, a red thread or some light is essential to venture safely along and through the journey of life.

In the Chartres labyrinth, in contrast to the Cretan labyrinth, the same motifs are treated from a Christian slant. According to the Chartres rendition, every woman and man is a pilgrim like Christ following the path in to and out of Jerusalem: that is into the living, dying and rising cycle of Jesus Christ. The Self can choose whether or not to pick up the red thread of intuition and love, as did Christ, or to take the clew from Theseus. Psyche is naturally drawn to the audacious aspect of the Self that has the courage to give one's life for others. One Respondent actually mentions the Chartres labyrinth that became an important symbol for a major meeting of her Congregation and a daily walking ritual for her:

> ...at our Chapter, we used the symbol of the labyrinth to represent our journey as religious. I was on the planning committee and had a small clay labyrinth made for each person in the Congregation. We also made a large one in the grounds of the venue where the Chapter was held. I used to walk it each day before the sessions began. The symbol of a journey and walking it together is comforting for me. (Rose)

Rose is describing and deepening in herself an initiation journey that has long been practiced by pilgrims. There are three stages to this journey, which originate in the mystic tradition. I suggest that Rose, in her daily walking of the labyrinth, was consciously or unconsciously engaging in those stages of purgation, illumination and integration. The first stage of purgation occurs as the pilgrim walks into the labyrinth with her desire to come to quietness and for inner healing.

The second stage of illumination happens as the pilgrim walks the path and reaches the centre. Waiting with heart open in that empty space, she accepts whatever comes in the stillness. It could be a new insight on a problem or concern. The third stage of integration occurs as the pilgrim leaves the centre and follows the same path out. As she walks, the pilgrim asks for help from the Greater Self to bring the new awareness she has been given into the rest of life...and some creative possibility surfaces.

I want to underline the difference between the Cretan and the Chartres version of the myth. There is a critical difference between the archetypal heroic pattern of behaviour in the Christian labyrinth and its precursor, the Cretan labyrinth. In the Chartres labyrinth, and as a symbol of the Self, Christ does not kill the enemy, as does the heroic Theseus. Christ gives a new twist to the archetypal pattern by offering his own life for others and not abandoning psyche. I think chaste celibacy and celibate love is a way (as Christianity was originally called) about unlearning an old pattern and learning a new way, Christ's way, to work with and transform complexes like projections, scapegoating and violence.

Truly beautiful, right at the Centre of the labyrinth, is the symbol of the Rose of Sharon. Dorothee Soelle reminds us that the Christian Way, the way of the Sacred Feminine, is about acknowledging fear, consenting to love and surrendering to the unknown:

> Those who at any moment know why and to what end they do this or that, have shut themselves off from the power of the rose that blooms without a why or wherefore…All religions testify to the intersections of Eros and religion that arise from a sacred power.[62]

---

62 Dorothee Soelle, *The Silent Cry: Mysticism and Resistance*, 113.

CHAPTER THREE

COMPLEX PSYCHOLOGY

I have mentioned some difficult complexes that people have to handle—like projections, scapegoating and aggression. In the language of depth psychology, complexes are human situations that affect us and are fundamental and recurring. As the name suggests, they hold people together and can also tie them into knots! Complexes show in a person's feelings, relationships, life situations and dreams. You can glimpse them in people's expressions and in their tone of voice. Complexes can be uncomfortably meaningful for the individual and for others. While they provoke and can awaken the person to look to another level of awareness, strong emotions can also be destructive of oneself and of others.

Celibacy and spirituality are two such aspects that are emotionally charged and affect the inner and the outer life of persons. They may appear as mature or immature complexes in the individual's life and surface in a myriad of ways. Analytical psychology, which is sometimes called complex psychology or archetypal psychology, is particularly helpful for looking at the complex phenomenon; and for our purposes, the effects of celibate chastity on persons' lives.

At the turn of the 20th century, Carl Jung developed this psychology of the complexes. He proposed an archetypal frame for understanding recurring psychological patterns that people feel, get caught in and try to humanize.[63] Jung took the term *archetype* from St. Augustine's use of the word. Jung pictured archetypes as energy taking form in the complexes and becoming visible in people's positive and negative behav-

---

63   C.G. Jung, "The Structure and Dynamics of the Psyche," CW 8, ¶¶ 194-219.

iours. "Arché" meaning "the beginning of" is exemplified in Plato's analogy of original images. For Jung they represented forming principles from which the complexes arise.

The individual's task is to become conscious of and responsive to what impels psyche behind the affects that arouse us. Awareness of typical human patterns is portrayed in myths like the Labyrinth and is a way of understanding and working with the complexes of celibate chastity. The unnerving potency of an archetype may be heard in the following song: *Is there someone singing my life in their words?* [64]

Taken from a recording that Roberta Flack made popular, the lyrics hint at the drive of an archetype, an image of affect that swamps us, as in this example, when we fall in love. So too in an individual's attraction to a life choice of celibate love, the magnetism can come from a deceptive inner voice or from an interior call to be oneself. How one clarifies the difference implies that individuals recognise when they are deeply affected by an experience, reflect on what impresses them and respond from this ground. Going deliberately into this realm of experiential knowledge is at personal cost. I risk trusting my own experience and taking responsibility for life decisions rather than depending on an outside authority that will bear the buck for my failures or achievements. It can be frightening to own that level of freedom.

Analytical psychology encourages individuals to step into the unknown, daring to trust that life has purpose in spite of fear of the contrary. It hypothesises that archetypal images residing in the unconscious are at work creatively in the individual and in the collective psyche across time and space. In *Celibacy and Soul,* I am exploring particular archetypal images that inform virginity and that lead individuals to consciously choose celibate chastity which also seems to choose them. In a later section we will stay longer with some of those archetypal images that have come through the questionnaires and interviews. Now I go further into Jung's perspective to see why his view is an appropriate framework with which to look at celibate chastity.

Jung's psychological work (1875-1961) is based on the interplay of archetypes in the psyche. He envisaged that there are predispositions

---

64   Roberta Flack, *Killing Me Softly*, CD.

behind the complexes that shape human identity, which he termed
"archetypes." Jung proposed they could take different forms in the life
of a person yet came out of a common creative source that wants our
psychic development.

The archetype, or pattern, of consecrated celibacy has a perennial
aspect while expressions of the archetype do and must change with different times and circumstances. Frank's comment takes account of the
shifts that have occurred in the way that women and men have expressed
the archetype of celibacy:

> *Celibates have been many during the past millennia and have
> done many beautiful things and given many services, particularly
> to the poor and needy.* (Frank)

This man notices the beauty and energy in people who authentically
live and grow into the archetype of celibacy. In *Symbols of Transformation*, Jung develops the energetic view of the archetypes with his concept
of libido as psychic energy. It was broader than Freud's view of libido.
Suffice to say here that Freud considered libido as sexual desire while
Jung widened that picture with his description of psychic energy as passionate desire.[65] This perspective on the nature of libido as energy coming from a deep source within the personal and collective unconscious
helps us psychologically to situate the choice of celibate commitment.

To connect with one's inner wellspring, Jung found that a symbolic
life is essential. He proposed a rediscovery of healing symbols through
recognizing the complexes that are rooted in the archetypes.

> The years...when I pursued the inner images were the most
> important time of my life...my entire life consisted in elabo-
> rating what had burst forth from the unconscious...the numi-
> nous beginning, which contained everything, was then..."[66]

To enrich with example, I want to return to that earlier extract from
Roberta Flack's song. The lyrics picture a complex of archetypal energies

---

65 C.G. Jung, "Freud and Psychoanalysis," CW 4, ¶ 252; C.G. Jung, "Symbols of
Transformation," CW 5, ¶¶ 185ff.
66 C.G. Jung, *The Red Book: Liber Novus*, vii.

that can spin one into projection and obsession that are both wonderful and consuming. When one is fascinated by someone or something, the intensity of feeling indicates that a complex and an underlying archetype are activated. It may be unclear as to whether the voice singing one's life is a call to love or to infatuation. Merging with the beloved or with a high ideal can be so attractive and exhilarating and yet destructive of authentic love, as Tim remarks:

> *I think that most religious whom I have known have spent some time of their lives in risky relationships (compromising romantic relationships)—and most have learned how to accept limits.*

It seems that for individuals to grow in mature love, there needs to be an acknowledgment of human vulnerability, and of some distance and courage to look seriously at reality. Identifying with an archetype, instead of exploring its meaning, can block the discovery of one's own potential and be destructive of others. I am saying that, for celibate chastity to be generative, individuals need to ponder how to embody this vocation to celibacy and spirituality. Frances reflects not only on how her understanding of celibacy has changed over time, but on how she has been changed:

> *From not doing something to doing and being something. From negative to positive. From denial to enjoyment (in spite of the hardships).*

What do symbols contribute to psyche and to the life dynamic? Now, as in earlier times, they offer forceful, indefinable psychic energies that can inspire and conspire against individuals and societies. They may no longer be acknowledged as a divine power yet their impact can be seen and felt. Their *unknown creative something* incites and is beyond words. We may experience their power in music as in the nocturnes of Liszt and Chopin, which are sometimes called "songs without words." Let me give another example of the power of symbol from my research. A few Respondents mentioned their profession ring as a simple and strong symbol that reminds them of their vowed celibate commitment. During this exploration, we will take up other symbols and images of celibacy and spirituality—including the title of this book—and see how they offer insight and voice to understanding the complexes of celibacy and spirituality.

Another important aspect from Analytical Psychology that is helpful for looking at *Celibacy and Soul* is that of paradox. In the Jungian framework the meeting of opposites is accepted as part of life and potentially creative. Any conflict is an opportunity for individual growth. Given that the subject of celibate chastity is controversial and that it generates a questioning and debate, accepting paradox or some inner conflict can make eminent sense to those who are searching and wanting to be open to growth.

I propose that encouraging those who find themselves struggling with celibacy to go deeper and search out its meaning allows space for a change of attitude and heart akin to a spiritual conversion that the Gospels call *metanoia*.[67] Jung preferred to call the process one of *individuation* where a deliberate going into the unknown is essential for any real inner transformation of the personality.[68] John Terry expresses both sides of paradox and the grace that can arise in working with positive and negative:

> *Celibacy is a starting point, a boundary, a condition that I make,*
> *do and live with. Though in itself a sterile state, I think for me*
> *it has been graced.*

The failure to take the inner journey, the journey to one's centre, to ask the difficult questions and to sit with 'I don't know' can also lead to a metamorphosis. Lack of courage to face difficulty can lead one into the shadow side of individuation, which is perversion: about which sexual abuse in the church is a grim reminder. To go into or to avoid facing one's life task has consequences. For those participating in such reflection, a healthy sacrifice of unhelpful binding patterns is implied. One comes to know, through personal experience, that growing in consciousness is creative and generative of one's being even if it can also be difficult. As Louise remarks:

---

67   Matthew 3:8 & Mark 1:4 in *The New Jerusalem Bible*.
68   C.G. Jung, Visions, Notes of the Seminars given in 1930-1934, vol. 1, 372.

Along the journey there have been fragile patches but basically my focus has been on God and returning to the centre. I have grown because of my failures...I can say like St. Augustine, "Oh! Happy fault!" The experience has made me more loving and understanding of myself and others.

This comment points back to the quest-i-on (the quest I am on!). In that sorting and sifting process, Jung identified a pivotal question: "What is the particular difficulty in life that disturbs and from which I try to escape?" That question prompts those who consciously want to face their personal dilemma to let go of an unhealthy narcissism and laziness and to take up their destiny. It is why I am searching out the value of celibate chastity.

A Dynamic View

In searching, questioning and understanding more of the choice for vowed chastity, Depth Psychology offers a dynamic view. It grew in response to people's asking questions about their lives that scientific rationalism could not satisfy. The discrediting of the sacred and the failure of religious institutions to meet the spiritual needs of individuals have not quashed the religious instinct. Although church attendances have dropped and there are fewer people seeking a vowed religious commitment, there is an abiding interest in spirituality. Pointing to the religious instinct, Jung noticed the factor of chance or accident that keeps popping up and prompts individuals to ask "Why?" when the unforeseen occurs. Let me illustrate with Catherine's help:

One experience in my life is outstanding. My niece was killed in a car accident when she was 17 and we were close. I couldn't believe God had let this happen and I was very angry with God. In my grief I called out to God one night, how could you let this happen after all I have done for you? (meaning a celibate way of life). I distinctly heard the answer...there are no bargains...it is not about you and I will do this and I will do that. It is about love. I had come through a real crisis of faith to a new understanding of my life choice—this was 22 years ago and is as real to me now as then.

The phenomenon of accidental happenings was viewed in many traditional cultures as reason to appease a threatening Spirit power. Jung saw chance events as meaningful coincidences whose synchronicity invited us to some new awareness. In the tragic circumstances that the previous Respondent described, Catherine tells of her struggle to make sense of her niece's death. Catherine had committed her life to God and found her vowed commitment did not save her family from tragedy. By staying with the grief of that event, she shifted from a sense of entitlement and a bargaining relationship with God to a deeper understanding of unconditional love. With a Jungian interpretation, there appears to be an intentional energy acting and prompting individuals and communities to wake up to some vital realization beyond our unconscious complexes and projections.[69]

A dynamic view of the psyche was shared by Jung, Freud and Adler. In the psychological framework that is progressively taking shape here, I am giving broad sweeps to each of their perspectives and to key psychological developments they inspired. As I reflect on celibacy, I am drawing on relevant aspects from these various psychological views, yet my anchoring and main thread for probing the transformative effects of celibate love is Jungian psychology. The latter seems in tune with the dynamism of life, of spirituality and of celibacy, as Peter endorses:

> *I have slowly moved from seeing celibacy as something static and negative to seeing it more as a positive dynamic process.*

Freud had pioneered a new consciousness in psychology. His psychoanalytical theory maintained that psychic development relied exclusively on the sexual character and the aggressive nature of libido that shaped psyche into an interacting structure of id, ego and superego.

This Freudian view emphasized the healing of emotional disturbance by discovering its unconscious and harmful sexual cause. The damaging complex calls for stronger ego-consciousness in dealing with the sexual problem. By avoiding the conflict, individuals repress energy and are left with nameless anxiety and/or other symptoms. In Freudian terms, the supposition is that the celibate woman or man is caught somewhere

---

69   C.G. Jung, "Civilization in Transition," CW 10, ¶ 118.

in an incestuous relationship with a castrating mother and a wrathful father: an Oedipal dilemma. To this implication, I let you hear Thomas' reply:

> *Rubbish! Religious are a mixed lot. Some may have variations in sexual drive at different times...It is beautiful to know those who are fully sexually alive and have dedicated their all to God—not a carcass!*

While Jung did not reject Freud's reductive approach to understanding inner conflict, he widened it. In Jung's "constructive" approach, which I am renaming a "generative" approach, he envisages that persons' struggles and their symbolic lives are expressing a desire for more life. Jung takes the human struggle beyond psyche's masked strivings to deal with human mortality. In psychic conflict, analytical psychology recognises our continuing efforts to re-connect with a creative inner source that lies in the unconscious and is reached and transformed by way of imagination. Rose expresses her growing through conflict in this way:

> *In my younger years as a religious woman...there was a constant theme that I wasn't good enough, that I should be different from who I was, a tension between how I experienced myself and the kind of person whom I thought others expected me to be. I haven't thought consciously about what celibacy means for a long time. I certainly feel freedom and fulfilment in many ways. I wonder if that is a function of being older and more accepting of myself?*

Another helpful perspective that views conflict as potentially meaningful for the individual comes from Adler's psychology.[70] He proposed that the power complex is at work in a person's unease, which shows if one constantly swings between extreme feelings of inferiority and superiority. Adler also drew attention to psychosomatic symptoms as symbolic expressions of being complexed. For example, some people come down with a bad back or maybe migraines when they feel stressed. The body often carries the shadow of psyche's tension.

Jung could accept emphases coming from different psychological perspectives because he saw that the sources of the psychic disturbance

---

70 Henri F. Ellenberger, *The Discovery of the Unconscious*, 571.

could come from a number of jarring complexes—including sex and power and, particularly for people in middle age, loss of a religious attitude. Victor White, friend of Jung and Dominican priest, was even more adamant that human development required inner conflict: as long as it is constructive.[71] To give an example, I asked Respondents in the questionnaire about their views on masturbation. Dominic describes an interim stage where one grows through this human conflict to a deeper chastity:

> *Masturbation is an offence against religious celibate chastity but many have to cope with loss of control and have to struggle to maintain or re-establish continence. This is part of life and it's a shame that religious formation seldom treats this question honestly.*

Dominic's comment about the lack of education in understanding celibacy is wisely Adlerian. Research supports the importance of psychosexual education. This gap is now being addressed by many Religious Orders and in priestly formation. Dominic's criticism raises questions of how one deals with shadow or uncomfortable material. In *The Interpretation of Dreams*, Freud proposed the existence of the personal unconscious that acted as a kind of refuse dump for what was inadmissible conflict in people's lives. Jung's clinical experience led him to suggest an additional supporting layer (that he called the collective unconscious) in the human psyche. Individuals could then access and work with the discarded aspect, which might then become the gold of new insight.

In facing the unconscious surfacing in our waking lives and dreams, Jung proposed that we meet not only a negative personal unconscious but the unknown Other from whom the individual may reclaim needed energy. For growing in integrity, we must ask tough questions and face the shadow of the unknown. Jung termed the shadow as one of the difficult archetypes of the unconscious whose positive and negative potential is neatly captured by Canadian poet and songwriter, Leonard Cohen, when he sings of the crack in all reality that allows in the light.[72]

---

71   Ann Conrad-Lammers, *In God's Shadow: The Collaboration of Victor White and C.G. Jung*, 203-215.

72   Leonard Cohen, "Anthem" in *More Best of Leonard Cohen*, CD.

The shadow can be helpful if one trusts one's instinctual warning to become alert to what is phoney in a situation. In meeting with the unknown, there comes a critical point when people see that they feel in a certain way and recognise pride, hatred and greed either in themselves or in another. I don't quite feel the exuberance of St. John of the Cross, who plunges into the dark night. It seems, however, that travelling into the dark night is essential.[73] I find that such a journey requires respect for me and for others. It involves being more truthful about my femininity, the importance of discovering my singular way along with a need for affection that does not seek dependence but more confidence in who I am. Louise makes a similar response:

> *I've lived a happy life—fulfilled. I think if I married at 20 when I entered the convent, I would have made a mess of it. I could happily marry now. I think I've learned to communicate and am more mature.*

In acknowledging personal shadow, there can be a new recognition where it is possible that the poison in the shadow can be taken out. Accompanying people in seeing reality empathically means helping them to observe themselves as they would observe others and carefully to put into words what they see even when that reality is unpleasant. When this occurs, there is the possibility that instead of living the shadow and being depleted of energy, individuals may find replenishment for their lives.

Forgiving is For Giving

Dividing the word *forgiving* into its salient parts of *for giving* shows how love and hurt can be linked. Synchronistically, I received a phone call from a friend when I was writing on this subject of for-giving and letting go. She was reflecting on a painful situation of rejection and could say many years after the event, *I am glad it happened. I wouldn't be the person I am now.*

---

73 St. John of the Cross, *The Spiritual Canticle and Poems*, stanzas 1, 5.

Self-reflection invites us to go beyond the darkness in personal experience and family history and learn from injury, illusion and unmet expectations. Searchers may gradually discover in themselves a capacity to trust again as they face what initially hurt and paralysed them. In conversation with Peter, one of the Respondents, I glimpsed this dynamic moving through his reflections. He spoke of how a strict family upbringing and a negative attitude to sex initially influenced his view of celibacy. Then he came to a choice of celibacy for its practicality. Peter is a missionary. It was the experience of falling in love that deeply changed him. For the first time, this man found himself choosing celibacy as a value in and for his life in spite of the pain involved. Why? And now I quote Peter: *ultimately I feel sure that celibacy is a call to happiness.*

To come to a place of forgiving and letting go, each person meets the shadow as adversary, as light-bringer and sometimes as the deep split to which one cannot be reconciled: I mean the darkness of the collective shadow which is shown in acts of racism, in the rigidity of fundamentalism and in the sexual abuse of vulnerable people. Those expressions of shadow that Jung described as situations of archetypal or unrelated evil cannot be accepted because they inflict mindless violence on others, oneself and the world. Yet even these circumstances can reinvigorate our values when we stand up and refuse to accept their brutality.

Elizabeth Kamarck Minnich, American philosopher and feminist scholar, writes of a transforming knowledge, which frees one's thinking and behaviour.[74] Mistakes and failures can either prompt people to be more aware and compassionate or cloud awareness and result in irretrievable damage. Picking up the guiding thread through *Celibacy and Soul*, I wonder: when is the shadow of celibacy generative, and when does it turn destructive?

From Freud and Jung's clinical work, it seems that when sexuality is covered over and repressed, Eros turns negative and becomes control, hatred and manipulation. Tragically, there are disturbing examples of celibate people perverting Eros and using their power to hurt innocent people—the grooming of children for sex, the rape of the vulnerable, the discrimination against women in the Catholic Church, the loss of faith

---

74   Elizabeth Kamarck Minnich, *Transforming Knowledge*, 190-191.

in community. There are also less dramatic examples of sexual activity, dishonesty and irresponsibility, which Peter articulates:

> *There are a number of priests whose culture accepts sex and having children as absolutely essential. They have been unable to break with their culture and although they have made a commitment to celibacy they live like married men. But unlike married men they don't take responsibility for their actions.*

The reality is that we all cause needless suffering and experience some measure of psychological splitting in our lives—whether or not we are celibate. Traumas of living that have not been properly worked through can warp thinking, attitudes and emotions. Wounded and wounding individuals can make others suffer because of unacknowledged pain. Referring to this phenomenon, Donald Kalsched draws an analogy of psyche's self-care system that turns destructive.[75] For the celibate and the non-celibate, distortion can show in a person's hardness, discontent and coldness. John Terry sees this danger in celibacy when *it colludes with an early tendency to withdraw from company and not relate.* Fear then hardens into a determination: *I will NEVER allow anyone to get that close again.*

Moving forward is more than acknowledging one's anger and hatred and forgiving significant others.[76] The process of letting go of these difficult emotions involves getting at what the anger and hatred are about. That exploration demands an honest and painful confrontation with the shadow in which it is important to have a trusted accompanier. This process takes, but it also goes beyond, ego-decision and ego-strength. It is not something that we can always give ourselves or get off a shelf. What happens relies on grace, personal good intent and the capacity to bear genuine suffering.

I want to spell out a confusion that can occur with forgiveness and reconciliation. There are situations where one may forgive and yet where reconciliation with an abusive Other may be impossible, inappropriate or even dangerous. It is a matter of self-care and common sense, just as you wouldn't rest your hand on the hotplate of a stove or go swimming

---

75 Donald Kalsched, *The Inner World of Trauma*, 2.
76 Jan Wiener, *The Therapeutic Relationship*, 493-508.

with a shark. That graciousness or grace can happen, and pardon and reconciliation can be possible, gives hope, restores inner peace and offers healing. These elements are heard in Louise's response. In her questionnaire she said that in therapy she had worked through many of her early difficulties with sexuality and intimacy that she names:

> *When I had an unhealthy sexual friendship I realised how sexual I was. The drive I believe came from my looking for un-met 'mother love' as my mother suffered PND (Postnatal Depression) when I was born.*

Figure 3: Story of the Wolves Within, by Dorothy Grills. Source: Image courtesy the artist. Reprinted with permission.

A story from the Cherokee Indians metaphorically conveys what is involved in this dynamic of forgiving and letting go. It goes like this:

Elder: "Grandson, within each one of us there are two wolves in our heart. Each wolf has a different diet. One wolf feeds on kindness, truth, honesty, loyalty, and generosity. The other wolf feeds on bullying, lies, snarling, anger, and disloyalty. In the end, only one wolf can live. The other dies."

Grandson: "Which one lives, Grandfather?"

Elder: "The one that you feed the most."[77]

---

77   Eva Solomon csj, Personal Sharing, 2014.

Com-Passion

Evolutionary philosopher, Brian Swimme, suggests that one takes a step into com-passion by simply waking up to a wonder in nature. Notice what captures your attention today. It can become a "contemplation of ultimacy" that sounds akin to the transformative movement that Wilfred Bion, British psychoanalyst, recognised as happening interiorly. That awareness of "the ultimate reality" in life deepens one's patience and empathy.[78] In his awakening, one Respondent named *the healing Christ* as key. Georg noticed that in contemplating this wounded healer, he became more accepting of himself and of people who are lonely and isolated. Patrick also recognises links between celibacy, feeling one's own vulnerability and compassion for others:

> *I can't live a celibate life on my own. It's only in relationship that it makes sense. It helps me know my own poverty and utter dependence on the living loving presence of God. This enables me to identify with others especially the downtrodden and outcast.*

In Christian terms, the Chartres labyrinth depicts the journey into compassion as the pilgrim metaphorically follows Jesus Christ through his living, death and resurrection: the Paschal mystery. In the questionnaires, Respondents consistently name Jesus Christ as drawing them into com-passion. Some refer to passages like that from Matthew's Gospel…"whatever you did to the least of these brothers and sisters of mine, you did it to me."[79] In a later section, we will look more closely at why Jesus Christ is an important archetype or recurring pattern for celibacy. For now, as an image of the deeper Self, and a compassionate presence, Thomas says it simply:

> *Not sure about Christ, but Jesus plays the role of down to earth and feet on the ground model. He's someone I can identify with in the human struggle.*

---

78   Brian Swimme, "Comprehensive Compassion," http://thegreatstory.org/SwimmeWIE.pdf. Retrieved June 8, 2014; Wilfred Bion, *Attention and Interpretation*, 26.

79   Matthew 25:35-46 in *The New Jerusalem Bible*.

What is the place of suffering in the process of individuation and becoming celibate? In explaining the individuation process, Jung refers to the symbol of the cross and I am reminded of the multi-coloured cross, with the golden figure of the Crucified that two friends gave me at the start of my writing journey. The cross is integral to Christian spirituality and to celibacy. "In the contemplation of the Crucified Christ… all vocations find their inspiration…and in particular, the gift of the consecrated life."[80] Several of the Respondents speak about the meaning of the Passion in their celibate lives especially at times of unavoidable suffering. As Catherine shared earlier, the compassion of God does not save from the cross of suffering. What stands out is a faithful love that is reflected in the Crucified and Risen Christ who "cannot disown his own self."[81] From this perspective, Jane reflected on her ordeal of surviving cancer and being emotionally abandoned by a good friend and also becoming aware of the love of the Other who would never abandon her:

> It was a painful but graced time because I realised that Christ, not this friend, was the centre of my life…During a recent retreat, the word 'surrender' became significant and I spent time reflecting on God's surrender to us in the act of creation, in Jesus' self-giving life, death and resurrection. I, in turn, am invited to 'surrender' to Christ by receiving this self-gift.

Peter gives another insight into how he stays in that creative place of suffering separateness and togetherness:

> What celibacy strives for is true solitude—even when I'm alone, I am most together with others. We have to suffer through our loneliness and turn it…into aloneness: solitude. Brother Stendl-Rast taught me this and I'm beginning to experience the truth of this in the Kalahari—in the aloneness of prayer I'm closer to the people I work for and can be lovingly with them. All this and yet I experience a yearning for a special Other and can be sexually

---

80   John Paul 11, *Vita Consecrata*, ¶ 26, http://www.vatican.va/roman_curia/congregations/ccscrlife/documents/hf_jp-ii_exh_25031996_vita-consecrata_en.html. Retrieved June 6, 2014.
81   2 Timothy 1:13, in *The New Jerusalem Bible*.

aroused. There is ambivalence or ambiguity in everything but I suppose we have to learn to love in the ambiguity.

This advice sounds rather like the importance of patiently holding the tension of opposing forces when one is feeling alone, in a dilemma or in a complex that seems unsolvable. For this reason, Jung refers to the psychological task as a work that can sometimes go against our nature. Who, apart from a masochist, wants times of suffering? When unavoidable suffering occurs in our lives, it takes a lot of trust and strength to wait in this space of "suspension" which is, according to the Christian view, the place of the cross.[82]

Is this a healthy attitude to take when celibate chastity is a burden? Frank's answer is *Yes, as long as the dynamic of the cross is recognised.* Suffering is not for its own sake but about coming to life and to love especially through experiences of vulnerability where we know that grace is somehow at work. Frank clarifies that holding the tension of opposites is essential to becoming oneself and in becoming celibate:

Earlier on, I tended to hold the image of Christ on his cross: now I hold the image of Jesus Christ come back into our flesh, His wounds showing. Earlier on, I thought of Jesus as Christ the Victor: now I know Jesus as the One of the Trinity who came into our flesh to fail...and he knows what we experience in our failures. Earlier on, I felt complete conviction that I was to make myself holy so that I could be his companion: now I recognise that he came to sinners, to me, a sinner, and I will grow holy when and how he chooses. And I am content.

In *Psychological Types,* Jung demonstrates another set of polarities that can be an experience of crucifixion. He describes polarities of attitude and of functioning within individuals that can feel like being stretched on a cross. It is a struggle to bear tensions in ourselves and in our interactions with others who might see life in another way because of differences in typology and experience. Sometimes, shadow emotions flare when people try to insist that their outlook is the only view.

---

82 C.G. Jung, "The Archetypes and the Collective Unconscious," CW 9, I, ¶ 574.

I can admit that in this work on *Celibacy and Soul: Exploring the Depths of Chastity*, I have become increasingly aware of the clash of opposites within me. There is a struggle between my organizing functions of thinking and feeling and my gathering functions of sensation and intuition. Finding a balance between quiet work and outer exploration and activity is a constant tension.[83] Writing requires strong attitudes of introversion. I also need extraversion, the psychological term for the more popular use of extroversion, which means enjoying the company of others. The play between the functions is an uphill battle. I can identify with Psyche, intent on and also a bit obsessed with completing the tasks of sorting, sifting, collecting and gathering: and she has good reason to stay on task. She wants to find Eros—and that is also my desire.

Another and most obvious polarity is the feminine and masculine. Out of their union, the child is born. Jung applied this generative synthesis of opposites to the inner as well as the outer world and he called these opposites *the animus in and for woman*, and *the anima in and for man*. That word "generative" is a bit cumbersome but it is full of meaning about a blossoming of life and we will gradually unpack this concept.

Just as in childhood, one learns from parents, family and culture what personality attributes are acceptable, so the child assimilates, adapts to and rebels against those learned ways of what it is to be woman or man in a particular setting. When a woman encounters the animus as an actual man, she gets a glimpse of her inner masculine. Similarly a man encounters his anima in an actual woman and so connects with his inner feminine aspects. Those authentic meetings bring celibate and non-celibate to ourselves. At times in this writing, my animus strength or inner masculine has felt focused, reliable and purposeful. At other times I have felt floundering and uncertain as to whether I could see the work through. Often I have needed to meet that Other in an actual man (and woman) and not only on an inner level. I am grateful to men and women friends who have helped me to stay inspired. It is essential that masculine and feminine energies find a way to meet, even if sexuality is not actively lived. I know that their meeting sparks off the passionate

---

83   Jane Wheelwright, *Death of a Woman*, 199.

energy of Eros, as this next woman also knows and voices her appreciation:

> *Having many male/female relationships, having an intimate relationship—knowing the intensity of deep sharing and receiving—and turning this love outward to others!*

In her comment we also hear an implication of what happens when relationship with the Other is lacking or destructive: the personality is hampered. Scientist-priest Teilhard de Chardin goes so far as to say it is a lie to suppress the sexual polarity of the Spirit.[84] Looking further afield at some historical figures that are spiritual and celibate, we see the remarkable benefits for society that come from the meeting of feminine and masculine energies. Examples include, Vincent de Paul and Louise de Marillac who pioneered a new concern for people in poverty, Teresa of Avila and John of the Cross who brought a renewal in spirituality, Mary MacKillop and Julian Tenison Woods who made education accessible to poor people in and beyond Australia's shores.

Passages in Life

I want to add to the snapshot I gave earlier, of stages in psyche's development with this section on Passages. By considering how depth psychology views these stages, I think the positive and negative potential of celibacy for people's lives becomes clearer. In a comment, Jan, a contemporary woman religious, points out that periods of celibacy occur for most people at some time in their lives.

In some older cultures, there are stages of life where celibacy is valued and even prescribed. For example in traditional Hindu culture, four stages of life were proposed: student, householder, forest dweller and ascetic. In Western society, the stages of life refer to what it means to be a child, an adolescent and adult. This comment by a Respondent shows his elderly father's experience. Because of medical reasons, Peter's father was no longer sleeping with his wife. He said:

---

84   Pierre Teilhard de Chardin, "The Evolution of Chastity," in *Toward the Future*, 72-79.

Son, I love your mother more with all my heart. I love her more
than ever before, when we were courting or newly married.
(Peter reflected) I would understand celibate love to be something
like this—a deeply human love transcending the 'genital-sexual'
love—a love more and more conformed to the love of Christ.

In contemporary society, the emphasis is on individuals. Psychosexual maturity is variously described by different schools of psychology. Freud identified progressive stages of individual psychic development as oral, anal, phallic, the latency period and genital phase, where each stage followed after successful transition from the former. For psychic development, there must be some interaction between the person's biological drives and his or her environment.

I have already mentioned Erikson's metaphor of generativity that will become a recurring motif. In describing the maturational path, Erikson describes eight stages of ego-development. According to this model, the individual gradually resolves trust over distrust and then faces some conflict over autonomy versus shame and from there meets another maturational task on the journey towards self-realization.[85] Similarly, Jung proposes that individuals have to face tasks set by their biological, sexual, aesthetic and spiritual make-up and their resolution affects people's subsequent development.

In the first stage of life, Jung describes the individual as appropriately youthful, naïve ("puer" or "puella") envisaging life's possibilities. One of the Respondents found in her life that people go through a similar developmental process when they vow celibacy:

Perhaps similar to the steps in a human relationship: you fall in
love, certain experiences of 'ensobering' (he is not always available
when I want, how I imagine etc.), temptation to leave him, new
and perhaps deeper love (accepting God's freedom). Or perhaps
one day even beginning once more at the beginning? (Judith)

Celibacy threatens to turn negative only when the limitations of what I am (and am not) are not accepted. Another Respondent makes

---

85   Erik Erikson, *Identity and the Life Cycle*, 247-269.

a similar observation about a gradual process of maturing into psycho-sexual celibacy:

> *The late developers need support and sympathy as they struggle to re-commit themselves to the vow/promise made, or to make an alternative choice if celibacy within the life chosen is no longer growthful for them.* (Elizabeth)

In psyche's development, the archetypes of animus and anima that we spoke of as polarities in the personality, act like a bridge to the Self.[86] Jung perceived the person's feminine side as the aspect of feeling, and his or her masculine aspect as thinking. These categories of Eros and Logos were not meant to thrust a reductive label onto the person because of gender or typology. They provide a blueprint, not a stereotype, of two different kinds of expanding consciousness that everyone needs to develop in subsequent interpersonal and intrapersonal relationships.

Jung recognised that psyche is shaped not only by our relationships and environment. He observed that psyche has access to an archetypal core and capacity to respond in a unique way to life's experience. There lies the hope. In the process of individuating, the potential and onus is on the individual to grow up, and out of unconscious conformity to set patterns. They include gender, class and racial stereotypes, and can shift as persons search out and choose their true ground.

When an unconscious content clearly comes to consciousness through a dream or relationship or life dilemma, the person needs to take an ego decision to act on his or her insight. Jung refers to this transcendent symbol as "the tertium non datur."[87] In religious language it is simply called "grace." As the third element, this transforming symbol brings together the conflicting opposites. One must take action or regress psychologically as Brendan describes:

> *Celibacy means freedom—after one goes through the anguish and crises of growth…It is a gift if one gives oneself totally to God in trust and goes where God leads us. It needs to be freely embraced/desired or it is not true celibacy.*

---

86 C.G. Jung, Visions, Notes of the Seminar Given in 1930-1934, vol.1, 203.
87 C.G. Jung, "The Structure and Dynamic of the Psyche," CW 8, ¶¶ 181ff.

The prompt which resolves psychic dilemma is a gift that comes from beyond the ego. It has a sense of grace because of its numinous dimension and hence a transcendent function. I recall those lovely lines in *The Divine Comedy*, where Dante describes grace appearing and transforming the personality. In the words of Virgil, "Love moved me and makes me speak."[88] In Jungian terms, Virgil is a shadow figure of Dante who prepares him for her whose name actually means "a blessing."

This blessing, Beatrice Portinari, comes to Dante because of the compassion of another feminine figure—the Virgin Mary. Yet even these anima and mediating figures transform. For Beatrice points them all to Christ as the One bringing Dante home to himself.[89] In the legend of the Dark Virgin that I shared at the beginning of this book, Mary appears to Diego asking him to build a church not for her but for Jesus Christ. The point is that the Virgin's role, the celibate's role, is to direct people's attention to the Other.

The transcendent aspect of the imago Dei in every psyche urges us to go through ignorance and blindness that St. John of the Cross describes as the way of "the darksome night…on love's journey."[90] Jane speaks in similar terms about Christ as an inner guiding figure of this Other:

Christ is the gate and the dark brightness in my heart.

The transforming movement comes from the Self and enables persons to make the inner passage to awareness and into a capacity for mature love. The result may not be a visible work of art but its touch can provoke an inner change in people that is undeniably aesthetic and simply beautiful.

While each person's situation is unique and particular, the symbolic world contained in myth and religion can bring light to one's personal dilemma and human destiny. So Jung speaks of living archetypes.[91] The problem of contemporary women and men is a sense of being alienated from their symbolic life and isolated from self and others. The archetyp-

---

88   Dante Alighieri, "Inferno," Canto I: 72, *The Divine Comedy*, Vol.1.

89   Dante Alighieri, "Paradiso," Canto XXXIII: 131-132, 142-145, *The Divine Comedy*, Vol.3.

90   St. John of the Cross, *Upon a Darksome Night*, stanza 1, 5.

91   C.G. Jung, "The Symbolic Life," CW 18, ¶ 1529.

al perspective of Jungian psychology accepts, appreciates and affirms the symbolic life for understanding identity, conflict and meaning in life. It is a view that is broad enough to give a psychological value to celibacy and its place in the post-modern world.

This psychological framework is especially valuable as I consider the Spirit of our times. The zeitgeist is increasingly shaped by a global capitalism and a communications revolution that have the potential to bring people closer together yet result in greater inequalities and repression. The confusing complexity can be gauged from the dilemmas in the European Union, in the Iridium Satellite system, in the inhumane treatment of refugees and in the paralysed power of forums for dialogue (like the United Nations) and in the terrible poverty in the world.

Progress in technological communications, bridging of geographical distances, military interventions and political strategies do not necessarily bring understanding. One social critic characterises this age as one of a malignant sadness that is often somatised by individuals. Statistics from the World Health Organization predict that major depression will be the world's second most debilitating disease in 2020.[92]

Drugs have helped many people predisposed to emotional and mental illness, and communication networks have opened new horizons. Yet they have not offered lasting relief to global greyness. In *Grand Design*, Professor Stephen Hawking and Leonard Mlodinow propose their solution through a unified theory of scientific laws that they term, "M Theory" which hypothesizes that the many universes are created out of nothing and go into nothing.[93] The new scientific mythology ramps up existential emptiness.

Against this backdrop, my clinical experience as a Jungian analyst points to archetypal patterns affecting and wanting to break through people's lives, and offer hope whether people are celibate or not celibate. This self-reflective passage takes time.

---

92   Anthea Lawson, "Four of these People are Depressed," in *The Times*, 18, May 8,1999; C.J. Murray & A.D. Lopez, *The Global Burden of Disease: a Comprehensive Assessment of Mortality and Disability from Diseases, Injuries and Risk Factors in 1990 and Projected to the Year 2020.*
93   S. Hawking & L. Mlodinow, *The Grand Design.*

I am not disparaging the need for necessary medication nor short-term therapies. The problem is when people do not become conscious of a deeper malaise and its constructive potential. In a telling phrase, psyche's ailments can be dumbed down and anaesthetized because the talking cure is costly in money and time. The dualism of body and Spirit seems to have shifted to the tendency to disregard both body and psyche.

In *Celibacy and Soul*, I am proposing a framework of Analytical Psychology to consider celibacy because its dynamic perspective recognises the interrelationship of body, soul and Spirit. It re-affirms what great religions have understood—that symbols are alive and active in the dreams, emotions and life situations of people. Given time and space to work, they can help us to make the passage and reconnect with our inner source of strength and meaning behind the complexes. Georg's story about his reason for choosing to become a celibate priest illustrates and shows the passages that wove through his life from childhood to the present because he picked up and followed the thread of love:

> *When I was a little boy...three years I think, I disappeared and everybody was afraid of what had happened to me...Then I came back with our cat in my arms. The family asked "Where were you?" I said "I was in the church and I prayed." "What did you pray for?" "I prayed for a man." (This man was a painter who was a friend of our family and he was very sick...Well he died. From what I learned, I think he died at the same time I was praying for him).*
>
> *...a little story but it was pretty typical. I was a very alive boy but I was also very religious...I think this was the reason...that when I came back from the War—I was a prisoner of war, I was 18 years old...that I started to study history, but after 2 semesters, I changed because I had a strong feeling that God wanted me to become a priest. First I didn't want this because I had a girlfriend at the time and I said "No, no this is not for me." Then after some months this resistance disappeared. More and more I thought I will do this...I became a priest. It was, I think, a strong emotional relationship to Jesus.*

CHAPTER FOUR

THE ART OF CONVERSATION AND
IMAGES BEHIND CELIBACY

In *Celibacy and Soul: Exploring the Depths of Chastity*, I have taken a cue from psychoanalysis by engaging in the art of conversation. The replies to the questionnaires and a dialogue with Respondents raised significant images of the archetype of virginity which lie behind celibacy. The conversational process gave creative space for the symbols to unfold.

If the intent of an archetype is to be embodied, this representative group of contemporary women and men are flesh and blood expressions of what happens when the vocation of the virgin archetype is deliberately lived.

> ...the living Spirit is eternally renewed through the history of (humanity)...changing blossoms on the stem of the eternal tree.[94]

Being a participant-observer gives me some freedom and some impartiality. As I look at celibacy and spirituality as a cross-cultural phenomenon, I see recurring patterns of celibacy and spirituality lived by individuals in many places and at various times in history.

In exploring the archetype behind consecrated celibacy, there is the problem of silence that comes with all areas of intimacy. The silence both protects and clouds the meaning of this archetypal expression. In the Prelude, I mentioned my own silence that has to do with an earlier

---

94 C.G. Jung, "Psychology and Religion: West and East," (1932-1952)," CW 11, ¶ 538.

defensiveness around criticism and a reticence that comes out of sensitivity about what is innermost in my life. Frank broaches this concern:

> *Secrecy is another problem. I suppose married people have their kind of difficulties talking about sexual experience, but the difficulty seems to be magnified for celibates.*

In contrast, the openness and generosity of this particular group of Respondents, women and men who share their experience of living celibate love, inform this narrative. Their contribution picks up issues triggered by other authors.[95] When such fringe dwellers dare to speak about what motivates and troubles people they can meet condemnation by the hierarchical church. As a celibate woman in a Religious Order, I feel a freedom from institutional silencing that also comes from my time in Jungian analysis. One man refers to the censuring problem with the almost un-discussable subject of:

> *Sexual preference: facing the discovery that one is homosexual. Where to take the problem! For example, the limited ability of individuals and communities to speak of psycho-sexual growth etc.* (Thomas)

In continuing to open closed subjects, I am trusting that there will emerge the mystery and the humanness into which many women and men have grown, not in spite of but because of their choosing a life of celibacy and spirituality. I am aware of personal limitations in dealing with the mercurial nature of unconscious material. As I engage in this work, I find that Jung's frequent remark (or is it prayer?) at challenging junctures comes to mind: "Deo concedente" or "God willing."[96]

My primary sources come from the Respondents and the literary, religious and psychological references deepen the meaning of the archetype. I take responsibility, however, for the way these pieces weave together and for coming to some conclusions about which you may or may not

---

95   Christian Cochini (1990), Janette Gray (1995), Michael H. Crosby (1996), Joan Chittister (1996), Richard A. Sipe (1996), Diarmuid O'Murchu (1999), Judith Merkle (1998), Sandra Schneiders (2011).

96   C.G. Jung, "The Practice of Psychotherapy" (1921-1951), CW 16, ¶ 385.

agree. Wherever the journey goes, I am delighted that we are in conversation about this subject of celibacy and spirituality.

The Virgin Archetype

The archetype of the virgin comes from another dimension that Eliade calls "at that time or in illo tempore."[97] While the recurring image and pattern of behaviour standing behind the celibate way of life is the virgin, I want to start our exploration of the virgin archetype with the notion of singular beauty!

Singular Beauty

When David says that celibacy is about *living a single life for sake of the kingdom of God*, he asserts that his being single has to do with God. *Aloneness* was another descriptor that Respondents mentioned, and so being singular gave a springboard for searching into images of celibacy. It prompted me initially to give this book the title, *Singular Beauty, Graced Friendship*.

Thinking about the phrase as an archetypal expression of celibacy—*living a single life for the sake of the kingdom of God*—I asked myself, is a celibate woman and man singular because s/he does not engage in genital sex with another person: even though s/he wants relationship with others? Is it fear that prevents sexual encounter? Why would one give up such pleasurable intimacy with another?

The priest who gave me this thread also gave the clew for his celibate decision. His choice for celibacy is about the kingdom of God, and that prompted me to unravel what this implied. Being singular emphasizes an aspect of Aloneness and of All Oneness reflected in the self-containment of someone like Mary of Guadalupe. Nevertheless, women and men who want to embody these qualities of the archetype are human and not mother of God. Moreover, positive and negative are signalled in those words: oneness, aloneness, all oneness and self-containment. The following Respondent makes quite clear that she is human, vulnerable

---

97   M. Eliade, *The Myth of the Eternal Return*, 4, 21.

but not fragile. Listen to her describing both the pros and cons of the aloneness of celibacy:

> *...perhaps because of the aloneness of celibacy and that there is*
> *no ONE person whom I can claim for myself alone, I feel that*
> *I can be not understood or perhaps dismissed...It's great when*
> *I am loved in return but it seems to me that in being celibate I*
> *can't really expect anything in return...On the other hand, being*
> *celibate means that when I have no one else to go to, I have found*
> *ways to accept the aloneness and allow that as part of my life and*
> *allow it to take me into stillness within me.* (Rose)

Words shift in meaning. I am finding that, in writing about singular beauty, I am claiming anew what singularity entails. Originally the name "singularitas" was given to a man who lived an unmarried and solitary life (which one Respondent saw symbolised in her single bed). Over time, "singularatis" applied also to women. The term was not always complimentary. For example, it was a criticism among the Sisters of St. Joseph to say *you are singular*. The implication was: *You are making too much of yourself.*

In the Syriac that derives from the Aramaic language spoken by Christ and his early followers, chastity also meant integrity and holiness: that is, there is goodness about being unashamedly singular.[98] Other variations on being singular are intimated in terms like "ascetic" and "agapetai." They point to a sense of integration, discipline and independence.

Lightening what could be a heavy emphasis on sexual abstinence, I recall those lines from *Desiderata* that counsel gentleness and a healthy discipline. That balance comes through remembering that I am part of all creation as this next Respondent came to realise. Rose observes how celibate people, beginning with herself, can be too hard on themselves, and as a result, be forgetful of offering that softer space to others:

> *...at the end of my yoga class the teacher reminds us to be gentle*
> *with ourselves, to have kind words on our lips, to honour the best*
> *in ourselves as well as the best in each other. I realise that is some-*
> *what unfamiliar for me generally—in my assessment of myself I*

---

98   Angelo Di Bernardino, *Encyclopedia of the Early Church*, 261.

*can often be judging or feel that I should be 'doing better.' In my
life as a celibate I don't often get nurtured—so I am trying to do
more of that for myself.*

This woman's comments signal the need for caring for the body and
having a caring community. These aspects surfaced in other comments.
David emphasized that being singular in his relationship with God relies
on real ties to the community, real friendships and a real work that sustains him. As I write, I am conscious of a singularity that I live and that
is supported by close friends, family, clients and religious community.

Genuine relationships are crucial and provide a supportive structure of interdependence. In this writing endeavour, I am conscious that
while living alone in this space for much of this time, I am sustained by
the prayer, loving and real connection face to face, and by email, text,
letter and mobile that give me daily inspiration and encouragement to
continue.

The aloneness aspect of being singular is described by Peter as being
all with the One. He adds disarmingly that it is a life style choice of being
like Jesus and "eunuchs for the kingdom."[99] I don't particularly like the
image that Jesus and Peter picked. There is no escaping that celibacy is a
radical choice to give a complete gift of oneself that another Respondent
describes as a *total self-offering*. In the 3rd century, around the regions of
what is now the Middle East, history tells of other singular people who
felt a calling to consecrated celibacy and a life of solitude and prayer.

What was it that these unusual people sought? As the historian Driot
clarifies, their lifestyle of "going apart" ("hesychia") was understood as
an expression of loving relationship with others and they were known
as Desert Fathers and Mothers.[100] I understand that same journey into
aloneness is motivating the priest from the Kalahari who spoke earlier
about all-oneness to "listen to the voice of the secret fire."[101]

That latter phrase conveys an image of spirituality and an experience
of mystery and singularity that is special and open to all people. All-
oneness can be fleetingly glimpsed when one is immersed in nature or

99   Matthew 19:12 in *The New Jerusalem Bible*.
100   Marcel Driot, *Fathers of the Desert*, 12.
101   Christian Jacq, *Ramses: The Son of Light*, 53.

is listening to a beautiful piece of music or is engaged in some creative work. In those moments, whether one is celibate or not, union with the Other and with creation can be experienced. In valuing that capacity to be all-one, we can learn to leave space for the unexpected to enter. Then an intimacy, where I allow room for the Other to come into my space on their terms, rather than on mine, may happen. It is the gift of Solitude.[102]

A friend pointed out this potentiality for soul-making. We were driving when she asked—not unkindly, *Why do you have to keep talking?* She was right. I was not allowing much space at that time in our friendship. Remarkable what comes out of moments of genuine sharing and silence! When aloneness morphs from lonesomeness to a constant loneliness, there are alarm bells. For while lonesomeness is part of the human condition as is occasional loneliness, it signals depression when that state becomes constant and the person feels walled up, unlovable and unloved. The next Respondent offers valuable insight into how loneliness led him to see the connection between spirituality and celibacy:

> *In the loneliness and desert of celibacy, there is a rich opportunity to search out the deeper truth and beauty of sexuality. There is a stripping away of everything to befriend sexuality and delight in its gift. For me celibacy doesn't make sense without spirituality because both are about relatedness, and celibacy enables me to search out the essence of sexuality.* (Patrick)

There can be resistance to being singular because the individual goes against the stream. In the collective view, the celibate woman or man can be perceived as a bit odd. Where group mentality rules, there is a danger of being reduced to the lowest common denominator and feeling insecure. What's wrong with being different? On the way of individuation where respect for the individual is valued, diversity and even some eccentricity are refreshing. A tension can arise between the individual and the group that is both necessary and painful for the *singularitas*. A community of individuals who discern the way of the Spirit models a very different kind of leadership from one of control, which does not

---

102   John Paul 11, *Man and Woman He Created Them*, ¶ 170.

allow creative tension between the individual and group. Jackie says of her choice of consecrated celibacy:

> *I sense the singleness of purpose in my life does allow me to be more available in terms of ministry to those in need. There is much more freedom available to me than if I were married and had children. Of course there is commitment to the Religious Order to which I belong…which of itself calls us to mature living and relationships.*

This Respondent describes what flows from being single "for the sake of the kingdom." It made me curious about this kingdom piece, which is more than fulfilling what Canon # 599 of the *Code of Canon Law* annotates about celibacy.[103] Again language matters. Unless people live in Lichtenstein, "kingdom" does not have much significance. Democracies like Australia have a different organizing principle from that of a monarchy who are anointed to their leading role. Yet when baptised Christians pray the "Our Father" as did Jesus, we pray that the kingdom, the reign, the will or the realm of God will come now.

We ask God to be the Organizing Principle on earth as it is in heaven. We do not ask for an elected leader but pray that "I am who I am" be the priority in life. Contemporary theologian, Denis Edwards, proposes that this Organizing Principle looks more like a trinitarian "God who is…Persons in Mutual Love."[104] Our prayer calls for a kind of mutuality rather than a subservience in our relationships. As Jesus reminds in the Scriptures, this kingdom is within all persons and can be claimed like a pearl of great price. In the parable of the merchant who finds a rare pearl and sells all he owns to buy it, the early church saw an image of virginity.[105]

I want to stay with that image of a pearl of great price. Each pearl is unique because of the natural and hidden transformational process it goes through. It starts to grow because a particle of dust lodges in the shell of the oyster. In trying to get rid of this irritant, the little mollusc

---

103   John Beal, James Conden, Thomas Green, *New Commentary on the Code of Canon Law*, 765.
104   Denis Edwards, *The God of Evolution*, 125.
105   Matthew 13:45-46 & Wisdom 7:7-14 in *The New Jerusalem Bible*.

coats the foreign matter with a nacreous substance that gradually creates the gem's lustre. It could be an image of one's deepest identity, or one's psyche, that is figuratively coming to birth through all the hassles of living. In Greek myth, that emergence is portrayed as the birth of Aphrodite, the goddess of love, from the ocean. The pearl of chastity and the birth of Eros are closely linked.

In Steinbeck's short story of *The Pearl*, we read about the hero's discovery of a priceless pearl. In his peaceful family and village, it awakens many responses which include envy, greed and violence. Taking the simile further, we note that chastity can visit creativity or destruction on individuals. The question is: "What does one do with the pearl of great price?" In the Gospel parable, it is not known what the merchant does with his lucky find, and that is key. The discovery of the treasure of God's kingdom makes one more compassionately human or unleashes destructive emotions.[106] Whatever the outcome, a change in one's inner landscape is inescapable.

During an interview, Frank referred to the image of the pearl as an analogy of the inner beauty that can evolve as one faces moral issues—similar to what celibate people face in growing into chaste love:

> *I think most of us go through a moral struggle and I think that it is inflicted on us by the sin that is in humanity. A father who doesn't teach a son how to be a male. A mother who is a close, binding, intimate mother, all of those things. An older person, a boy or girl who teaches a younger one to masturbate, or something like that. Those are realities that are visited on us when we are growing up and most of us have one or Other and some of us have the lot of them.*
>
> *We have to handle those as we grow. If we choose to grow whole, we have to grow over them. The way I came to think of it was: there is this flaw in the oyster and that if I grow around it, it will become a pearl. That's how I think of the struggles that most of us have. We're accustomed to saying if you overcome this, you will be stronger than you were. That's good, that's one image. If you can accept this you can become more whole. That's another*

---

106 John Steinbeck, *The Pearl*, 94.

good image. Another basic image is that this is a struggle I have.
So I'll grow around it and I'll become a more beautiful person.
I like that idea of beauty. I think it may be what we need to re-
conceive in our day.

Frank speaks of re-imagining beauty, living into the aesthetics of
chastity that is critical for his life as a celibate person and member of the
wider society. The kingdom of God is sited in no particular geographical
place or time. It is an attitude, a dynamic or environment where relationships of truth, justice, and love matter. Peter gives another understanding of what that realm of God could be like:

the reign of God is where God is single-mindedly sought and
served, and others sought and served for and in God.

From an analytical perspective, to be singular for the kingdom of
God points to a process like individuation. It is not about individual-
ism where one is self-absorbed, unrelated and even unconcerned about
others. My thoughts go to the Jungfrau ("the Maiden") which is the
highest mountain in Switzerland. It is symbolic of both reaching up to
the divine and being potentially remote. In *Vita Consecrata*, John Paul
II encourages vowed celibates to take as an icon for prayer the Transfiguration of Jesus Christ on the mountain. He reminds that celibacy
must include both glory and suffering. Impishly, one of the Respondents picked up that point and said he hasn't seen too much of the glory
of celibacy! The point is that (celibate love) involves both "going up the
mountain" and "coming down the mountain."[107]

In their reflections, I hear the Respondents describing a spiritual
journey that longs for an inner marriage relevant for everyone: partnered, single, celibate. I hear a common quest for community where
caring relationships with others and with the earth are growing. Where
do celibacy and being singular fit? I think David pinpoints the combi-
nation when he suggests that a touch both of Zorba the Greek and of
divine madness is essential for this way of loving:

---

107   John Paul 11, "Vita Consecrata,"par.14, http://www.vatican.va/roman_cu-
      ria/congregations/ccscrlife/documents/hf_jp-ii_exh_25031996_vita-consecrata_
      en.html. Retrieved June 6, 2014.

> *Loving God as a single person where this is seen as the way I am called to live this love. Loving others in genuine friendships and loving the church community in preaching and teaching and in theology…I don't think I would defend celibacy much but describe it as 'some kind of madness' that only makes sense in being in love with God and being called to love in this way.*

I agree that there are aspects in consecrated life that can prompt vowed celibate women and men to disconnection and remoteness in their relationships with others. The damage caused by some who have misused the power of their call and taken advantage of others' trust has cast a long shadow on church credibility.

It was a gift when a singular man, Bishop Geoffrey Robinson, named issues of power and silence in the church as major factors contributing to sexual abuse. He actually showed singular qualities of integrity, all oneness, self-containment. Robinson's forthrightness on matters of celibacy and sexuality has met with stonewalling from some Catholic leaders. It takes a deep faith to trust that disparate pieces of one's life are being woven into a bigger tapestry of beauty and meaning for the sake of the kingdom.

Jesus Christ: Expression of the Self

My niece asked what motivates me to work assiduously on *Celibacy and Soul: Exploring the Depths of Chastity.* My motivation is the reason most Respondents gave for their ongoing celibate commitment: the person of Jesus Christ. This man of Middle-Eastern culture is more than a sign, symbol or metaphor. In theological terms, Christ is called the Word and Sacrament of God's unconditional love. In personal terms, he is someone I love. Jackie has a delightful image for a personal relationship that is growing:

> *In my room I have two figurines in conversation; they symbolise for me the Christ and me in constant conversation.*

For the vowed celibate, Jesus Christ embodies the Way saying enigmatically, "we must be born again." What could this mean? Note that the Greek word for *way* is *hodos*, a feminine noun. In the Second Testament account of the conversation between Jesus and Nicodemus, we hear about the difference that this new way makes to a person.[108] The Pharisee flippantly asks Jesus how one manages a return to the womb. In reply, Jesus dismisses any regressive move to childish innocence but indicates a spiritual birth, a psychological virginity that other traditions also take up in myths of the twice-born. The latter were often associated with divine figures that died and rose again and are significant for ordinary people.[109]

Jesus describes how we become the twice-born through water, fire and the Spirit.[110] Taking the theological perspective of Metropolitan John Zizioulas, theologian Pat Fox sees the action of the Holy Spirit opening to all creation this way "of personhood in which the distance of individuals is turned into the communion of persons."[111] With that kinship in mind, vowed celibates can make a choice to embody Christ's life, death and resurrection in their lives. This choice is an ongoing initiation into their baptism. Jung described this sacrament as a passage where something from above, namely the Holy Spirit, comes to the initiates who stand in the water of the unconscious and open themselves like little children to the kingdom of God.[112]

Jung is speaking as psychologist when he describes Christ as an archetypal expression of the Self.[113] As such, Christ could be either a freeing figure or a threat to consciousness.[114] I understand that connection becomes freeing rather than restrictive when individuals take personal responsibility for their following of Jesus Christ. A number of Respondents spoke of Jesus Christ as friend and companion. He comes across as a compelling someone more than an archetypal figure as Judith spells out:

---

108 John 3 in *The New Jerusalem Bible*.
109 Gertrude Jobes, *Dictionary of Mythology*, Part 1, 447.
110 John 3:3-8 in *The New Jerusalem Bible*.
111 Patricia Fox, *God as Communion*, 46.
112 C.G. Jung, *Visions 1*, 192; Luke 3:16 & Matthew 18:2-4 in *The New Jerusalem Bible*.
113 C.G. Jung, "Aion," CW 9ii, ¶¶ 70 ff.
114 C.G. Jung, "Aion," CW 9ii, ¶ 230.

Christ is my friend, a brother, a person challenging me, entrusting me with certain things to do.

I will return to those key elements of being friend and brother of Christ. Many Respondents observed that their relationship with Christ changed over time from enthusiasm to an imperative for justice and a living presence in and through creation. John Terry traced that movement, and Jane notes that hard times have actually taken her to another depth:

> *All our relationships change over time. When my father died at a youngish age, I was shocked and saddened, naively believing that my relationship with God (Christ) would shield me from human grief and deep sense of loss. I felt affronted by pious platitudes which seem to roll off many tongues. Months later while reflecting on Jesus' post-resurrection appearance to Mary Magdalene, I had a sense of the presence of Christ even in the emptiness of my grief. The image of Christ as lover has always been appealing but it is stronger now.*

Analytical Psychology emphasizes that opening oneself to be re-made in tune with the unique Self at the centre of one's being is a work of grace and a possibility for everyone. Fifty years ago, the Second Vatican Council (1962-1965) highlighted that the vocation of all Christians is to that same holiness. While consecrated celibacy is a *charism* (*a gift from the Holy Spirit*) it is a specific vocation among other vocations for moving towards wholeness.[115] As the document emphasizes, chastity is a blessing in one's life that is meant for others. It is a radical expression of what every Christian's baptism entails: a blessing for being and loving like Christ rather than a life focused on denial, penance and austerity.

In the Second Testament, Jesus' call to celibate chastity is first expressed with his invitation to the disciples: "Follow me."[116] Two Respondents actually named themselves as itinerant disciples travelling through life in a celibate way because of Christ. Why? Because as this man says:

---

115 Walter Abbott, "Lumen Gentium," 41-43 & "Perfectae Caritatis," 1, 12 in *Documents of Vatican*, 11.

116 Mark 1:13 in *The New Jerusalem Bible*.

Yes!!! In deep. (Juan)

These comments take me to the aesthetic of celibacy that happens in meeting the eyes of an Other who shifts the conversation from mere observation to an emotional connection.[117] I understand what Janice means when she says that when you are aware of the Invisible Other everyone and everything takes on a different shade:

> *Christ is the centre and deepest core of my being—unifying presence—leading and directing through the Spirit of loving and so I meet the eyes of Jesus through God's people.*

As an archetype of the Self, Jesus Christ is an incarnation of God's love and wisdom. His life makes sense of celibacy and spirituality. I agree with Peter's comment in his questionnaire, where he explains that Christ is the ultimate reason for being and staying celibate. Choosing this distinctive path of consecrated celibacy, I revisit and do not avoid asking more about the "why."

The journey into celibacy does entail sacrifice which again raises questions. Why do it? Jane remarks, *the crucifix is a potent symbol of self giving—a reminder that love costs.* I think she is right. Many of the Respondents mentioned this element of sacrifice in their self-giving. It is important to articulate what is particular to the suffering of celibacy that resounds right through our body selves. Timothy Radcliffe describes some of what is entailed in the loss of genitality and the gift of our corporeality:

> *The immense pain of celibacy is that we renounce a moment of intense bodiliness when bodies are given to each other, without reserve. Here the body is seen in its profound identity...as a sacrament of presence. The sexual act expresses, makes flesh and blood, our deep desire to share our lives. That is why it is a sacrament of Christ's unity with the church. As celibates too, in our corporeality, we can make Christ present in our way...the Word to expression, not just in his or her words, but in all that we are.*

---

117   Della Thompson, *The Concise Oxford Dictionary*, 2.

God's compassion seeks to become flesh and blood in us, in our
tenderness, even in our faces.[118]

As Radcliffe observes, love changes every aspect of our being and softens or hardens us. Whether celibate, married or in another partnership, some healthy sacrifice is intrinsic. It may not be dramatic. A friend shared this story of a married couple who at their Golden Jubilee were asked,

"What is the secret of such a long relationship?"

The old fellow answered. "It's all in how you make the gravy!"

"Yes," replied the elderly woman. "When I make the gravy I make it thick because that's how he likes it."

Her husband replied, "And when I make the gravy I make it runny and thin because that is how she likes it."[119]

The parable of the gravy illustrates that the essence of loving is in little sacrifices of going beyond self for the ones we love. In light of married love, another Respondent clarifies the serious sacrifice of family and sexual companionship that vowed celibacy carries:

Not having children has been the most difficult part of celibacy
for me and now at this age not being a grandmother has hurt.
(Jackie)

For women and men who vow celibacy, even if their sexual drive lessens with ageing, there remain the loneliness and aloneness that can get in the way of true solitude. Loss and grief need to be acknowledged rather than evaded. In an enabling and loving environment, people can grow in the attitude of Christ, who shows celibate and non-celibate how to be willing to bear the tension of opposites in a sacrificial way where emotion is worked with rather than killed. While the libido may not be

---

118   Timothy Radcliffe, *The Promise of Life*, http:/dominicans.ca/Documents/masters/Radcliffe/promise_life.html. Retrieved June 8, 2014.
119   Katrina Brill rsj, Personal Communication, January 22, 2012.

lived out actively in genital or possessive relationships, the energy can be transformed. This attitude is conveyed in Tim's image of celibacy:

> *(Celibacy) suggests above all—a complete but willing gift of myself to God.* (Tim)

Eucharist and Prayer: Circles of Remembering and Transformation

Some Respondents wrote that prayer and Eucharist are strong symbols of celibacy for them. As I reflect on these as archetypal expressions of celibacy, it strikes me that prayer and Eucharist are intimate conversations of a person with God about their relationship with the Self, with others and with the world. I am aware that insights the Respondents have shared are like a Eucharist. Note Frank's remark:

> *I have put a lot of things here which are deeply personal. I hesitated about a number of them...but they are gifts to me and not for myself only. I hope they will help you help others. I am trusting you with a lot.*

Frank's gift of making himself vulnerable, his generosity and concern are obvious. Jane also hints at the Eucharistic reason for her choice of celibacy and for sharing aspects of her celibate experience with us. It is about Christ and this mystery in her life...of being taken, blessed, broken and given to others:

> *Celibacy suggests to me Christ in the Eucharist which symbolises Jesus' self-gift on Calvary. Jesus' life was a continual Eucharistic action of being taken, blessed and broken and given for all humanity...I am called to take my life, my whole being and pour out myself in loving service to the Other...I become my best and true self by this commitment.*

These responses indicate the connection between Eucharist and celibate commitment, and echo in Christ's words of consecration:

"Take this, all of you, and eat of it: for this is my body which will be given up for you. In a similar way...and once more giving thanks, he gave (the chalice) to his disciples, saying: Take this, all of you, and drink from it: for this is the chalice of my blood, the blood of the new and eternal covenant, which will be poured out for you and for many for the forgiveness of sins. Do this in memory of me."[120]

In the busyness of life, it is easy to forget priorities. In the Eucharistic circle of Christ's self-giving, the ritual celebrates what creation does naturally and what all people who are in touch with God desire to do.

If evolution is, as John Haught suggests, the "transformative drama of life...of creation, incarnation and redemption," Eucharist makes present that drama.[121] The ritual is more than a personal prayer of remembering Jesus Christ. People gather together for a liturgy that reminds that communion with God is about communion with others and with the world: "a spirituality of communion."[122] The person brings her/himself to Eucharist to be transformed just as the bread and wine are transformed into Christ. The next step is bringing that altered consciousness into the rest of life. I am aware that sometimes the reality of Eucharist can be masked because people either are not welcomed to participate fully in the Mass or feel excluded. It is difficult to get below the distancing style of liturgy or past the personality of presider to enter into what Jane recognises as a mystery of transformation.

Taking up an evolutionary perspective, Frank's next comment recognises that, in opening to nature, awareness can come of the great life source flowing through the body of the universe—past, present and future. Realization of the Spirit in matter and celebrating creation's evolving interrelatedness are traces of silk that Teilhard de Chardin wanted to leave to others and that Frank reiterates.[123]

---

120 "Eucharistic Prayers I-IV," in *The Roman Missal*, 2011.
121 John Haught, *Making Sense of Evolution*, 53.
122 Congregation of Institutes of Consecrated Life and Societies of Apostolic Life, *Starting Afresh from Christ*, ¶ 29.
123 Ursula King, *Teilhard de Chardin and Eastern Religions*, 15.

I should perhaps add the symbolism of nature. I am an outdoor man and often hike and camp. Friends and I have celebrated Mass on mountains and in deserts, and these celebrations somehow mean to me that the truths of Jesus Christ's revelation dwell in nature and bring it to its fulfilment. This, I suppose, is not unrelated to American nature mysticism, and it explicitly is de Chardin's insights which I share with my closest friends.

There were other circles of prayer that Respondents named as central to their chaste commitment. In mundane and at problematic times, they spoke of circles of friends who helped them. Patrick maps the developmental movement that has happened to him because of being part of a circle of contemplative pray-ers:

From a vague infantile understanding both of sexuality and celibacy, through the pain and struggle of sexual intercourse and relationships, searching for my vocation and finding a place where I know my true happiness abides. Enabling me to face deep intimate relationships while having a small community with whom I pray and reflect on life.

The experiences of spirituality that Respondents mention go beyond conventional church circles. Rose finds her support with close family and with colleagues and friends who meet over a meal to discuss work and their lives. A few Respondents mentioned significant relationships with nieces and nephews. Catherine, John Terry and Karen describe the importance of these radiating circles. Frank, Jane and Thomas speak of their intentional commitment to a local community of religious. Others, like Tim, single out parish and special interest circles.

As Becky voices, these circles of friendship and reflection, where people can drop their persona and be themselves, are essential: *Their care and concern keep me able to live a religious life.* In my searching, I also found that celibate chastity is itself sometimes imaged as a circle of fire. In trying to understand what that image could mean, I began with Jung's comment about mandalas, or sacred circles, arising when psyche is seeking equilibrium.[124]

---

124   C.G. Jung, "Psychology and Alchemy," CW 12, ¶ 123.

As I stayed with the circle of fire and allowed the symbol room to work, these associations came to mind. One was of the sun and its familiar journey across the sky. Thoughts went to Martini's painting where, if you look carefully at Figure 4, you can see the fiery wheel of the Spirit in the scene.

Figure 4: The Annunciation with St. Ansano and St. Giulitta, by Simone Martini and Lippo Memmi. Source :ARAS Online Archive. Reprinted with permission.

I remembered other circles like the megolithic circle of Newgrange where spirals carved in stone speak of the cycle of life, death and resurrection. I recalled *The Divine Comedy,* and Dante's pilgrimage through the icy and fiery circles of the Inferno, to Purgatorio and to Paradiso. On reaching his final destination, Dante faces an image of the Trinity—in circles of threeness and yet substantially one:

"three circles of three colours and one magnitude."[125]

In coming to this mysterious vision of God, the pilgrims had to pass through hell and purgatory. Similarly, the life journey for the celibate and non-celibate person passes through all terrains that include experiences of the presence and the absence of God and can lead either to deeper trust or to despair. Celibacy can be a place of depression or transformation. Dante describes moving through such circles where the shadow of life can purify and transform. He views the love of God stirring the cosmos and leading persons to self-surrender. I think of those Respondents who speak of their commitment as one of self-giving and not primarily about sacrifice, ministry or availability. As Frank observed:

> The chastity that results from self-control is really quite beautiful, and a strong and spiritual way to live. It brings a sense of integrity and calmness.

No wonder the circle of fire is an evocative symbol for many mystics. Teilhard de Chardin exclaims about the divine presence, "See the universe is ablaze."[126] This image of psychic energy is picked up by analytical psychology. In the Visions seminars, Jung speaks of the spiralling kundalini energy in the body that coils like a snake about to strike.[127] The serpent image suggests an energy that is both creative and dangerous. In Hatha yoga, kundalini is pictured as energy flowing from the base of the spine through the body and in its dynamic passage bringing a change of consciousness that can awaken or overwhelm the individual.

Similarly, the Chinese practice of Qi Gong offers a balancing of the body's meridians by releasing blocked chi energy. This vital cosmic energy is always available and flows through creation; many Australian Aborigines recognise this in the Rainbow Serpent Dreaming. Taking time to walk, especially in some area that is unspoilt, can replenish psyche with some of the energy that nature freely gives:

---

125 Dante Alighieri, "Paradiso," Canto XXXII: 116-117, 144-145. *The Divine Comedy*, Vol.3.
126 Ursula King, *Teilhard de Chardin and Eastern Religions*, 119.
127 C.G. Jung, *Visions*, vol. 1, xix.

Become aware of a beam of light passing from heaven through you into the earth and then the energy from the earth coming up through you to heaven.[128]

Early in *Celibacy and Soul,* with the idea of pilgrimage and circumambulation and transformation, I introduced the symbol of the labyrinth. This is an image for helping to traverse the unknown to the centre of the circle: and in this instance to the heart of celibacy. As a sacred circle or mandala of initiation, the labyrinth reminds, encourages and gives clues about going through life and dying into a renewal of attitude.

Constellating Virgo

It is time to take up the virgin archetype from a cosmic angle with the constellation of Virgo. To bridge into this archetypal expression of the virgin, I return to the Respondent who speaks of all-oneness. My reason for choosing Peter's comment to lead into Virgo is because it is discordant. The virgin is usually a term identified with women and not often claimed by men. For just as there are not many accolades for being celibate and singular, there is not a lot going for identifying as a virgin in the 21st century. Nevertheless, Peter says:

Celibacy is a life commitment to being alone—'all with the One' and 'one with all.' Caelos single, alone. It is a call to become more virginal, for example, disposable to the will of God.

It is intriguing that this rugged missionary equates virginity and celibacy with becoming more attuned to following the will of God. In October 2010, Dr. Paul Bishop was giving a seminar in Zurich on Jung's view of the Stages of Life through Goethe's poem, *Primal Words*. Thanks to Paul's scholarship, I have more of an idea about the meaning of the will of God that is refined through Goethe's poetic insight. In the following stanzas, do you hear intimations about what it means to be singular, virginal and obeying an inner law?

---

128 Karen Schindler, Personal Communication, 1999.

....You must be
None but yourself, from self you cannot flee
No time there is, no power can decompose
The minted form that lives and living grows.[129]

Someone with a sense of vocation, be it to celibacy or to another path, is listening to an inner law that comes from attending to another voice, the voice of an Other, the Self. As I listen to the Respondents, I am conscious of this sensibility that enables them to become more open and malleable to the will of God.

After many conversations with the Respondent whom I call Peter, I became aware of someone who has become virginal past his own wants and whims. As a person of the Gospel, he shows care for other people who are struggling to survive, and his life reflects the message that people are loved by God as God loves Christ. Louis Gendron, a Jesuit priest and recent Province Leader of China, prompted my reflection further. Apparently in the writings of St. Ignatius of Loyola, the saint returns to the following Scriptural passage about the will of God:

> ... looking round at those sitting in a circle about him, Jesus said, 'Here are my mother and my brothers. Anyone who does the will of God, that person is my brother and sister and mother.'[130]

Louis spoke of this text as motivating Ignatius to build up the family of God instead of devoting himself to a family of his own.[131] That motivation still stirs many celibate women and men to describe celibate chastity as *a call to give their all*. At the negative end of the spectrum, for some vowed celibates and at some stages in life, the archetypal or recurring image of the Virgin can point to a regressive innocence and naiveté. Without the responsibilities of children and partner, they can slip into being accountable to no one. Self-centredness and incapacity for relating can take over instead of generous love. Let's hear Peter on that note,

---

129   Johann Wolfgang van Goethe, "Primal Words, Orphic" in *Selected Poems*, 123.
130   Mark 3: 34-35 in *The New Jerusalem Bible*.
131   Louis Gendron, SJ Personal Communication, 2012.

as he reminds us of the potential for both healthy and unhealthy aspects in consecrated celibacy:

> *For many years I didn't know how to relate properly to women—scared of intimacy. Married people mature in marriage where religious life seemed to keep some of us immature for a long time.*

Peter recognises and addresses this shadowy propensity in him-self. By voicing that tendency, he articulates its root cause as fear of intimacy and then chooses vulnerability over un-relatedness. In Jungian circles, childish attributes of the virgin are suggested by terms like "puella" for a woman and "puer" for a man. Literally these Latin words translate as "girl" and "boy." While it may be excusable to act childishly as a teenager, it is unpleasant in an adult. I am not downplaying a place for healthy escape and fantasy, but to remain permanently in that zone is to be neurotic.

In the current Western context, the archetypal temptation to remain at the fountain of youth attracts many—celibates and non-celibates. Advertising and marketing encourage consumers to become obsessive and invest huge amounts to hide signs of ageing. It seems that delayed adolescence among some celibates appears to manifest more in risky behaviours like drinking to excess, rigid conformity to the rules, inappropriate sexual behaviour and rebellious attention seeking.

While the constellation of Virgo is not my star sign and may not be yours either, it can add to an appreciation of the virgin archetype. Considered astrologically, Virgo is the sixth house of the Zodiac that comes into prominence around August 23 until September 23. She appears as a figure in the night sky, holding in her hand what seems like a wheat sheaf or a palm.

This motif of Virgo became identified in Christianity with the Virgin Mary whose title was "Star of the Sea." Reminiscent of the Dark Virgin of Tepeyac, early icons like the Virgin Hodigritia or the woman of Mercy depict Mary with a star on her forehead leading the way. According to church tradition, these icons were originally inspired by images of the Virgin painted by St. Luke, the evangelist.[132] That guiding motif of

---

132   Maria Giovanna Muzj, *Transfiguration*, 42-48.

Virgo intimates the problematic ideal of virginity if the accompanying dark context is not included. The shadow needs to find safe expression otherwise it will break out in unexpected ways.

Virgo has another important aspect to her identity as the goddess of justice. According to this archetypal pattern, justice belongs to the nature of virginity but the passion for justice goes further than mediation. There are numerous examples of religious women and men who are at the forefront of issues about right relationships. Patrick says:

> *The amazing thing about celibate love is that it creates energy to go out to others and care for those who seem to have no one to care for them, "to give and not count the cost."*

To further understand Virgo's character, it helps to know that the Greek word for justice includes compassion. That latter word links love, non-violent action and patience. What does this imply for the virgin? Sandra Schneiders spells it out when she identifies prophetic compassion as a defining quality in those truly living consecrated celibacy. The title of her most recent book underlines witness and virginity: *Prophets in Their Own Country, Women Bearing Witness to the Gospel in a Troubled Church*. Schneiders singles out and identifies Virgo's prophetic stance in the gracious way women religious met the recent investigation by the Vatican of women's Apostolic Congregations in America.[133]

In the Christian and this post-Christian era, the constellation of the virgin carrying a palm branch can still be seen in those who give their lives to Christ in service of others. Like the pointer stars of the Southern Cross, their lives speak of the cross of transformation and its promise of resurrection as Jan Williamson depicts in her painting of *Mary of the Southern Cross*.

The justice of the old law is replaced with a new law about mercy. So Debra explains how living celibacy awakens compassion in her:

> *Sometimes I feel a sense of powerlessness because I cannot change the situation because of many factors...Many poor people amaze me in how they find joy in simple experiences and I need to*

---

133   Sandra Schneiders, *Prophets in Their Own Country*, 24.

remember that...I can learn to look for the joy in what I have
and not dwell on what I don't have.

On the other hand, Virgo can have unpleasant tendencies that flow
out of an unpredictable side. If celibates get caught in this shadow side
of virginity, they can turn cold, be passively aggressive or controlling.
Juan described some celibate people who repress their sexuality in ways
that cripple their own lives and block relationship.

...they are retarded or impoverished in their relating as they spend
so much energy in NOT doing.

Such juxtapositions remind me of other unusual combinations. In
ancient Greece, the bright star of Venus was Aphrodite. She was the virgin goddess of spiritual and passionate love. This pairing may seem paradoxical. In the classic story of *Psyche and Eros* that you read at the beginning of *Celibacy and Soul*, Aphrodite's role, although initially adverse,
proves to be creative. Aphrodite guides the action by pushing Psyche on
the individuation path.

Exemplifying this mythic situation, the following Respondent had
to contend with inner difficulties to grow in celibate love. In the gift of
friendship, both she and her friend seemed to be spiritual guide for each
other as they grew through infatuation and into love. Catherine wrote:

In my 30s and 40s I wanted to be number one, the most special
one. To lose my possessiveness was not easy...He is not mine. He
is my dear friend though. This awareness is a recent gift—maybe
4 or 5 years old... My friend says this is the gift I have given him.
He has given me the gift of patience and forgiveness and magna-
nimity of soul. So we have given each other away only to receive
back more than we ever imagined.

From Catherine's comment, we can trace the motif of the guiding
star of unselfish love leading the virginal soul into integrity and transformation. This is relevant in Buddhism where Buddha's enlightenment
comes through the light of a star. After spending yet another night in
meditation, Gautama looks up in the sky and sees there the Morning
Star. At the moment of dawn, Gautama perceives and becomes what the
name of Buddha signifies: the awakened one.

Figure 5: Mary of the Southern Cross, by Jan Williamson. Source: Image courtesy the artist. Reprinted with permission.

In Indo-Tibetan Buddhism, Tara offers a variation on this theme of enlightenment that includes compassion and the feminine. According to one creation myth, the Tibetan people emerged from the tears of Tara. Aware of the need to overcome prejudice, Tara made a deliberate choice to become enlightened as a woman. Now for a gem! While women are often considered morally inferior in Eastern as in many Western traditions, there is also a Tibetan belief that if a woman contemplative is genuine, she is exemplary. I hear that transformative effect in Louise's reflection which is not about superiority or inferiority but her individuation through vulnerability:

> Celibacy has made for wholeness in my life—but I've suffered a lot of brokenness on the way. The brokenness has enriched me—I became more human and compassionate.

Compassion through vulnerability was shown by the remarkable Buddhist monk, who was Tibet's first Dalai Lama. Naming Tara as Supreme Deity, he encouraged others to rediscover feminine compassion and feminine strength and to view all others as sisters or brothers.[134] From the perspective of analytical psychology, I am aware of the healing effect that Tara portrays in compassionately seeing and simply being with another. It is the quality of celibate love about which Judith speaks:

> I see celibate love as different to other love in that it is love for God and a non-possessive love for the other person that leaves others free to answer.

In Middle-Eastern tradition, the guiding and compassionate star of Virgo can be recognised in the yearning of the Jewish psyche for the Messiah. In the Book of Numbers, the star is associated with the Promised One who will bring universal peace.[135] Yet in this symbol of the star, we meet also the suffering servant of God. Such a witness confronted humanity anew during the Nazi period when Jews were forced to wear the Star of David.

---

134   His Holiness the Dalai Lama, *The Art of Happiness*, 113.
135   Numbers 24: 17 in *The New Jerusalem Bible*.

Figure 6: Star of David (Judenstern), by anonymous artist. Source:
Courtesy © Art Resource. Reprinted with permission.

In Matthew's Gospel, the evangelist traces that messianic theme and the intersection of life and death with the story of the magi.[136] The magi read and understood the import of stellar configurations. Their journey implied that Christ's birth holds a cosmic significance that can bring the opposites together—the masculine and feminine and the creation and destruction of innocents. That evolving sense of God present in the universe and in all events, even the inexplicable, is what Louise has found important:

The Cosmic Christ—Creation spirituality fills my soul.

136　Matthew 2:1-12 in *The New Jerusalem Bible*.

In the 19th century the Catholic Church, acknowledging the Aurora Australis visible in the night sky, identified Mary as patroness of Australia. The constellations remind us what the star-goddesses of other times and cultures signify. How do I rediscover the attributes of the Virgin-Mother of Mercy in myself? In psychological language, those following a virginal way need gradually to withdraw projections on others, and come to see all beauty as reflections of the Greater Self who is "the first star."[137] In the light of his experience, David can say:

> ...*struggling with difficulties in loving human persons has led eventually to being in love with God in a new way.*

Like our mythic forebears, storytellers, poets and artists are still recognised as those who can perceive and point out this inner and cosmic radiance. In parts of the world where the connection with nature is strong, people recognise the stars as divine beings. I am reminded of van der Post's description of a young mother tenderly holding her baby aloft one starlit night in the Kalahari Desert.[138] This African woman was conscious of a pure and cosmic place within and beyond our being: the virginal place. She was receptive to that energy and bonded her child to that deep source. Carl Jung picks up and describes individuation as our becoming aware of that guiding aspect of the star within and calling us to surrender to its prompting.

In psychological terms, Jung recognised the critical connection between meditation, imagination and action. He realised individuals need to keep an eye on their star. With this awareness of their origin and destiny, individuals can perceive within themselves something of the divine spark and choose to attend to that essence:

> ...the Light of Nature has been brought by the stars...(it) is the quinta essentia, extracted by God himself from the four elements and dwelling in our hearts...enkindled by the Holy Spirit.[139]

---

137   Dante Alighieri, "Paradiso," Canto II: 28-30, *The Divine Comedy*, Vol.3.
138   Laurens van der Post, *The Heart of the Hunter*, 43.
139   C.G. Jung, "Alchemical Studies," CW 18, ¶ 148.

The constellation of Virgo suggests that persons and the world need the prophetic light and merciful love that Virgo carries. The actual beauty of the night sky speaks of the Self while the Respondents often reflect that their compassion comes from an Other who sustains them. It reminds me of my companion on this journey. I am travelling in the company of Mary of Guadalupe, the woman wearing a dress patterned with roses and a veil patterned with stars. She is an expression of the Black Virgin whose image and expression of the virgin archetype and of celibacy I want to take up now.

The Black Virgin

The image of Mary as purest of virgins can be an unattainable ideal for women and men who embrace celibate chastity. Instead of companion, Mary can be put on a pedestal disconnected from the human struggle. I am aware that both Mary and the Greek goddess, Athene, call themselves "handmaid of the Lord."[140] Yet when "servant of God" implies unthinking loyalty to the patriarchy, it is pernicious. Although gifted with wisdom, Athene became caught in hierarchical constraints and betrayed the feminine. Chaste celibate women and men can face this same threat. Finding ways to voice disagreement on issues that matter is both essential and difficult for celibate and non-celibate. Respondents point to the importance of debate and cite the subjects of priesthood and power in the Catholic Church. All spoke against an imposed celibacy, and to quote Thomas:

> While celibate priesthood has a place in church life, there are other possibilities as in other churches. We need mutual support to explore relevant issues together. The Catholic Church badly needs the feminine voice in all issues and at all levels both in governance and in daily life.

I want to return to the archetypal figure of the Black Virgin because she can be of particular relevance for celibate women and men. Let me start by saying that I know the Virgin Mary is not a goddess: not Athene nor Artemis. She has qualities associated with the Greek archetypal fig-

---

140 Ann Shearer, *Athene: Image and Energy*, 123,129.

ures of Sophia and midwife and with which many celibate and non-celibate persons relate.

Unfortunately Mary has been anaesthetized. In his fresco of the Annunciation, Fra Angelico shows a tempering of the Other worldly ideal of Mary as the chaste virgin by painting a shadow in the scene. Is it hers or the overshadowing of the Spirit?

Figure 7: The Annunciation, by Fra Beato Angelico. Source: © Art Resource. Reprinted with permission.

Scripture indicates that Mary's "fiat" to bearing Christ was uttered with trepidation rather than with certainty.[141] Going to the *Song of Songs*, I discover that the dark woman associated with both the Virgin Mary (and Mary Magdalene) was called the Rose of Sharon:

> I am black but lovely, daughters of Jerusalem…
>
> I am the Rose of Sharon,
>
> the lily of the valleys.[142]

---

141   Luke 1:38 in *The New Jerusalem Bible*.
142   *Song of Songs* 1:5, 2:1 in *The New Jerusalem Bible*.

This stanza with its sensual imagery celebrates the love of King Solomon and a Shulamite woman. In the Jewish tradition, their relationship was taken as an allegory of the love between God and the soul and between God and humanity.[143] Later in the Christian tradition, this analogy was also applied to God and the Virgin Mary.

Characteristics of the virgin which are "good taste" ("Sapientia") and "wisdom" ("Sophia") are palpably present in devotion to the Black Virgin—and by extension to be cultivated by celibate men and women![144] This veneration has early origins. In Asia, there are echoes in the cult of Artemis Ephesia which celebrates divine feminine and natural energy. Not surprisingly, Christian tradition has Ephesus as the place where the Virgin Mary lived with St. John and from where Mary was assumed into heaven.

In AD 431, this city was the site of the third Ecumenical Council of the Christian Church. At this assembly, the Virgin Mary was declared to be the Mother of God, and her son declared to be man and God. Human and divine, masculine and feminine are acknowledged as meeting in this archetypal image of Mary as the Virgin-Mother.

Often artists can convey something in image better than any written word. An icon called the Greatness of God in Toplou, Crete, portrays universal redemption and a conjunction of opposites. The Virgin Mary is sitting on a throne between Adam and Eve. The Christ Child is on her lap and with her left hand Mary reaches out and takes hold of Eve's arm. The mothering-virgin welcomes the feminine in both women and men that can feel burdened with guilt and shame. She embodies the acceptance and reconciliation of nature and Spirit that lie at the heart of the cult of the Black Virgin.

Devotion to the Black Virgin is both worldwide and culturally specific. This image of Mary as a maternal black woman (who in terms of class, gender and race holds no worldly power) is held in great affection. It seems that a positive relationship with the Black Madonna provides a balance for the image of the untouchable Virgin. To fill out this picture of the quiet potential of the Black Virgin-Mother, I give a general back-

---

143 Wisdom 7:27, 9:9 in *The New Jerusalem Bible*.
144 Gertrude Jobes, *Dictionary of Mythology, Folklore and Symbols*, Part 2, 1475.

ground, hone in on the Black Virgin of Einsiedeln, and reconsider her relevance for celibate women and men.

Let's travel out from the site of the Christian labyrinth. In the Cathedral of Chartres, in a chapel near the famous labyrinth, is an image of the Black Madonna. Over the border in Spain, is her shrine in the Benedictine Abbey of Montserrat. Here the dark Virgin is called "Little Browny" by couples who come to ask her blessing on their marriage. It is the same shrine where Ignatius of Loyola prayed and put down his sword and his worldly prestige. In Australia, in the Catholic Cathedral of Darwin, Mary is portrayed as an Aboriginal woman with child poised traditionally on her shoulder. It is as though the Black Virgin and Mother opens a comfortable space for people to bring all of themselves—light and shadow—to someone who cares and in whom they can trust.

I became familiar with Mary under this archetypal expression during analytical training in Zurich. One of the places for pilgrimage is the site of the Black Virgin in a chapel within the Benedictine Monastery of Einsiedeln deep in the Romansch area. Strategically, Einsiedeln stands at the beginning of the Swiss path to Santiago de Compostela which marks the burial site of St James the Apostle. During the Crusades, Compostela, the field of the Star, took the place of Jerusalem for pilgrimage.

The story of Einsiedeln's Black Virgin goes back to the 9th century and to a hermit called Meinrad. A singular man, he had gone into this area, known as the Dark Forest, to live a life of prayer, holiness and solitude. In such marginal places, it was common for Mary to be invoked as patroness.[145]

This archetypal image of the Black Virgin is like the Indian figure of Shakti who invites people to come and find the strength they need. More earthy parallels of the Black Virgin are Isis and Kali whose names mean "the Black One" and who destroy evil and ignorance.[146] Irrepressibly, the Shakti of nature and of the dark feminine is active and thousands of pilgrims pray for and receive her help at shrines like Einsiedeln.

---

145   J. Salzgeber, *Einsiedeln*, 3-15.
146   Gertrude Jobes, *Dictionary of Mythology, Folklore and Symbols*, Parts 1 & 2, 903.

What does the Black Virgin bring to the image of the virgin and to celibacy? In a seminar entitled, *Looking at Sacred Image*, Dr. Cornelia Vogelsanger, then Curator of the Zurich Ethnology Museum, referred to the black Kali and the feminine strength that she inspires.[147] The Kali myth communicates a quality of fortitude that comes out of deep reflection. Although this age is actually called the age of Kali, the characteristics of feminine strength and energy are hard to locate in Christianity except in the Black Virgin.[148]

Jung calls for a rediscovery of the devalued feminine, the unconscious and the bringing together of conflicting opposites that the Black Virgin embodies.[149] This virginal element is in touch with the ordinary human situation. In contemporary justice and spirituality movements, we hear that awareness of woman, sexuality and the earth of which Elizabeth Johnson speaks:

> For the Spirit creates what is physical—stars, planets, plants, animals, ecological communities, bodies, senses, sexuality—and moves in these every bit as vigorously as in souls, minds, ideas.[150]

The Black Virgin was also associated with the rose: both the Rose of Sharon and the mystical rose. In beauty and fragrance, the rose was thought to hold purifying and curing attributes. Many of the early monasteries that also doubled as hospitals cultivated roses. A Capuchin convent on Lake Zurich still has a rose garden and gives the name of rose to the village of Rapperswil that surrounds it.

In Aboriginal dreaming stories, the lotus is seen as a variant of the rose. In Eastern symbolism, it is the throne on which both Buddha and Tara sit and from where they are ready to spring to the help of those who call. Jungian psychology and alchemy take up the image of the red and the white rose and regard it as a symbol of striving towards one Self, the golden flower. For in the centre of the single rose is found the philoso-

---

147   Cornelia Vogelsanger, Personal Communication, April 23, 1999.
148   Nancy Qualls-Corbett, *The Sacred Prostitute*, 46-47.
149   C.G. Jung, "Psychology and Alchemy," CW 12, ¶¶ 192-193.
150   Elizabeth A Johnson, "An Ecological Theology of the Holy Spirit," http://www. duq.edu/events/holy-spirit-lecture-and-colloquium/2008. Retrieved June 7, 2014.

pher's stone. It is a reminder that one's true identity is found in connecting with one's self.[151] Dante seemed to understand these connotations:
in *Paradiso*, when Beatrice eventually leads the pilgrim home to where
God resides, the image of the single white rose appears.[152]

I began this section with the Christian labyrinth of Chartres. Could
we now return to that labyrinth whose centre point is an image of the
mystical rose? Reflectively walking towards the centre, pilgrims open to
a change of heart: a life, death and resurrection experience. Their prayer
asks the Black Virgin for a new insight that they can integrate into the
rest of life. It could explain why this Respondent writes that over time
her relationship with God has changed and she too has changed—in a
way that reflects the aesthetic of celibacy:

> *Growing in intensity and compassion without fear! The reality of
> God's unconditional love of me calls to mind patience and heal-
> ing!* (Janice)

As an archetypal expression of the virgin, the Black Virgin is simply self-giving love…"a rose needs no 'why;' she blooms because she
blooms."[153]

Virgin Land: Gardens and Deserts

Without symbols, visions and dreams, our lives lose their vibrancy.
There are many metaphors that deepen the meaning of the virgin archetype and call for inclusion. My gathering of those recurring motifs can
be selective rather than exhaustive. From early times people knew also
the power of metaphor to arouse Spirit. As the psalmist wrote:

> I will speak to you in poetry, unfold the mysteries of the
> past.[154]

Such an approach is at home with Jung's imaginal perspective of
psyche. On the global scene, I see increasing awareness of the world's

---

151   C.G. Jung, "Psychology and Alchemy," CW 12, ¶ 101.
152   T.S. Eliot, "Ash Wednesday," in *Collected Poems*, 98.
153   Angelus Silesius, unknown source.
154   Psalm 78:1 in *The New Jerusalem Bible*.

scarce resources that raises the virgin image to consciousness. Pristine spaces, unpolluted by greed and exploitation—virgin forest, virgin land, and endangered species—are gaining attention. Thanks to conservation and heritage movements, the sustainability and integrity of our planet are major issues. Worldwide concern underlines that it is the thread of love that holds our fourteen-billion-year-old world together. Have you noticed that women and men religious are active in these ecological movements? Many have a deep spiritual awareness of creation, as Patrick articulates:

> Love for me is an extraordinary energy of presence within every atom as in 'the world is charged with the Grandeur of God' (or love) wrote G.M. Hopkins. It is the triune God in and through all creation. Celibate love is an unconditional yes consenting to the transformation of this love at the heart of life.

Many old tales intuit the untarnished aspect present in the individual and in the collective psyche as does this story told by ethnologist, Karl Kerenyi.[155] I think of this anecdote about psychological virginity as the Artemis factor. It clarifies the importance of feminine strength in both women and men for the survival of our world.

With Ovid as his source, Kerenyi recounts a section of the myth where the three-year-old Artemis is sitting on Zeus' knee. Her father promises anything she desires. Artemis wishes for a never ending virginity (*parthenia*) and untamed space. Some would say here is the image of woman who desires an unending puella existence: little girl who refuses to grow up. On the contrary, I am suggesting that the Artemis aspect brings something uniquely feminine to humanity and this quality goes back to the request that she makes of her father and which Zeus grants.

Kerenyi takes the story as an explanation of the importance of the life stage of parthenia for women and for the future of society. This period of a woman's life refers not only to virginity but to a transitional time for the young girl who was moving into the next stage of her development as woman.[156] While touching on the maturational rites from a woman's perspective, I include commentaries from male as well as

155 Karl Kerenyi, *Athene*.
156 Karl Kerenyi, *Athene*, 41.

female Respondents so that you can see this feminine Artemis factor is essential for both genders.

In Greece, initiation rites for girls and boys were observed. The one of Arktoi might be seen as an extended celebration of Christian baptism and confirmation. Initially, the girls were formally introduced to their relatives and were given gifts. The second transition came in their ninth year (which Freud called the latency period) when they were considered as entering adolescence. Attic girls were then consecrated to the Goddess so that they could become aware of the spontaneous energy which Artemis represented.

In this mystery cult, Kerenyi wondered (as perhaps you are wondering): What could young girls take from an aggressive image of Artemis?" His conclusion was: "The spirit of parthenia." Its untamed or wild character represented instinctual strength and feminine independence that women need to integrate in order to cope with childbirth, childcare and for helping others to give birth.[157] Where might this image be helpful for celibates?

At the last General Chapter of the Sisters of St. Joseph (2013), I watched Artemis energy take form. Those women knew what it meant to assist others in bringing to life new ministries in schools, hospitals, prisons, aged care, NGOs and what Thomas Berry noted as the most pressing matter of all: care of the universe.[158] In effecting change, Louise can articulate more about this midwife capacity:

> *I think I have the courage to enter into the lives of others, especially those impoverished and in need. My life is enriched by just being with the person. If I can walk the journey with them there is a 'giving or a loss of me' and I can truly be there for the Other. My sexuality is enhanced. I become a more loving person. Spirituality in the depths of my soul.*

The lighting of the torch for each Olympic Games displays vestiges of the ancient ritual as a group of contemporary women take the flame from the cauldron. In this re-enactment, I see a reminder of Artemis

---

157   Karl Kerenyi, *Athene*, 85.
158   Thomas Berry, *The Christian Future and Fate of the Earth*, 68-80.

energy highlighting what is critical for our universe and our individual lives. This next Respondent connects with this Artemis factor in himself:

> *As I come alive to the deeper realms of love, I awaken to the violence and unjust structures in our culture and in our world. Celibate love quickens my mind and heart to listen to the poor and broken ones. Here in this land…the Aboriginal people, the homeless and jobless, the mentally ill and the afflicted also within the church.*

I have come to understand more about Artemis and her link to the border. Various Respondents spoke about needing to go to far-flung places for revitalising themselves and in answer to need. Jackie mentioned her working and studying in areas that *I doubt would have been open to me if I had not joined a Religious Congregation.* Those border places may not be comfortable and yet have a raw beauty. Often women and men vowed to celibate love are willing to go there for the love of God and for others. Let's hear Patrick on that issue:

> *If a person really works at the physical, mental and spiritual side of relationship and is open to the call of love beyond oneself, there is a blossoming and fruitfulness in the whole life. Tomorrow I will be at 'Z' Centre with the Detainees. In that setting we celebrate the oneness of being, and something of us as sexual beings enables us to touch the core of being.*

Underneath real feminine strength in man and in woman is love. It impels Patrick to minister to asylum seekers, and other women and men to engage compassionately in their border ministries. As feminist analysis reveals, there appears to be a relationship between treatment of the feminine and the state of the land.[159] In older societies, and it still holds true for many Aboriginal Australians, people know that they have to return to the virginal state of wilderness for personal and for social transformation. It is not surprising that people feel drawn to go on pilgrimage, to desert experiences, or to follow dreaming tracks with that same desire. The natural strength and independence of the virgin

---

159   Elizabeth A. Johnson, "An Ecological Theology of the Holy Spirit," http://www. duq.edu/events/holy-spirit-lecture-and-colloquium/2008. Retrieved June 7, 2014.

Artemis could symbolise what many women and men feel is lacking: a natural longing for making "God's birth…a continual process."[160]

With this kind of perspective, the mystery of the Incarnation is recognised daily in and around us. In locating her inner midwife and being that enabler for others, Louise is helped by her celibate commitment. She refers to her work as a chaplain in a psychiatric hospital and speaks of a creativity and warmth for those in need because of seeing celibacy as:

> *Open, creative, loving and bringing to new life those who struggle and suffer. I have a great opportunity to enter into the mental struggle of persons in my ministry. Listening and promoting life.*

While I am referring to comments made by those vowing celibacy, let me emphasize that the classical tales convey that psychological integrity—the virgin land—applies to everyone and goes beyond a physical state of virginity. Even the rigid St. Jerome emphasized that physical virginity did not characterize someone as truly virginal. In his letter to Eustochium, Jerome refers to a spiritual virginity whose purpose was *holiness*: a word whose root comes from *wholeness*.[161] To be a virgin meant a rediscovery of the original condition into which everyone is born and the integrity that people can regain throughout their lives. Along these lines, Jungian analysts and authors, Diane Cousineau-Brutsche and Christine Downing have described a virginal aspect of the soul that can never be spoilt.[162] The message can be healing for those overburdened with guilt and shame.

The archetypal motifs of the enclosed garden ("hortus conclusis") take up and develop virgin land with a slightly different slant from that of the wilderness or the edge spaces. In the *City of Djinns*, Walter Dalrymple compares the garden with its sealed fountain to paradise. Etymologically, *paradise* came from two Persian words that meant *a wall around*. The Western world can thank Xenophon, early historian and

---

160   C.G. Jung, "Psychological Types," CW 6, ¶ 428.

161   St. Jerome, "Letter XXII. To Eustochium." http://www.ccel.org/ccel/schaff/npnf206.v.XXII.html. Retrieved June 8, 2014.

162   Diane Cousineau-Brutsche, *Le Paradox de L'ame*; Christine Downing, *The Goddess: Mythological Images of the Feminine.*

writer, for bringing garden, as in paradise, to our consciousness. It was a place of bliss as are the garden oases created in the desert.[163]

In Genesis, we read that Yahweh planted "a garden in Eden...(in which God) settled man and woman...to cultivate and take care of it."[164] The garden is portrayed as an idyllic setting somewhere in the east and situated near four rivers. In this place, humanity could find an eternal and happy home but apparently failed their first test. The problem was that in this paradise lived the equivocal snake and that fateful tree of the knowledge of good and evil to which woman, and then man at her prompting, succumbed. If Yahweh had not wanted humanity to wake up to good and evil, there would have been no phallic snake, no receptive feminine and no tree of life right in the middle of the garden! That was the original garden, original sin and original grace.

Later in Scripture, Israel and the individual soul are both referred to as the enclosed garden and the virgin daughter of Zion.[165] These images, especially in the harsh environment of the Middle-East, would have communicated much more than a sense of vulnerability, sensual delight and oasis. They would have replayed ambivalent themes such as refuge and temptation, weakness and strength. In the Second Testament, paradoxical connotations of the garden as a sacred and a suffering place continue. The garden of Gethsemane and the garden of Christ's burial link the motifs of suffering, death and resurrection. Poignantly in John's Gospel, Mary of Magdala, when she goes to anoint his dead body, mistakes the risen Christ for the gardener.[166]

In this garden where she expected to find death, Mary re-discovers life. I wonder if it was not a case of mistaken identity but rather an understanding (that Mary had intuited at a deeper level) of the nature of the One she sought and loved. According to Latin tradition, Mary Magdalene was a former prostitute who experienced the loving forgiveness of Christ. When this man who had given her freedom and autonomy spoke her name, Mary knew him. Taking these Scriptural texts psychologically, it is the knowing and strong woman (considered in the Eastern

---

163 William Dalrymple, *City of Djinns*, 236-237.
164 Genesis 2:8,15 in *The New Jerusalem Bible*.
165 *Song of Songs* 4:14; 2; Kings 19:20 in *The New Jerusalem Bible*.
166 John 18:1-2; John 19:41 in *The New Jerusalem Bible*.

Church as disreputable) who is the first one to recognise Christ and is sent to proclaim the resurrection.[167]

In Christian tradition, the Virgin Mary was personified as the enclosed garden, made fruitful or generative through the Holy Spirit. St. John of the Cross takes up this metaphor of the rediscovered garden for all who respond to God. I imagine he could have in mind the Alhambra or even the more modest gardens that lie behind the gates of Spanish dwellings. In such an inner landscape, the soul and God can meet. While St. John speaks in erotic imagery, another Respondent, Ruth, can also say *this love still possesses me totally.*

An enclosed garden with its suggestions of Eden, Gethsemane and Resurrection is often found inside monasteries. It stands as a physical reminder to the occupants of their dedication to Christ. In *Paradiso*, Beatrice picks up this soul-garden motif when she tells Dante to look beyond his rapture for her to see the interior garden where Christ waits.

As in Beatrice and Dante, the virgin in everyone needs to keep a focus on the source of all beauty. One of the Respondents remarks that emotions can overpower but wisdom can be learned through mistakes. Another woman Respondent gives instances in her 30s where two close friendships took on a more intense, sexual nature that left her stressed and confused. It is a developmental journey, as Frank tells from his experience:

> From what I've learned as religious and priests told me their stories through the years, I believe that the celibate who does not pray regularly has violated a boundary, or has let life violate their boundaries. The celibate who uses another person for his or her own needs, whether those needs are material, psychological or include physical activities, has violated a boundary—by putting themselves before God in front of that person.

If the Artemis factor of midwifing life and cultivating the inner garden are important aspects of virginity, where does the desert image add to an understanding of the virgin soul? As we touched in the symbol of being singular, the image of the desert attracted many early Desert

---

167   John 20:17 in *The New Jerusalem Bible.*

Fathers and Mothers. These radical celibates sought God at the edge of society in order to be, as one Respondent described, *in the bundus with the little people* (Peter). Many women and men religious work in outback areas of Australia and in all parts of the world—often in a metaphorical kind of desert—to be where human need calls.

The border or desert place could be a healthy space where Religious Orders and their members are finding and redefining themselves. Thomas Berry considered the ecological crisis as the area where vowed religious are taking leadership. He observed that, "women are attuned to the voices of the Earth in a way especially needed as we move into a future less dominated by the plundering processes of the industrial nations."[168] Nowadays, Religious Congregations tend to be at the edge of the official church. Rather than holding status and power in big institutions, they might well be in a restorative position.

In the past, corrosive attitudes to sexuality and celibacy grew as Christianity and vowed celibates became more identified with secular power. Christianity was not immune then nor is it innocent now. In a more balanced view, the early monastics identify pride as the worst transgression against celibacy, and counsel genuine humility.[169]

In its derivation, humility suggests an attitude of an unpretentious modesty that does not call attention to oneself but acknowledges the One who is the source of life. That attitude grows through seeing the beauty of life and of others in spite of failure, powerlessness and suffering. The next Respondent sees the vow of celibacy in this light rather than accenting genital or non-genital behaviour:

> God is Maker, Keeper, Lover. My call in life to connect, accompany, include. (Jane)

As I want to emphasize, archetypes like virginity contain opposites that individuals and groups have to balance so that the new third thing can arise. Pride and humility are an example of such opposites that vowed celibates have to address in themselves. With a sense of psychological virginity comes a recognition of the holiness in all creation

---

168   Thomas Berry, *The Christian Future and Fate of the Earth*, 79-80.
169   Marcel Driot, *Fathers of the Desert*, 137.

including, and especially, in the dignity of each person. I am reminded of St. Basil's words that are quoted in the introductory sequence of the film, *Dead Man Walking*, and that point to the power and beauty of truly embodied celibate love:

Annunciations are frequent but incarnations are rare.[170]

Graced Friendship

In the words of Ruth:

> *So back to celibacy, I realised that with the experience of God's love being the most important thing in my life, I couldn't think of sex with just one person; God has become too distracting. Is my need for intimacy met? The short answer is 'Yes'…Celibacy is not in order for anything…for example, not to answer a call. It is simply who I am. The inner life heads inexorably to the outer life of mission.*

Ruth's experience invites us to open up another archetypal expression of celibacy, the gift of *Graced Friendship*. What do celibate love and graced friendship mean? Many of the Respondents described celibacy as a gift for loving freely. They suggested that graced friendship or celibate love expresses itself in a myriad of beautiful ways…by *presence, warmly, genuinely, non-possessively, non-selfishly, playfully, in trust, in kindness, concern for others, not seeking our own fulfilment either physically or emotionally, in prayer, in conversation, in meals, in walks, in openness to the moment and to the sacred, in ministry, in mutual respect, in care of oneself, in sharing of deeper life issues, with embrace and affection, in silence, non-genitally, through the eyes, in compassion, in commitment, in laughter and tears, in sacrifice, in delight, unconditionally,* and the list of blessings continues…

What stands behind graced friendship? Ruth says it is the grace of God's love that captures and compels her: not something she does, not even a sense of call. *Simply who I am.* It's about identity and a love for God that affects all of her life.

170　Tim Robbins, *Dead Man Walking*, DVD.

The Second Vatican Council described the charism of celibate chastity as a gift of the Spirit to individuals in order to benefit others. As I write, I am conscious that the women and men whose voices you are hearing in this work offer a rich and diverse blessing. Among them are missionaries, hospital chaplains, teachers, parish priests, counsellors, a psychologist, and administrators, those ministering in aged care and congregation leadership, spiritual directors, theologians, community workers, pastoral directors, professors. Their lives enhance others.

I am re-emphasizing that psychological virginity, the diamond aspect, is a grace from the Greater Self in everyone. Those who vow celibate chastity are pointing to this star aspect within all people for showing the graced friendship of unconditional love to others. Another awareness of this angle may be seen in a current trend among people entering religious life and priesthood. Candidates tend to be older than in previous generations. Those now considering or choosing a vowed celibate life often have been in sexual partnerships, in a marriage and may be parents or grandparents. They know that celibate chastity, virginity of soul, is not the preserve only of those who are physically virginal. They are drawn by the generous love of God which they desire to share with others. Frank underlines the freedom of choice in this gift:

> My experience of the choice of celibacy is a decision to love God first and all in God. And then to love others for the sake of their human fulfilment without demanding that their fulfilment promote my own. Now at 67, what does celibacy mean? It is wholeness to me, a kind of integrity...celibacy has also let me feel the full burden of brokenness in our humanness. It has given me a kind of clarity about being a person among persons and about being an individual person, uncoupled and in some ineluctable way solitary.

Joan Chittister intimates in *Fire in these Ashes* that graced friendship is an archetypal expression that goes right to our poetic roots.[171] I have heard people talk about befriending the shadow; I think graced friendship is about noticing and befriending grace as she constantly steps into and enriches our lives. Keeping the fire alight is no new phenomenon

---

171 Joan Chittister, *Fire in These Ashes*, 1996.

reserved to the Christian religion. Long ago in the Greek-speaking world, tending the fire was the responsibility of the virgin goddess, Hestia. In every ancient Greek and Roman home was an altar to the protectress of children, and there the sacred flame was revered. Before and after each meal, this mothering goddess was invoked.[172] The Respondent, Janice, appears to connect in her dreaming with this aspect of offering hospitality and friendship to others:

> My dreams often are celebrating and enjoying food and friend-
> ships—always many people and much food…When I awake
> I have a sense of unity, loving freely. I have sexual dreams too
> which I take as living example of intensity and spiritual growth.

I know that there are many contemporary female and male Hestias who gather people around the hearth, offering them nourishment, peace and community. In old Roman times, it was considered a disaster if the actual fire died. There was even a custom in some places where fathers handed the fire to their sons at the time of their marriage. In this way the fire was ritually passed from generation to generation. They were conscious of its gift and its cost. People were prepared to keep and defend the hearth and all it symbolised of home, relationship and identity.

The mythic example of Hestia gave rise to such cults as the vestal virgins. These vestal virgins did not freely choose celibacy. It was an imposition; not the freely chosen gift that many of the Respondents emphasize as essential for their celibate life. As a service to the existing social order, the celibacy of the vestals was about loyalty to the empire not about original or end times as celibate chastity came to be seen in Christianity. The old order was not a threat to the respectable power structures as sometimes Religious Congregations were and are perceived as such by church and State now.[173]

In their imposed celibacy, vestal virgins had to live as exceptions to what was considered woman's destiny for marriage and bearing children. Yet the role of these archetypal virginal figures was to remind people

---

172   Robert Graves, *The Greek Myths*, vol. 1, 74-76.
173   Peter Brown, *The Body and Society*, 8.

that they were all carriers of a divine spark that came from an invisible and reconciling source. Along these lines and in contrast, one of the Respondents suggests that his energy to give to others comes from his freely chosen and generative celibate commitment:

> *It may be that my creativity and compassion for those in need is released or enhanced by celibacy.*

Tim gives the impression that growing into one's vocation gives one a sense of compassion for others and for oneself or what I understand as graced friendship. Whether one accepts the gift of celibacy or marriage or another partnership, Tim raises this important question, "Where do I find the joy and freedom to be truly myself with God and with others?" I am delighted that the next Respondent also speaks of celibacy, graced friendship, as being about finding happiness and as well as about giving joy and blessing to others:

> *Since celibacy is a vocation for happiness, unless I discover within myself somehow, in a clear-sighted moment, that I will be happiest myself as celibate, I simply have not a vocation to be a celibate…so unless this celibate vocation has this real 'blessedness' for me, I don't have this vocation.* (Peter)

The message coming to light is that the blessing of chastity is to give and to share friendship. This gift of friendship points to the divine Other who loves us. For this reason, Dominican, Timothy Radcliffe, entitles one of his books *I Call You Friends*. Their remarks indicate that many of the Respondents have taken to heart the invitation to discipleship as one of friendship. Ed says that he tries to walk and talk with Christ *in my waking moments* especially when it is hard going. Hear another Respondent, David, speak about his understanding of friendship and its impact on his life as a priest:

> *I find close friendships further my spiritual life because my friends are on a similar journey and we support each other…loving others has opened me to the love of God.*

The poet, Kahlil Gibran, knew this potential as we hear in his letters to Mary Haskell. Gibran knew the intimate and fruitful space that connects spiritual friends. What the poet recognises and names is that graced friendship creates room for the third, the Transcendent, to enter.

That consciousness of leaving space for the third in graced friendship is voiced by many Respondents. I am thinking of Debra who spoke of her overwhelming sense of God's love experienced through the love of another. It freed an inner capacity in her to see and accept her vulnerability like the jealousies and possessiveness that are part of human nature. As a celibate woman, Debra spoke of being gifted with a friendship that is based on love, respect, trust and openness. In this regard, I want to mention the place of a spiritual accompanier. While I address the role of spiritual guide in more detail in a later section, like other expressions of graced friendship, it is invaluable. Rose writes of her experience over the five years when she was living in another country:

> ...I used to talk to a spiritual director who was very supportive of me personally as well as in relation to my spiritual journey. She has been a wonderful help to me and I stay in contact with her.

This kind of friendship predates and is wider than Christianity. In the *Metamorphoses*, Ovid speaks about a flow of separateness and deepening intimacy between friends that happens through conversation. Like Ovid, Plato is thought to have deliberately written in the form of a dialogue because he wanted to create the possibility for others to enter into what he called "a literary garden."[174] I imagine that the Scriptural *Song of Songs* and John of the Cross' *Spiritual Canticle* also take the form of a dialogue to invite and to point to a growing intimacy between the person and the inner Self.

I notice that the dialogue moves from spoken words to songs between the soul and the Self. The reality of graced friendship changes everything, for awareness of God's love opens us to see others and the world in a new light. That sensibility is not easy to convey, and again requires the touch of the poet, musician or artist which is the language of aesthetics, the language of love. Quoting some lyrics composed by Canadian artist, Loreena McKennitt, Frank describes celibacy as imaged in song:

---

174   Kenneth M. Sayre, *Plato's Literary Garden*, xv; Scott Buchanan, *The Portable Plato*; Virginia Hilu, *Beloved Prophet*.

Another whole set of personal symbols are in song: "while Love is Lord of heaven and earth/ How can I keep from singing." I do, a lot, except when I am desolate.

In my experience of Jungian analysis, I find that client and analyst also meet in an allegorical enclosed space where conversation is important and graced friendship grows. In alchemy, this place was called the vessel of the virgin and "the rose garden of the philosophers."[175] In the contained space of analysis, individuals can and do meet their virginal side that not only wants to sing, but needs to express the shadow aspects, the difficult stuff of life. Both sides need space to speak so that the work of transformation can find an impetus. Ideally this place provides what Jane describes as the meaning of celibate love and room for:

Loving freely, openly, allowing others to come and go.

Alchemy and the Brother-Sister Relationship

In Analytical Psychology, the space where client and analyst meet is called an alchemical vessel. The alchemical work is a metaphor for an inner change that happens through a psychological and spiritual process.[176] The goal of the work is symbolised as the transformation of lead into gold where the shadow of neglected and negative aspects of personality become freed energy.

For Carl Jung, alchemical imagery illustrated the transformative stages of individuation.[177] Describing the relationship between client and analyst, Jung refers to the virgin archetype.[178] Client and analyst engage in a reciprocal relationship where the focus is on the dilemma the client is addressing, not on the client or the analyst. Janice takes this attitude to her friendships and knows how her celibate commitment affects her relating:

---

175 C.G. Jung, "Psychology and Alchemy," CW 12, ¶ 235.
176 C.G. Jung, "The Practice of Psychotherapy," CW 16, ¶¶ 385-386.
177 C.G. Jung, "Mysterium Coniunctionis," CW 14, ¶ 792.
178 Joanne Stroud, *Images of the Untouched*, 167-168.

...having many male and female relationships and having an
intimate relationship—knowing the intensity of deep sharing
and receiving—and turning that love outwards to others.

Jung called the rapport between client and analyst, the transference.
It is akin to Mircea Eliade's description of the alchemist's role. Other
terms, like the interactive field, indicate there is a kind of magnetic field
in the therapeutic engagement.[179] This differs from the Freudian outlook of viewing the psychoanalysis as a problem of shared unconsciousness although this happens at times. Winnicott took an attitude to this
dynamic as transitional space for moving through a psychological or
emotional block.[180] "...The potential achievement, if it can be maintained—if the conscious mind does not lose touch with the centre—
means a renewal of personality."[181]

Jung saw that, by staying with paradox in their lives, individuals
could become amenable to the dark feminine that he also described
as the wisdom of the Holy Spirit. This is the Sophia that the alchemists sought in their work and was attributed to the Virgin Mary or
to Hermes. It required of aspirants a virginal attitude of dedication to
inner and outer transformation. Rose reflects on her experience of living
celibacy that has changed her:

I have often experienced celibacy as a lonely thing, an empty space
within me, but in more recent years I've been able to appreciate
that empty space more—to see it as OK and with the potential to
deepen my relationship with God and the spiritual.

That key player of Hermes (Mercurius) in the alchemical opus was
also described as "one out of the rock heap."[182] This trickster could lead
one through and into all kinds of situations. It was this character who
changed the lead into gold. Hermes represents Spirit. In Christianity,
these mercurial aspects are again seen as belonging to the Holy Spirit, to

179 Jan Wiener, *The Therapeutic Relationship*, 73.
180 D.W. Winnicott, *The Maturational Processes and the Facilitating Environment*,
      53.
181 C.G. Jung, "Psychology and Alchemy," CW 12, ¶¶ 187-188.
182 C.G. Jung, "Alchemical Studies," CW 13, ¶ 243; Rafael Lopes-Pedraza, *Hermes
      and His Children*, 13.

Mary and to Christ, "the stone that the builders rejected."[183] I noticed that Frances refers to Christ as the rock on which she builds her life:

> *He's the rock on which my life is based. He's the one who gives meaning to my life.*

The alchemists gave the name of "the lapis" ("the stone") to their transformational work. The stone represents that elusive and enduring Spirit of one's Self, which brings consciousness.[184] The work depends on the Holy Spirit because human effort alone cannot change the dross of our lives into gold. Applying the symbol of alchemy to chastity, individual or communal efforts are not sufficient. Grace needs to enter to change one's heart.

In this intense work that goes through periods of confusion, it is necessary to grow in a deep trust in the Self who is guiding the process. Frank describes the paradoxes of celibacy that affect and challenge him:

> *Celibacy has left me both more and less vulnerable in my relations with and love for others. Too great a love, or even too much liking, for another can draw me, I'm afraid all too easily, away from my first love, for God. Yet, this same God has made it very clear that I love God by loving others. This is one of the several paradoxes celibacy involves.*

Alchemy accepts the necessity of complementarity, which it expresses in sexual imagery. For something new to emerge, the marriage of opposites needs to occur ("coniunctio oppositorum").[185] In sexual union, there is a very physical joining of female and male. Can that intimacy of feminine and masculine happen when not expressed genitally? Respondents Debra, Peter and Frank said yes:

> *I think having close, respectful humanly intimate relationships with others is a help to satisfying sexual urges while remaining celibate. At least I have experienced such relationships—they were sexual in the sense of physical but not getting into bed...I believe*

---

183   Mark 12:10 in *The New Jerusalem Bible*.
184   C.G. Jung, "The Archetypes and the Collective Unconscious," CW 9i, ¶ 683.
185   C.G, Jung, "Mysterium Coniunctionis," CW 14, ¶ 726.

I have somehow experienced that real intimacy lies beyond the simply physical and we can become celibate lovers. (Peter)

The Respondents do not show rigidity in their comments. Rose describes what is happening for her as potential. Peter's remark is sensible and Frank speaks of vulnerability rather than feelings of inadequacy in his celibate choice.

Remaining celibate has involved a lot of denials in my life, as married life would have. I haven't felt sexually inadequate. Just inactive. (Frank)

Traditionally, the alchemical work demanded that two people co-operated in the endeavour. They were called the "soror mystica" ("mystical sister") and the adept. The implication of a brother-sister relationship was seen as integral to the work of transformation. Hear Catherine describe the mutual coming together and separation in her relationship with her friend:

It is a great gift I do not take it lightly. It is a treasure. There is a powerful level of communion that we have. At times, my friend is my guide and support and at other times I am his. We have learned to let go of expectations and focus on our life together and apart from each other.

Why is the brother-sister archetype especially important for celibate men and women? For enabling me to know something of this relationship, I am grateful to my own sister and brothers. The sister and brother archetype is a psychic pattern for knowing what equality and complementarity mean. In Jungian terminology, a shadow figure often appears as someone or something of the same gender.

In Religious Congregations, female members are also called "sisters" because of their sharing a common founding Spirit, a story. It grows deeper as a community life, often not under the same roof, is shared. These sisters show the best and weaker aspects of my personality. They are essential for psychological and spiritual development as well as support. In Jungian terms, there are many faces of the animus. For a woman, brothers and fathers are early manifestations of the Other. Psyche learns that reaching out to the Other is essential. For the celibate woman, the fraternal connection is especially rich. She has an unusual kind of development that has to do with the brother rather than with the husband.

The celibate man similarly finds his connection with the sister rather than wife. She offers him a disinterested warmth and understanding. St. Francis of Assisi saw himself as brother of all of creation, which, in turn, was his sister or brother. The sister-brother connection experienced by St. Clare and St. Francis offered them affection and inspiration. I saw that fraternity with God in all creation in a group of Franciscan brothers living in Zurich. There was something brotherly in their reaching out to others. In what was euphemistically called "Needle Park," these brothers befriended and assisted people whom many others would consider the dregs of society. In learning to live sexuality as celibate women or men, brothers and sisters have much to offer.

A realization of the power of the sibling dyad came at different stages of this research where I experienced assistance from the Respondents. The latter, whom I did not know except through the Co-researchers, were prepared to share intimate aspects of their lives because they were generous and open. I had a sense of belonging to a community intent on helping others.

I would describe this relationship as did Jungian analyst and friend, Dr. Henry Abramovitch: the brother-sister transference.[186] It can be important for being affirmed in one's uniqueness while other factors, like rivalry and jealousy, can also be present and affect the dynamics. Where there is growing trust, persons can risk self-disclosure without fear of being rejected. Brotherhood and sisterhood can bring a freedom to take up one's destiny. Jane says she is grateful to her religious sisters because she sees their deep and faithful commitment, while Frances looks to and speaks of a brother relationship where:

> *I have a friend, a male religious, whom I love deeply and this experience of loving and being loved has opened up a whole new world to me and has given me a whole new insight into God's love for me.* (Frances)

---

186   Henry Abramovitch, "Brothers and Sisters: Archetypal and Personal Dynamics," lecture at the C.G. Jung Institute, Kusnacht, Zurich, June 1999.

What I hear through all these remarks is that celibate chastity is a matter of the heart, where people are learning through vulnerability to become compassionate:

> *I have come to some newer understanding of (my vulnerability).*
> *I know boundaries support and assist me. I'm not afraid to love*
> *emotionally out of my true self.* (Louise)

CHAPTER FIVE

THE SECOND MOVEMENT
A LARGER TAPESTRY

Eros: The Fire and Spirit of Love

In this second movement of *Celibacy and Soul*, I want to reflect on the mercurial aspect of the Holy Spirit, source of Eros, who gets psyche moving and who brings the blessing of celibate love into collective consciousness. In the eco-spirituality that is emerging globally, the image of God as fire and Spirit fits. The circle of fire intimates what drives renewal. Palaeontologist and Jesuit priest, Pierre Teilhard de Chardin, envisaged a vitality released around both those who put themselves at the service of God and the evolution of the world. His cosmology and anthropology predicts that:

> ...after harnessing space, the winds gravitation, we shall harness for God the energies of love. And on that day for the second time in the history of the world, (we) will have discovered fire.[187]

Fire is an elemental symbol of the Self. It pictures a divine radiance moving within the microcosm and macrocosm of creation. Taking fire as an expression of the Self, we can look to Egypt where the Sun God was revered. It is impossible to ignore the incandescent ball that looms up, governs and then descends at the end of the day. In Australia, the Aboriginal dreaming of the Kaurna people of the Adelaide plains personifies fire as their ancestor. *In illo tempore*, Tjilbruke, whose name

---

187 Pierre Teilhard de Chardin, "The Evolution of Chastity," in *Toward the Future*, 86-87.

means "hidden fire," carried the body of his nephew to the island of Spirits.[188] On his journey of compassion, the mythic hero created healing places for men and fertility places for women that their descendants continue to walk and respect.[189] Like that of St. Paul, Tjilbruke's story reminds psyche that she carries a treasure that is also meant to be life-giving for others. Jackie commented:

> Celibacy is still about my relationship with God but it also involves my relationship with others.

Fire triggers growth as the Australian bush declares each summer. We know to stand in awe of its nature. In the Scripture the burning bush, miraculously not burnt up by its blaze, was the place where Moses learned the eternal being of God and whose name is about being: WHO I AM.[190]

At the Easter Vigil, all those present for the ceremony witness the lighting of the new fire and the Paschal candle that represents the Risen Christ. Those gathered light individual candles from this source and are reminded to hand that energy to others. In the Second Testament, Christ speaks of himself as bringing fire to the earth and longing to see it raging. As an image of the Self, Christ points to his desire that others engage in the transformation by divine fire. Janice expresses this possibility in her understanding of celibacy:

> It is a gift that frees me to love, to be, to create and to live with intense passion and energy.

While transformation is God's work, mystics like Catherine of Siena, own that their "nature is fire."[191] Were these people fanatics? Or is everyone invited to enter into this passion? If enthusiasm means to be filled with the god, how do we experience such quickening? When I asked Respondents about experiences and images of God, many identified an insight into God's love which had a developmental aspect. Hear what Peter says:

188   M. Eliade, *The Myth of the Eternal Return*, 4, 21.
189   Lewis O'Brien, *Tjilbruke the Ibis Man*, 1988.
190   Exodus 3:14 in *The New Jerusalem Bible*.
191   Catherine M. Meade, *My Nature is Fire*, 167.

When a kid it was 'Dadda Jesus.' Then: 'sweet Jesus.' Then: 'Jesus, God.' Then: 'Jesus, friend, lover'.…And now very much mine and humanity's breakthrough into God—'the Omega point.'

This Respondent picks up Teilhard de Chardin's expression of God as "the Omega point…(for) emergence…the via tertia."[192] The dynamic takes one from being tentative like the disciples who met Jesus on the way to Emmaus to finding their "hearts…burning within them."[193]

The responses tell of taking time to reflect and letting wisdom take root in action:

To love is to be vulnerable. Jesus' love meant lepers and prostitutes could approach him. This love makes me gateless and opens me beyond structures, boundaries and beliefs. (Patrick)

Patrick describes how he is stirred by the people and the events of his life to embody Christ's attitude to life. Something within the person is fired, cooked and primed for transformation. I want to illustrate with the words from a dream. At the beginning of analysis, I usually ask the client if there is a dream that is staying with them. In the analytical process such initial dreams give a snapshot of the unfolding work.

During my selection interviews for psychoanalytic training, one of the panel asked if I could recall a recent dream. I replied…*I can recall putting some swan-shaped pastries into the oven.* At the time, it made no sense. Now as an analyst I have another appreciation. I suppose that the interviewing analyst recognised that my unconscious was in the state of preparation. Maybe she made an association to the motif of the swan in the Grail legend. In that scenario, the innocent had shot a swan. I will not even try to enumerate what I had shot down! In the legend of Parsifal, the naïve one needs to wake up to compassion and to be softened by life in order to be ready the second time around to ask the question: Whom does the Grail serve? Like Parsifal, I needed to wake up to, *Whom do I serve?*

---

192 Ursula King, *Teilhard de Chardin and Eastern Religions*, 219-221.
193 Luke 24:13-35 in *The New Jerusalem Bible*.

A daily response to such a question needs visible form... allowing "the word to become flesh."[194] There are other influences that can get in the way. A thought that can find its way into the mentality of some women and men, and has done so, is that celibate chastity is about not daring to love anyone. What takes hold is a parody of celibate love, which indicates a misunderstanding of human development, of chastity and an impoverished theology of religious life.

I recall one woman who spoke of the guilt she still carries after confessing to masturbation. On the other hand, Georg who works with alcoholic religious remarked, *we were told to cut off instead of thinking the thought to the end.* Thinking things through rather than dissociating gives psyche space, or pause, to reflect on whether or not that looks great—but not for me. In contrast to splitting off and dissociating, Rose has noticed an integrating movement within herself:

> I'm more connected to myself and more connected to God within me...perhaps the spiritual and the human are more merged in me, like they have come together and are not separate.

Fire in Earthen Vessels

The capacity we carry to love is conveyed in St. Paul's metaphor of our holding a treasure: what he calls "fire in earthen vessels."[195] In accenting fire, I want to convey the Spirit in reality and in sexuality, which are capable of giving light, life and warmth and can also turn cold. Ignatian Spirituality takes this consciousness into account by advising persons to pay attention to which Spirits motivate and then to make choices out of that realization.

The image of the earthen vessel suggests receptivity in every man and woman. What sustains ardour? Another Scripture story gives a clue. In Luke's account, when Mary goes to help her pregnant cousin, she greets Elizabeth saying, "My soul proclaims the greatness of God."[196] The vir-

---

194   John 1:14 in *The New Jerusalem Bible*.
195   2 Corinthians. 4:7 in *The New Jerusalem Bible*.
196   Luke 1:46; 1 Samuel 1:10 in *The New Jerusalem Bible*.

gin is aware of being the Grail, the earthen vessel of God, and she gives
an inkling of the meaning of chastity which shows itself:

> … *in commitment, in compassion, in giving freedom, through*
> *the eyes, with an embrace, in words, with silence, with everything*
> *I am.* (Brendan)

The different versions of the Grail legend that come from Oriental
and Celtic sources point to the healing associated with this sacred symbol.[197] Emma Jung and M-L von Franz refer to Chrestien De Troyes and
von Eschenbach who associate the power of the Grail with Christ's Last
Supper when this vessel held the Body and Blood of Christ.

Jung was moved by the legend because it brings together the feminine Grail of Consent with the masculine Spear of Destiny. The story
symbolically reconciles a paradox of sexuality. The opposites of male and
female are not denied and yet unite on another level in the lives of Kun-
dry, the deranged woman, and Parsifal, the poor fool, who both undergo a transformation. These protagonists realise a capacity to choose their
destiny rather than be victims of fate. I think this recognition is what
Frank means as loving detachment and which Frances expresses.

> …*I think (celibate love) has to do with not being exclusive. For*
> *me the love of a married couple is exclusive: they belong to each*
> *other in a special, exclusive way—this is not so in celibate love. I*
> *can have a special deep love for someone who also loves me, but I*
> *can't expect that he or she love only me. He or she doesn't 'belong'*
> *to me, in spite of a very deep relationship…it's as though celibate*
> *love is more far reaching without detracting from its profundity.*

This aspect is communicated in some sculptures and paintings where
the Virgin Mother is depicted as seated confidently, holding the lance
of divinity in one hand and the Christ Child in the other. This uniting
in a real way is at the heart of celibate chastity and takes a long time to
learn. Peter gives us an idea of how celibacy has changed and deepened
his capacity to give and receive. His background had caused a wounding
in his sexuality. As we hear in Peter's account, the celibate journey had

---

197   Emma Jung & Marie-Louise von Franz, *The Grail Legend*, 1-38.

taken him from being non-sexual, into awakening and into a freedom to love in this way:

> *Originally I think I chose celibacy from a wrong motive. I feared intimacy. I was brought up very strictly re sex. Later I chose celibacy for its practicality. Still later (as a priest) when I had really fallen in love for the first time, I believe I chose it as a value—in spite of the pain involved. And so I am not so devastated by my falls and imperfections but can struggle along because ultimately I feel sure that celibacy is a call to happiness.*

This transformation is described by St. John of the Cross as "a wounding" of the Spirit.[198] He likens the soul to a log of wood that is consumed by the fire of God's love. The journey of individuation, catching and holding the fire, is open to all.

In coming to know the fire of love through celibate chastity, a client went straight to the kernel when she asked, *Can the yearning to love and be loved be met in religious life?* I don't know what her personal answer will be as she continues to work with that question. It is also the subject of my work. The desire for erotic relationship that naturally arises in us is not easy to handle. In times of stress and loneliness, the yearning can be strong and come into conflict with a vow or promise of fidelity to another. The struggle is real for one vowed to celibate love or to another partnership.

David notes that there are some people who have felt needy of the sexual companionship of marriage and left the priesthood or religious life. More in reflecting than questioning, he wonders if there happens to be more a need of companionship and intimacy than of sexual closeness. Falling in love can be an opportunity, not only a crisis, for growing in love. Whatever one's decision, it seems to proffer what St. John of the Cross terms, a journey through "the dark night of the soul"[199] where one is faced with holding or losing the fire, as Debra observes:

> *While some may be sad, aloof, frustrated, cold or confused, others stay in the struggle trying to love and discover how to do this in*

---

198   Kurt F. Reinhardt, *The Dark Night of the Soul*, 199.
199   Kurt F. Reinhardt, *The Dark Night of the Soul*, 199.

the context of a vowed life, very grateful for the love they have been given.

Celibacy in Cross-Cultural Contexts

While celibacy is not the norm for any society, it can be more difficult in some settings. An anthropologist and priest from the Catholic University of Eastern Africa writes that in traditional African societies, it is vital for a man or woman to have children.[200] Some of the Respondents who have worked in South America and Africa confirm this view. Peter comments that many are incredulous and think *you're either a bit weird or having someone on the side.*

In many cultural environments, being mother or father of a family is seen as respecting one's place in creation and being like the Creator in giving life to others. Often, the sacredness of sexual activity is emphasized by religious rites that impress what it means to be responsible women or men in their society. That awareness and healthier valuing of sexuality seems to be slowly registering within the Catholic Church.

In many older societies, sexual activity and procreating were envisaged as performing one's duty without much mention of pleasure. To be childless was a terrible punishment and shame and, in many parts of the world, it is still so. Virginity might be all right before marriage, but the future of oneself and the community depended on having children. For this reason, polygamous marriage could be acceptable (but usually for men, not for women!). From such a perspective, celibacy appeared detrimental to identity and in conflict with the individual's relationship with God and the community. Frances confirms this collective imperative from her missionary experience:

> *I found that, in South America, many people don't understand choosing celibacy—because having children is so important.*

Appreciating the impact of culture is crucial in order to support an individual's celibate choice and to respect social context. When celibacy is seen as anti-cultural not just counter-cultural, Shorter turns to Vic-

---

200 Aylward Shorter, *Celibacy and African Culture*, 16.

tor Turner and Arnold van Gennep's ideas of "liminality" and "rites of passage."[201] Through this anthropological lens, a commitment to celibacy could be reframed as a long initiation process into which individuals knowingly enter to become mature and productive members of their community. What is then demanded of people vowing celibacy is courage, responsibility, support from the community, and grace, to grow through their threshold situation.

Similar difficulties with celibacy and its effects on individuals can be seen in contemporary Western society. The emphasis on sexual activity and performance is promoted by social media and a discrediting of celibacy in the wake of sex abuse scandals. In my analytical work, I am aware of self-doubt that arises for some women and men religious about their celibate commitment in the current social climate. Frank describes the situation in America that seems to apply in Australia and Europe:

> Today, U.S. celibates have another problem evoked by the current cultural attitude toward celibacy. We interject cultural attitudes, and right now, our culture values celibacy about the way it values manual labour. This means that celibates have the problem of self-appreciation.

Yet even in traditional cultures, the archetype of the virgin that lies behind celibacy manifests at crucial times. Among the Arapesh of New Guinea, it is believed that temporary celibacy during pregnancy enhances the developing child's life. Important energies, both physiological and metaphysical, are seen as redirected into the child's growth by the parents' abstinence. The decision of the parents to be celibate until the child is born is considered as safeguarding the life of the child, the well-being of the parents and the life of the community.[202]

In some societies, shamans who act as mediators with the Spirit world for their community, practice temporary sexual abstinence. During their religious preparation, shamans underwent a rigorous initiation

---

201   Victor Turner & Edith Turner, *Image and Pilgrimage in Christian Culture*, 36; Arnold van Gennep, *The Rites of Passage*.
202   M. Eliade, *Encyclopedia of Religion*, 144.

that included celibacy. Taking up Jung's observations, celibate commitment could be re-considered as a shamanic journey.[203]

As in these older mystery religions, vowed celibates express the desire to grow into the likeness of God. Yet, as one of the Respondents clarifies, people need to avoid any unhealthy inflation. There is a danger in trying to be too good and the focus is key. Tim spoke of identifying with the compassion of Christ and his vulnerability rather than any Messianic ideal:

> *Celibate love in Christ is being drawn to increasing identification with Christ's compassion: Matthew 25 is a good exposition of celibate love and in this sense celibacy is modelling generous love.*

Shamans, or religious professionals, were respected because of their initiation into a spiritual world and their ability to read its signs. Irrespective of whether they were real or fake, shamans carried projections of the healer. Religious celibates are also initiated—ordained and professed—into a spiritual service of God and the community. They too can attract projections of the healer that can be difficult to handle. Those who identify with the healer archetype can lose their individuality and humanity. Those who know themselves as vulnerable human beings at the service of God and of others tread carefully. As Juan suggests,

> *the ministry of souls is not a job or a function…It requires such an effort and dedication as keeping a family.*

Regardless of cultural setting, it is prudent for persons to doubt, in the sense of question, whether their living of their vocation is genuine. I am thinking of the warning against pride that the Desert mothers and fathers gave to celibates. Some Respondents, like Thomas, suggest that in their choice of a religious vocation, celibate commitment has not come easily but was more like an evolution:

> *My 'choice' for celibacy was very gradual—not sure when or if I really made it. It sort of happened!*

---

203   C.G. Jung, "Civilization in Transition," CW 10.

In considering the impact of environment, I find that Victor White's comment about the necessity of a doubting process is reassuring. White compared it to a disentangling of knots that is integral to soul making.[204] Other Respondents came to a similar conclusion about examining uncertainties and working with paradox in their lives. In the following description of celibate chastity, Thomas allows us to glimpse his working with doubt in a lyrical way:

> *Celibacy does free yet it holds captive; it is gift (otherwise it's impossible) and it is burden; it is fulfilment (I feel more or less fulfilled) but there are regrets at time—that is, for me, part of the human struggle.*

Reluctantly Celibate

I baulked at one Respondent's reference to celibacy as a choice to be *"eunuchs for the kingdom of God."*[205] Strong reactions indicate a complex and it is relevant to consider and clarify my response, which might also have been yours. The figure of the eunuch and hermaphrodite reveals some of the fascination, the feared and despised aspects with which celibacy is associated.

Physically, for women a eunuch could be the girl or woman who has not developed and who cannot bear a child. Psychologically, a woman may be a eunuch because she is not attracted by or is estranged from her inner masculine or animus. With men, the physical eunuch is someone who does not go through puberty. Psychologically, the eunuch could be the man who feels unmoved and cut off from his feminine or anima aspect. For women and men in these situations, it poses questions about sexuality and spirituality. Rose's response shows a valuing of sexuality and yet no self-diminishment because of choosing celibacy:

> *Can't the sexual expression and the spiritual both exist together and even enhance each other? I don't have a very convincing response...Being celibate and being a religious is right for me*

---

204   Victor White, *Kinds of Opposites*, 148.
205   Matthew 19:12 in *The New Jerusalem Bible*.

*now at this stage of my life. And in my heart it feels right for me
and I believe it has helped me find depth and happiness in my
life. But I don't know how to explain it to others.*

The hermaphrodite is someone who has both male and female genitals. As the derivation of the Greek word suggests, Hermes and Aphrodite were two powerful gods who were seen as uniting in the person
who was born with bisexual characteristics. In tracing this image and its
relevance for celibacy, I want to turn to India.

In the Hindu texts of the Vedas, dating from the second millennium
BC, both eunuchs and hermaphrodites were called "hijras." Castration
was deemed the worst of degradations. It relegated the person to the
lowest level of humanity: literally Untouchable. Patrick reflects on what
could be similarly castrating in celibacy:

*When first becoming a priest…celibacy was like a 'chastity belt'
protecting me.*

In the Mahabharata, eunuchs born or made that way became scape-
goats. Like lepers or people now living with AIDS, hirjas were ostracized
from the local social and religious life. Yet they could hold a ritual role.
Metaphorically, hirjas carried the sins of the people.[206] Their notoriety as
freaks of nature marginalized them. This setting apart can also happen
to vowed celibates: either being put on a pedestal, or as Jane notes of her
treatment as a nun:

*I don't want to be thought of as strange, not fulfilled, nor a
freak—which are some reactions.*

The Islamic world held a particular view on those born or made
impotent. While the Prophet Muhammad had forbidden castration,
eunuchs were made guardians of sacred shrines. They were seen as safe
because of no longer being bound by sexuality. From this angle, some
Respondents noticed that people's reactions to them as celibates could
swing from one of being trusted and respected to being viewed with
suspicion or even a target for sex, as Brendan found:

---

206 Dominique Lapierre, *City of Joy*, 373-376.

It depends...some think celibacy is strange and it creates barriers, others show respect and it leads to sharing and trust. Sometimes celibacy makes one seem available.

In the Scriptural accounts, Jesus Christ was aware of the insult levelled at him and his followers of being impotent or castrated because of their radical dedication to the kingdom of God. He accepted this offence and turned it to align himself and God's kingdom with those who were most shunned in society.

Christ goes further. He speaks about voluntary and involuntary eunuchs contrasting the celibacy that is imposed by biology and life circumstance with a freely chosen commitment. He is not reluctant to take up this motif from which I shrank. Judith takes up this point and says how vowed celibacy connects her to:

...those in need: I feel more solidarity with people who have to live a life of a single even though they would prefer a partnership.

The Christian tradition adopted some symbols of radical celibacy. Up until the late 60s, the symbol of tonsured hair was retained in priestly ordination and within the religious profession ceremony. The tonsure was a sign of the person's dedication to God. At the time of taking first religious vows when just a little of my hair was symbolically cut, I remember feeling a sense of shock and loss.

In the book of the same name, Germaine Greer amplifies the image of the female eunuch as one of independence. She encourages women to overthrow institutionalized constraints and to freely and confidently express their sexuality. Greer's comment prompts me to ask myself, 'Are those who make themselves eunuchs "for the sake of the kingdom" drab people who are metaphorically castrated and have lost their freedom and creativity?'[207] 'Are they receptive to Christ's message of another life because their present life has little to offer them?' As we have heard the Respondents express, it is difficult to handle some of the stereotypes that desexualize and dehumanize the celibate person. Listen to Debra:

---

207   Matthew 19:12 in *The New Jerusalem Bible.*

One person referred to me as a neuter which was most hurtful and some just do not expect me to have deep feelings of love for a person, especially a man.

There are celibate women who are feminine, warm and real, and male celibates who are manly and virile. Their lives point towards integrity, a kind of psychological androgyny. The latter is not a blurring of genders or indeterminate sexuality. It describes people coming closer to their contra sexual aspect that means their being more at home with their inner feminine and inner masculine.

In the remarks of the Respondents, I hear them express a yearning for wholeness and their sense of vulnerability. I do not sense their being impotent and loveless human beings. Quite the reverse, I have the impression that they want to live fully while accepting their personal limitations: rediscovering the aesthetics of chastity.

CHAPTER SIX

A SOCIOLOGICAL VIEW: CELIBACY IN EARLY JEWISH AND CHRISTIAN CULTURES

Situating celibacy in the framework of Jewish and Christian culture adds to the understanding of celibate commitment. In ancient and mainstream Israel, perpetual virginity was a disgrace and an insult to the Creator. There are many stories of women lamenting their virginity and God's merciful intervention.

In the Second Testament, a major shift occurs when virginity becomes a choice instead of a life sentence. With the figures of Mary and Joseph, celibate chastity is deliberately and quietly portrayed as a possible vocation rather than condemnation. Like other Respondents, Debra speaks of its value while Roger accents choosing:

Joy of service to others.

To clarify this cultural shift in Judaeo-Christian culture, I want to trace some historical, biblical and popular stories of groups of women and men who chose "to be eunuchs for the sake of the kingdom."[208]

Essenes and Therapeutae

Although a minority in Jewish culture, there were religious communities of celibate women and men. Classical sources give descriptions of two Jewish sects, the Essenes and Therapeutae.[209]

Josephus dates the Essenes as prior to the 2nd century BC and their demise around 68 AD. The name "Essene" came from Syriac-Hebrew

---

208 Matthew 19:12 in *The New Jerusalem Bible*.
209 Geza Vermes & Martin D. Goodman, *The Essenes: According to Classical Sources*, 2.

roots and meant "healer." According to early texts, the Essenes numbered over four thousand and were scattered throughout Palestine. Pliny describes them as communities that were dedicated to the Torah and to God's word. They showed trust in God's providence by withdrawing to the wilderness. The Dead Sea Scrolls give more details of the Qumran community. The monastic groups were led by a priest and modelled on the twelve tribes of Israel. Their members believed that everyone had an immortal soul and was destined for life after death. Their life in common aimed at holiness and was based on regular study, meetings, prayer and a communion meal that celebrated the Covenant of God with the people.

Although equality seemed characteristic of the brotherhood, women were obvious by their absence. Archaeological evidence around the gravesites substantiates their exclusion. The members lived an ascetic and simple lifestyle accenting the healing and prophetic gifts of individuals. After baptism came a three-year initiation and purification after which the candidates could be admitted to full membership. The communities stressed the celibacy of their adherents and saw marriage, women and sexuality as belonging to this world.

Hippolytus, who was a Roman bishop (170-236 AD), describes one branch of the Essenes who did advocate marriage and admit women. They prescribed an initial testing of three years for women that ascertained their fidelity and ability to bear children.[210] Such circles continue till today. A derogatory view of woman, the body and sexuality has created an exclusive system in the Catholic Church. The reluctance of ecclesial authorities to recognise the equality of woman is mentioned by many Respondents. Thomas and Patrick write about Catholicism's complex with sex, woman and power:

> *There is nothing, I believe, against married priests—except the church's long history of sex-phobia based in the power of a celibate clergy.* (Thomas)

---

210   Geza Vermes & Martin D. Goodman, (Ed.). *The Essenes: According to the Classical Sources*, 73.

Authority and the right to exercise power have been restricted to a male celibate clergy. In this way, ecclesial documents and pronouncements evade issues of human sexuality instead of asking people to participate in a re-visioning of sexuality and spirituality. There are priests, like the following Respondent, who offer constructive suggestions for an inclusive model of church:

> *(there is) need for a renewed anthropology, a positive understanding of sexuality, a new sense of our purpose and calling as well as a renewed spirituality of marriage.* (John Terry)

The Therapeutae offered a more inclusive picture. I have a professional reason for including them as members of the psychoanalytical profession are sometimes called therapists. In the 1st century AD, Philo of Alexandria writes of these celibate women and men who lived in Egypt and identified themselves as "disciples of Moses."[211] In contrast to traditional healers who cared for physical ailments, the Therapeutae attended to the soul angst.[212]

There is no evidence of an initiation rite. While the communities were mixed, women and men had separate buildings and they met in an enclosure on the seventh day of the week. (An echo of the enclosed garden metaphor and innuendos of the Genesis account of Creation). The Therapeutae valued a rhythm of quiet, prayer and community life. Their monasteries provided space for sharing prayer and meals while each person had his or her sanctuary for solitude, work and study. They seemed to understand what Teilhard de Chardin later articulates about an aesthetic or spiritual life: that is, to increase the strength of your Spirit—nourish yourself.[213]

In contrast to the Essenes and in tune with the brother-sister archetype, women were honoured. They were considered like Moses' sister, Miriam. As the Exodus story recounts, Miriam came through a tough time with God and her brothers but she was not abandoned by them. It

---

211   Geza Vermes & Martin D. Goodman, *The Essenes: According to Classical Sources*, 15.

212   Joan Taylor, *Jewish Women Philosophers*, 7.

213   Pierre Teilhard de Chardin, "The Evolution of Chastity," in *Toward the Future*, 69.

meant that, in the world of the Therapeutae, women were considered as having a right to live this way.

Like the Essenes, Therapeutae shared their goods and lived a moderate life style. Their prayer followed a rhythm that celebrated the passage of the sun with the singing of the Hebrew Scriptures. Later that pattern was adopted by Christian monastics. I recognise something of the Therapeutae in Becky's reflection:

> *I have found celibacy a gift, a freeing…permission and an acceptance to work, interact, counsel and to be with people of both sexes.*

According to Philo, their healing capacity came from having an education in wholeness.[214] While the Theraputae may have had other problems, they did not get bound up with the shadow side of misogyny into which the Essenes fell. I find it intriguing that one of the latest encyclicals encourages women and men religious to offer "a spiritual therapy" for these times.[215] This next Respondent has discovered a freedom to relate in that generous way:

> *I guess my friend's love connected me with God's love and we were companions in mission together. I didn't get into many either/or situations—either him or God…Recently I reflected on my call and remembered that early on I was drawn to give my life over to God…once I experienced God's love, I wanted to share that experience with others.* (Catherine)

Sibyls and Prophets

The sibyls were virgins whose oracles inspired action.[216] During antiquity many prophetesses made their way to the sacred centre of Delphi in Greece. In Hebrew tradition, Sibyl was the wandering daughter of Noah

---

214   Geza Vermes & Martin D. Goodman, *The Essenes: According to Classical Sources*, 77.

215   Congregation for Institutes of Consecrated Life and Societies of Apostolic Life. *Starting Afresh from Christ*, Part 1, ¶ 6.

216   Gertrude Jobes, *Dictionary of Mythology, Folklore and Symbols*, 1446.

and famous for her gift of revelation.[217] What light do these seers shed on celibate chastity?

I remember looking at Michelangelo's depiction of the Sybils on the ceiling of the Sistine Chapel. He had pictured them at significant junctions in the Judaeo-Christian myth of salvation. One of these seers is the Cumaean Sibyl who had foretold that God would be born of a virgin and would bring reconciliation.

The image of the virgin with the cornucopia of peace and plenty suggests a God-given capacity to share with others. In the words of the evangelist, "you will be able to tell them by their fruits…and the greatest of them is love."[218] Rose describes what prompts her self-giving:

> *In my work with children and families and the school communi-*
> *ty, I feel that there's a capacity to be very present with them, very*
> *available, and I hope I'm not driven by my own ego and my own*
> *needs. Perhaps that capacity is enhanced by the celibate life I live.*

In the First and Second Testaments, the lives of other formidable prophets give another appreciation of the prophetic voice. Judith mentions Jeremiah who was a priest in Israel around 587 BC. This prophet preached God's love for the Jewish people in which he saw mirrored his marital situation. It was a disarming message from a disinclined celibate and prophet. Jeremiah compared God to a potter moulding clay and desiring psyche's recreating.[219] This symbol was mentioned by Jackie as one that comforts and challenges her:

> *The Clay and the Potter—where I am formed and reformed by*
> *the Potter.*

In the Second Testament, another imposing prophet is Jesus Christ's cousin whose name epitomizes his character: Yahweh has been gracious.[220] It may seem strange that John the Baptist was named the protector of Florence which Proust identifies as the birthplace of the Renaissance and the city of lilies. Historically Firenze brims with beauty and

---

217   Gertrude Jobes, *Dictionary of Mythology, Folklore and Symbols*, 1446.
218   Matthew 7:15; 1 Corinthians 13:13 in *The New Jerusalem Bible*.
219   Jeremiah 16 in *The New Jerusalem Bible*.
220   Jeremiah 31: 3-4 in *The New Jerusalem Bible*.

creativity.[221] This place of beauty and its guardian are virginal because they point to the mystery of God.[222] I hear similar overtones from many of the Respondents:

> *Celibacy helped me to be more available to be sent anywhere at any time. Now celibacy throws me more and more into desire for God.* (Peter)

Earlier I mentioned a prophetic woman from the Second Testament who is a strong and tender expression of celibate love. Let me put Mary Magdalene in the context of another story. I was watching a documentary about a black African woman whose name I was too late to discover but whose remark registered, *I may not be better than anyone else but I am as good as anyone else.* She cut through gender and race and class stereotypes.

That is how I see Mary Magdalene as she washes Jesus' feet while others are contemptuous and fail to show him courtesy. In this act of love, Mary gives a clew to celibate and non-celibate about touching others. The jar of rich perfume which she carried to anoint Christ's body is emblematic of this woman. Regardless of Scriptural debate as to her actual identity, Mary Magdalene is immortalized as the woman who has "shown such great love."[223]

In psychological language, the feminine shows a true ego-position before the Self. Mary embodies an attitude for every woman and man where ego is at the service of the Self. Theologians pondered why Mary remained with Christ at the Crucifixion while the other disciples ran away. Meister Eckhart concluded that she had no other place to go because Christ was her life. It fits the Scriptural account where Christ acknowledges Mary's devotion and makes her the first witness of His resurrection.[224] Catherine, along with other Respondents, mentions Mary Magdalene:

---

221   Marcel Proust, *In Search of Lost Time: Swann's Way*, vol. 1, 552.
222   John 1:19-34; Matthew 11:11 in *The New Jerusalem Bible*.
223   Luke 7:47 in *The New Jerusalem Bible*.
224   John 20:11-18 in *The New Jerusalem Bible*.

...the itinerant preacher—Mary Magdalene...Words and deeds.
Like her, I preach and only sometimes I use words.

Virgin Martyrs and Saints

A recent film, written and directed by Xavier Beauvois, *Of Gods and Men,* shows where celibate love can lead. This winner of the 2010 Cannes Festival tells of the martyrdom of a group of Trappist monks from the Monastery of Tibhirine, in Algeria, during the 1990s.[225]

That same integrity and courage that virginity can engender are illustrated by many women martyrs. St. Cecilia who was named the patron of musicians was born of an aristocratic Roman family. During the 3rd century during one of the persecutions, she refused to convert from her Christian faith and was killed. In 1599, Maderno immortalized this woman in a sculpture which can be seen in St. Cecilia's Church in Rome. It depicts the body of a graceful young woman lying like one of the clay figures of Eros that mark some graves in Crete. Martyrs still challenge a world of violence with the possibility of a society that is not determined by power, wealth or gender roles. A radical faith and belief in transformation prompted them to give up their lives. When individuals go against accepted social patterns, they usually have to pay a price. David's response conveys something of this sense:

> *Celibacy is a dangerous way of life. It only makes sense as being in love and expressing this in commitment to those around.*

There are other saints who bring an understanding of consecrated celibacy. Some women and men are recognised by the Catholic Church and others have no formal accolades. In passing, I want to mention Australia's first canonised Saint—Mary of the Cross MacKillop—and the man who inspired her—Father Julian Tenison-Woods. They often come to mind in this process of writing. The website of the Sisters of St. Joseph gives access to resources that tell the story of this woman and man who have shaped Australian spirituality and continue to influence it.

---

225 Xavier Beauvois, *Of Gods and Men,* DVD.

Two saints whose writings continue to impress are St. Teresa of Avila and St. John of the Cross. They lived and communicated a spirituality of intimacy with God. Bernini's sculpture of Teresa conveys something of the soul's wounding by divine love. Study the expressions of Teresa and the angel. It might stir memories of the tale of *Psyche and Eros*, verses from the *Song of Songs* and Parsifal's quest. All these associations gather in this sculpture and hint of Teresa's overwhelming experience.

A woman of great heart, her journey speaks of grace, Spirit and common sense. The eldest child of a devout Spanish family, Teresa De Ahumada had a deep love for God and for others. Her desire for religious life led her to take vows of chastity, poverty and obedience. Teresa candidly describes her conflict with vocation:

> My natural feelings arose with such force that…without God's support I would not have taken one more step. God gave me courage in spite of myself and I set out.[226]

For John of the Cross, the awakening to God's love seemed to have come in two phases which he called the night of the senses and of the Spirit. He described his union with God in a place deep within where God alone dwells.[227] John affirms that for every person, celibate or not, the inner journey requires a willingness to go through the darkness in order to come to know the Other who resides in our depths.

As Judith clarifies, there are many saints who are sensitive and sensible guides, and she refers to those who particularly give her inspiration in her celibate vocation to be strong and passionately alive:

> *I could also add Catherine of Siena and Mechtilde of Magdeburg. Mechtilde is important because she had a very intimate and tender relation to Christ as did Catherine of Siena.*

---

226 St. Teresa of Avila, *The Collected Works of St. Teresa of Avila*, 4, 1.
227 St. John of the Cross, *The Spiritual Canticle and Poems*, 448.

Figure 8: Ecstasy of St. Teresa, by Gian Lorenzo Bernini. Source:
ARAS online archive. Reprinted with permission.

Celibacy: In Major Religious Traditions

After studying Hinduism, Buddhism, and Christianity, Eliade could say that celibacy by its existence points to the significance of sexuality for society.[228] As I peruse these traditions, Frank's comment about the blessing and beauty of celibacy stays with me. I want to explore it in big brush strokes:

> *Celibacy is a great tradition in the world's religions that expresses the uniqueness of each person's relationship and the relationship of the whole community with the Holy One...*

Hinduism: Living in Awareness

From the Hindu perspective, there are four paths to the Spirit that a person travels. One way through celibacy and contemplation is called Brahmacharya, "a state of consciousness beyond time when...Being and Consciousness and Joy are One."[229] Marriage and the time of retirement are two recognised paths, and the fourth stage occurs when the individual sets aside family and material concerns.

Whether or not individuals went through these stages, it was essential for them to keep growing in awareness of God in everything. The purpose of brahmacharya, the choice of celibacy, is awakening to this reality. Under the care of a teacher, brahmachari practice a lifestyle of simplicity, austerity and detachment.

Initiates were taught to cope with their feelings by considering and respecting all women as mothers and men as their fathers. Kindness to others was seen as the way to moderate one's sexual attraction to other women and men. This Respondent reflects a similar constructive approach to sexuality after an adverse introduction to celibacy and sexuality:

> *...Sexuality is part of me and I don't want to cut it off and I don't want to suppress it. But I want to transform it, but this is*

---

228   M. Eliade, *The Encyclopedia of Religion*, 44.
229   Juan Mascaro, (Trans.), *The Bhagavad Gita*, 15.

not so easy. I think it was very unhealthy our attitude to sexuality in the past...When you have a sexual thought I think you have to accept it because it is a feeling like other things. And all the feelings are good. The question is what you do with the feeling. Maybe when you are attracted by the body of a woman then I think it's important to see the woman as a whole person. But this was not possible in the past when they told us cut off, cut off. You cut but you didn't think the whole thought to the end. The Latin is rispettare. Spettare—'to look-again.' 'Again look,' but not only at the breast but the whole personality of the woman. (Georg)

The brahmachari were members of ashrams or communities that offered encouragement rather than dependence. An experience in Bede Griffiths' ashram in India helped one Respondent who has since fostered a contemplative community that gives vitality to a number of people, celibate and non-celibate. Patrick could write:

Today I would describe celibacy as a radical way of loving. A deep and rich way of loving that is both intimate and affectionate without genital intercourse.

If sexual desire became too overwhelming for an initiate into brahmacharya, it was taken as an indication that the person was called to the householder's path. That did not mean that brahmachari were expected not to struggle with their passions but rather to acknowledge any natural conflict to themselves if to no one else. I like this healthy approach for dealing with the shadow of disconcerting emotions. In one of her responses Jane shows that attitude:

When I feel sexual tension, which may manifest in sexual attraction or an aching aloneness, I try and go 'deeper' to be intimately connected and interconnected with all people. At times, this is just theory and I feel the desire for a bodily flesh and blood contact with another. All I can do is simply invite God into my yearning and ask God to help me realise that my yearning is actually for the More, the ultimate, the One who alone can satisfy the desires of my hungry heart.

By seeing themselves as the servants of Krishna, the brahmachari found their inspiration. This spiritual relationship was considered primary. As they listened to their own experience and that of others, brahmacharis were encouraged to think, speak and act from a place of equanimity. While the choice for celibacy is respected in Hinduism as one way to inner freedom, it is considered as rarely attained. The loneliness of this path, the hypocrisy of some of its adherents and the suspicion it has aroused in others, seem not only Western phenomena.

The congruence and dissonance between ideal and practice raise the question for women and men whether they are Hindu, Christian or Buddhist. In choosing celibate chastity, can I face unlived aspects of my sexuality without others paying the price? This next Respondent gives an insight into the degree of honesty, struggle and humanness that his living unconditional love demands:

> *When I was younger, celibacy left me with a terrible problem of what to do with the powerful drive for sexual intimacy. As for any red-blooded person, celibacy was a problem area—curiosity, natural sexual urges and the fact it was forbidden fruit. I would agree with some who say that you can only really become celibate after 50 years. I believe that you could avoid sexual activity but to be really celibate? As I grew older the sexual drive became less but the dross of loneliness remains and needs to be purged as it gets in the way of true solitude and aloneness—which I have in a small way experienced as 'blessed.'* (Peter)

Buddhism: Surrender to the One

Rose mentioned that Buddhist spirituality was helping her to live in the present moment. In Buddhism, everything has its roots in the concept of Oneness. Buddhist nuns and monks practice meditation and celibacy to help them surrender to the One. Awakening comes through three treasures. Those core elements are the Buddha, the Dharma (truth) and the Sangha (community). While Buddhist practice accentuates the Oneness of life, it recognises the cycle of creation and cosmic interdependence coming through death and renewal. It offers a persuasive argument for eco-spirituality.

The source of universal energy was associated with the goddess, Kundalini. The latter, symbolised by a snake coiled up at the base of the spine, represented a sacred and inner potential that overcomes fear of letting go and fear of death. As individuals surrender to this feminine potential, they do not need to cling to what is ephemeral. From clinical practice, I find that one needs to have a strong ego, so that "letting go" can happen.

Aptly, Buddhism described a person's decision for celibacy as leaving home. The detachment of itinerancy or, as I heard it described, "the readiness to go where one is sent," is central to becoming a member of an apostolic Religious Congregation. It reminds me of Luke's Gospel story of Jesus' miracle of the draught of fishes and of those first disciples who "left everything and followed Him."[230]

This risk of going into the unknown is an image for the journey of transformation. I am reminded of the introduction to a film called *Broken Silence*. The Carthusian monk, being sent to Asia by his community, begins his account with a quote from Pascal: "when we leave home, our troubles begin."[231] We see how the protagonist's letting go of the familiar was a critical step in his process of individuation and that of others.

One of the Respondents shared a similar experience of leaving and homecoming. In Georg's 40s, he fell in love with a woman and they became sexually involved. Yet Georg's feeling of closeness to Christ held him in the priesthood. During a retreat he came across Rembrandt's picture of the homecoming of the prodigal son. The artist's depiction of the father's love moved Georg. Rembrandt paints the father with a masculine left hand and a finer right hand that rests on the boy's shoulders.

The image conveyed to Georg something of the male and female in God and God's extravagant love for us. This sense of God's embrace was healing for Georg:

---

230   Luke 5:11 in *The New Jerusalem Bible*.
231   Wolfgang Panzer, *Broken Silence*, DVD.

It felt like a homecoming...It's very important for me. There's the prodigal son and there is the father and he is very tender with him. And it moves me very much because I see myself in this young man. I am not so young. I think it was good for me to run away so I could come home.

Figure 9: Heimkehr des Verlorenen Sohnes (The Homecoming of the Prodigal Son) by Rembrandt Harmenszoon van Rijn. Source: ARAS Online Archive. Reprinted with permission.

Protestant and Ecumenical Christianity—One Among Equals

In the Protestant tradition, there are communities who practice celibacy. The Shakers in the United States of America owe their origins to 18th century Methodist dissenters in England. They broke away from Anglicanism and formed a new community. These individuals were attracted by the teachings of the Quakers and would meet and pray in silence for the coming of the Holy Spirit. As their Pentecostal worship included speaking in tongues, singing and dancing, they became known as "the Shakers."

Brother Arnold belongs to the five Sabbath day Lake Shakers in Maine, New England. Arnold describes his experience of being a member of this little Christian community who consciously value and show that gender equality and spiritual communion are possible:

> *Our life…serves as a positive reinforcement for the celibate life. We help each other in our struggles whatever they may be and share our humanness with each other…We practice an equality of the sexes as we find ourselves not superior to the Other, but equals.*[232]

Near the village of Taizé in eastern France, there is a monastic community of men from various Christian traditions who profess celibacy. This ecumenical community was founded in 1940 by Brother Roger Schultz (1905-2005). The young Swiss left his homeland and offered shelter to Jewish and political refugees. In 1944, Brother Roger and other monks vowed celibacy, simplicity and reconciliation. They continue to reach out to people in need across North and South America, in Africa and in Asia.

In 1996, looking for somewhere to spend an Easter retreat, I found my way to Taizé. It was not an experience of solitude as had been my original intention. I was amazed to be among thousands of young people who had gathered there to meet and to share their lives. Not only the religious brothers but also those religious sisters who offered hospitality impressed me. I saw how celibate chastity can provide a generous

---

232   Brother Arnold Hadd. Personal communication, 2011.

and reconciling place for others irrespective of faith traditions. Brother Roger's commitment has helped to create:

> a community where kindness of heart and simplicity could be the centre of everything.[233]

233   Brother Roger. Personal communication with Brother Emile, January 31, 2012.

CHAPTER SEVEN

THE THIRD MOVEMENT: TOWARDS AN INCLUSIVE THEOLOGY

A Way of Embodying Eros

In the introduction to *Celibacy and Soul*, I propose that sexuality, what it means to be a woman or a man, is integral to identity. Celibate chastity is one way of expressing one's sexuality. Regardless of a person's path in life, celibate love is about giving and receiving intimacy and affection in a non-genital and non-possessive way. I am conscious that people can be physically celibate and yet avoid the disposition of living with God as the centre of their life. Celibate chastity is more than abstinence. The latter can be an excuse to put others into a bind because someone does not relate well.

One of the Respondents spoke of the need for a new theology of sexuality for celibacy and for marriage. I am not a theologian and I look to theologians to articulate that ground behind celibacy and spirituality. From 1979 to 1984, Pope John Paul II gave 129 Papal audiences on *Theology of the Body* that are published as "Man and Woman: He created them."[234] It is a work that alludes to Scripture, philosophy, and spirituality. As the title acknowledges, man and woman are named as God's creation: separate, equal and complementing each other.

While I am not developing an understanding of sexuality lived in marriage, it is important to see marriage and celibacy as complementary rather than competing. John Paul describes marriage and sexual companionship as the best image of the inner life of God. He describes celibate chastity as a "precious gift of divine grace...and an undivided

---

234   Brian J. Bransfield, *The Human Person, According to John Paul II*.

heart."[235] Judith Merkle, a teacher in religious studies, describes celibate love as a transformation of how one loves God and other people.[236] I hear another Respondent pick up that theme:

> *Personally, celibacy means an awareness of my self and sexuality in relationship to God so that I do not isolate myself from others while not seeking or eliciting from them sexual gratification or commitment. Theologically, seeking to be open to God and the direction of God in my life in the solitariness of being human, created for union with God.* (Jan)

Sandra Schneiders writes in *Finding the Treasure* that celibacy is at the heart of vowed religious life.[237] In tune with human development, Sandra describes the emergence of different forms of the archetype. Respondent, John Terry, notes that he has found help in the reflections of Eugen Drewermann, who takes up the affective dimension and reminds me to keep focusing on the beauty of celibacy:

> Theology and psychology need one another…Jesus avoided speaking the language of the theologians of his day. (It is liberating to) hear something about God in the words of poetry…in the music of Mozart and Beethoven or in the pictures of van Gogh…[238]

Aware of the importance of aesthetics, Donald Goergen proposed re-engaging Scriptural sources, theologians and prophetic figures for appreciating celibacy.[239] Goergen's framework follows five threads: Genesis, the *Song of Songs*, Matthew's Gospel, and the writings of Paul and Augustine. While I take up his clew, I am influenced by other writers and the contributions of the Respondents. Taken together they contribute to an Incarnational and Trinitarian view that deepens and re-balances Christian attitudes to sexuality, to the body and to the feminine.

---

235 Brian J. Bransfield, *The Human Person, According to John Paul II*, Talk 73.

236 J. Merkle, *A Different Touch*, 234.

237 Sandra Schneiders, *Finding the Treasure*, 129.

238 E. Drewermann, Lecture, May 21, 1977.

239 D. Goergen, *The Sexual Celibate*, 13ff.

The Genesis perspective, that predates the Christian era by 950 years, provides the earliest Judaeo-Christian appreciation of sexuality. In the creation accounts, sexuality is proclaimed as a blessing and obligation. God does not want man to be alone and woman is his complementary and equal partner. This view of what John Paul II calls "original inno-cence" is portrayed in Michelangelo's painting of the creation of first man and woman in the Sistine Chapel.[240]

Figure 10: The Creation of Adam (and Eve)
by Michelangelo Buonarroti. Source: ARAS Online Archive.
Reprinted with permission.

Giving the spark of life to Adam, the Creator's other arm is tenderly holding Eve. Enfolded by God, Eve gazes diffidently at man. God lov-ingly embraces woman and the look of love connects the Creator with Adam as they both stretch out their hands to each other. In a delightful twist to the myth, the fresco gives the impression that Eve has emerged from the side of God.

In that story, humanity received another gift besides "original inno-cence, original solitude, original nakedness and original depth."[241] It is the gift of freedom. In giving humanity the capacity to choose, the Cre-ator allows self-centredness, alienation and violence: a disorder some-times called sin. As the Genesis story relates, that happy fault triggers

240   Brian J. Bransfield, *The Human Person, According to John Paul II*, Talk 3.
241   John Paul II, *Man & Woman He Created Them*, 161-176.

the love story of God for a distraught creation. In his response, Frank describes how this myth resurfaces in everyone's life:

> *Here is the passionately loving detachment that God the Creator*
> *shows to each person by leaving us free to love God or not. It is*
> *a love fraught with risk…But it seems to me that God will be*
> *the infinite Holy One whether any of us loves God or not: the*
> *celibate has to love that way—that the Other be whole with the*
> *contribution of the celibate's love, but the celibate person will*
> *remain whole whether the Other loves her or him…This is how I*
> *experience celibate love.*

Frank brings home the message of the myth. Each of us loves God through our treatment of others. That message has often been distorted and the shadow and responsibility of sin displaced on to woman for leading man into temptation at the bidding of Satan. The suspicion of body and of the feminine was emphasized by Christianity even though its roots go back to earlier traditions.[242] What I hear often in my clinical work is psyche's desire for a healing of the rupture that Genesis reflects.

The story of God's love and of humanity's search is told in the *Song of Songs*. Apologists take up the canticle to understand the quest and the meaning of sexuality. The Song can be translated on many levels. It may be interpreted as a canticle of the love existing between Israel and God. Others consider that it is a celebration of human love or as a metaphor of God's love for the human soul. One perspective need not exclude others.

In the 3ʳᵈ century, Origen treated this canticle as an allegory. He suggests that the Bridegroom is the Word of God that attracts and seduces the bride who is the current reader of the poem into recognition of the mystery of God's love. Do this song and this language speak to people now? In various instances, the Respondents refer to the *Song of Songs* as expressive of their vocation and their desire. For example, Patrick writes:

> *I see celibacy as an evolving reality. From being nothing in the*
> *beginning to an extraordinary gift that is still unfolding. My*

---

242   Luise Schottroff, Silvia Schroer, Marie-Theres Wacker, *Feminist Interpretation: The Bible in Women's Perspective*, 227.

breaks from time to time are signs of already but not yet...Own-
ing the espousal love to the beloved, the gift of the beloved towards
our fulfilment.

Continuing with Goergen's framework, I go to Matthew's Gospel.
New insights into celibacy come through this person of Jesus Christ
who sees sexuality in the light of the kingdom of God. When asked His
priority, Jesus makes clear one needs to embody love of God and love
others as oneself: to this "all are equally called."[243] Counter culturally,
Christ introduces a radical possibility of choosing celibacy for the kingdom as an option to marriage.

While Jesus reiterates the Genesis perspective that the physical union
of woman and man mirrors God's fidelity, Christ embodies celibate love.
He clarifies that at the core of both marriage and chastity is self-giving
which is at the heart of life and transformation. Judith has a similar view
of what celibacy and marriage mirror:

> *Celibacy means for me to find a deeper love for Christ. But I*
> *am also very scared to say such things. For I think in marriage*
> *it can absolutely be the same. If the person understands her love*
> *as a deep love coming from God, taking part in God's love, it is*
> *absolutely the same.*

In the Gospel debate about marriage and celibacy, Jesus affirms that
each choice has its advantages and its joys, its renunciations and its
challenges for expressing the love of God. Christ refuses to compare
one with the other. His emphasis stays with the meaning behind each
path.[244] What is paramount is how individuals with their nature and circumstances can freely love God and others especially those who are dis-
possessed.[245] Catherine finds her words for that directive as Agape love:

> *...celibate love frees me to reach out to the most impoverished*
> *and to go where they are and help them.*

---

243   John Paul II, *Vita Consecrata*, ¶ 15, http://www.vatican.va/roman_curia/con-
      gregations/ccscrlife/documents/hf_jp-ii_exh_25031996_vita-consecrata_en.html.
      Retrieved June 6, 2014.
244   Matthew 19:1-12; Mark 10:1-12; Matthew 19:10-12 in *The New Jerusalem Bible.*
245   Matthew 25:35-36 in *The New Jerusalem Bible.*

Matthew, the evangelist, makes clear that celibate love is a matter of the heart, which Christ clarifies as service of others.[246] It has both a present and not-yet dimension that the parables portray. This realm of the heart is reflected in those who live an inner life that affects the outer world and yet is not concerned with appearances. From this perspective, how one expresses sexuality is not as important as fidelity to one's inner being which affects and shines through relationships. In contrast to obsessive media coverage of people's lives, the Scriptures give little description of the sexual life of Jesus and Mary and the other disciples. What is emphasized is Christ's relationship with Abba and the Holy Spirit and the love he shows to others, or as Frank asserts:

> *The only real scriptural warrant that supports my experience of a call to celibacy is Jesus' life.*

How does Jesus' life of celibate love look? Scriptural accounts portray someone who instils in others their dignity as daughters and sons of God. They tell of a contemplative, attractive human being whose friendships with women and men were intense, warm and compassionate.[247] While this man firmly befriended the vulnerable, he did not hesitate to show anger, disappointment and frustration with others who were hypocritical.

The Scripture narrative reveals that Jesus Christ was aware of evil and suffering. He goes to the limits by insisting that loving others included enemies. He was not afraid to touch or be touched. He offered healing and forgiveness for sins. In showing the way, He gives His own body and blood as an ongoing memorial. Condemned to die as blasphemer, Christ faces temptation to despair. In the space of abandonment, He entrusts His Spirit to God. Then, the Gospel story tells of this man's resurrection and of the spiritual transformation of terrified believers. As one of the Respondents commented, this love embodied by Jesus Christ shapes his celibate life:

> *Well, I think if it wasn't for Jesus I wouldn't be a celibate. The more I read the Gospels the more I fall in love with this man; the*

---

246   Matthew 23:1-12; Matthew 25 in *The New Jerusalem Bible.*
247   Philippians 2:7 in *The New Jerusalem Bible.*

more I am inspired by His single-minded devotion to the will of the Father and His universal and very human love for us. He must have been the most sexual of men and He chose celibacy.
(Peter)

The fourth part of Goergen's framework looks to St. Paul's writing. Paul shows an ambivalent attitude to sexuality, a patriarchal opinion of women and a personal preference for celibacy. As the Christian community believed the end times were imminent, sexual abstinence was stressed. Even though Paul appears stuck in a conservative view of women, he supported some autonomy. He encouraged Thecla to choose celibacy rather than the respectable route of marriage. In Paul's opposition to this aspect of the social order, he went against the prevailing belief that women were biologically and spiritually inferior to men and that their only task was populating the empire.[248]

What was distinctive in Paul's attitude? Underhill suggests that Paul went beyond gender restrictions and recognised everyone's potential for gradual transformation into the likeness of Christ.[249] Refreshingly, Radcliffe explains Paul's perspective as moving from sex as a function to seeing sexuality and celibacy as about presence and union. Whether women and men choose sexual companionship or celibate chastity, they belong to the Body of Christ.[250]

In language reminiscent of the image of psyche as butterfly, Paul affirms that, as members of this Body, all people are called to become themselves. Transformation goes deeper than gender, cultural, social or marital status. The Acts of the Apostles hints at this new sexual ethic that was developing.

The original Christian community in Jerusalem apparently consisted of celibates and non-celibates. What distinguished them was not their sexuality but their faith in the Risen Christ and a unity of "heart and soul."[251] It led them to share with each other what they owned and while

---

248   Peter Brown, *The Body and Society*, 9.
249   Evelyn Underhill, *The Mystic Way*, 135-136.
250   Timothy Radcliffe, *I Call You Friends*, 326-7.
251   Acts 4:32; 5:12 in *The New Jerusalem Bible*.

it was not based on religious vows, it was grounded in the spirit of evangelical chastity, poverty and obedience.

As well as traditional families, there were women and men who lived together as brothers and sisters and these virginal women were known as *Agapetae* or *Beloved*. Women who were virgins and lived with clerics were recognised as Ascetics. In Celtic Christianity there was a growing practice of celibate men and women who lived together. It could happen that when a woman converted to the Christian faith, she was rejected by her family. Men often needed the help of these women. I do not mean in the sense of sexual favours or serving new masters: though this possibly happened too. In the Second Testament, Paul indicates a diaconate of some women when he refers to the church that gathered in the house of Aquila and Prisca.[252] In these emerging expressions of living celibate love, I hear some echoes from Respondents. There was Peter's reference to his parents and how in their final years their intimacy had taken the form of celibate love.

The fifth strand in Goergen's frame takes me to the 2nd century and to Clement of Alexandria. This church father wrote in praise of both marriage and celibacy and criticized those who took extremist views. There was ambivalence towards sexuality among some Roman intellectuals, including Tertullian. They considered that sexuality lowered the fire of the spirit.[253]

St. Augustine's contribution to the debate left sexuality, the body and women in a problematic light. Augustine was a Neoplatonist who was strongly influenced by Plotinus. He became a bishop and reformer in the Catholic Church of the 4th century. Although Augustine's stance was more nuanced, he was blamed for a view which saw human beings as caught in the existential dilemma of souls imprisoned in their bodies. Later, Thomas Aquinas attempted to restore the balance by developing Aristotle's notion that the soul cannot reach its natural perfection without the body. Aquinas emphasized that other sins (like malice) were more serious than those committed by passion.[254] Increasingly those more temperate views of the body and sexuality were lost.

---

252   Romans 16:1; 1 Corinthians 16:19 in *The New Jerusalem Bible*.
253   Ann Shearer, *Athene, Image and Energy*, 99.
254   Victor White, *God and the Unconscious*, 128.

History offers some explanation. Augustine, for example, had sub-
scribed as a young man to the Epicurean philosophy of pleasure, which
changed after his conversion to Christianity. Through St. Ambrose,
Augustine was introduced to the Rule of St. Basil and the reflections of
the Desert monks. With zeal and eloquence, Augustine wrote on many
subjects including marriage, virginity and the Trinity. Contemporary
Dominican theologian, Timothy Radcliffe, points out that while Augustine advocated the ideal of celibacy, especially for the clergy, he clearly
knew the struggle involved, where:

> …the only possible justification for the vow of chastity is
> that it makes us happy. That was St. Augustine's view. He
> asks, 'Who can consciously embrace something that does
> not delight him?' Dom Sebastian Moore wrote that if Freud
> thought that God was all about sex, then Augustine thought
> that sex was all about God. Chastity is an entry to the utter
> and incomprehensible joy of the Father in the Son and the
> Son in the Father, which is the Holy Spirit. It is true that
> some deep pleasures take time to learn. It took me years to
> learn to love whisky, but I stuck at it. I am still working at
> chastity![255]

A Christian community that opposed excess gathered around Augustine. Many were oppressed by a reality where women and slaves did not
have legal rights and were prey to violent abuse.[256] Christianity attracted
many such people because it offered safety and a dignity denied them in
the old system. Jung identified that such conditions are ripe for a swing
to their opposite expression (an enantiodromia).[257]

The collective attitude became restrained about sexuality and body.
Human weakness was highlighted and overshadowed the joy of sensuality. Augustine's caution that sexual activity could be a danger for the
spiritual person gave prominence to celibate chastity. Yet Radcliffe is
adamant that Augustine's intention was to present:

---

255 Timothy Radcliffe, "Religious Life in the World that is Coming To Be," August,
      2003. http://www.marianist.com/articles/radcliffe.pdf. Retrieved June 10, 2014.
256 J. Herrin, *The Formation of Christendom*, 68.
257 C.G. Jung, "Symbols of transformation," CW 5, ¶ 341.

…chastity (as) the liberation of desire from…the temptation to make ourselves God and to rule and possess other people.[258]

The challenge is integrating the contributions of Augustine with "the Word become flesh."[259] To choose celibacy is both a physical and spiritual commitment: I mean facing and letting go of the shadow of pride and possessiveness while holding onto passion that flows and is felt in one's body. A challenge for vowed people is acclaiming their physicality as women and men. In his prayer, Augustine allows us to glimpse such a transforming of passion when one opens to grace: "Late have I loved Thee, O Beauty so ancient and so new…"[260] Frances suggests an understanding of this attitude in her life:

> *The deepest, most intimate desire of the human heart is union with God. 'Our hearts are restless until they rest in Thee.' (St. Augustine)*

Trinitarian Theology

Theology describes one's relationship with God. According to Patricia Fox, it aims "to illuminate the mystery of God, and to promote the full humanity of all people and the integrity of creation."[261] In *Vita Consecrata*, John Paul II picks up this thread and describes the lives of consecrated celibates as intending to make visible the beauty of the Trinity.[262]

This image of divine beauty awakening us to the beauty in ourselves and in our relationships was familiar to Origen. He had a theological view of the Trinity as "the archai of all things in the universe."[263] The

---

258 Timothy Radcliffe, "Religious Life in the World that is Coming To Be," August, 2003. http://www.marianist.com/articles/radcliffe.pdf. Retrieved June 10, 2014.

259 John 1:14 in *The New Jerusalem Bible.*

260 *The Confessions of St. Augustine*, 236.

261 Patricia Fox, *God as Communion*, 20.

262 John Paul II, *Vita Consecrata*, ¶ 19, http://www.vatican.va/roman_curia/congregations/ccscrlife/documents/hf_jp-ii_exh_25031996_vita-consecrata_en.html. Retrieved June 6, 2014.

263 Charles Kannengiesser & William L. Petersen (Trans.) *Origen of Alexandria: His World and His Legacy*, 248.

word "archai" brings to mind the Jungian notion of the arche-types and the potential they hold.[264] Imagining this essence unfolding, Jung gives the analogy of a crystal which contains in its core a myriad of possibilities that environment shapes.

I see a parallel in Christianity where the source of divine (and human) beauty is "in a trinity of persons."[265] How does this make a difference to people's lives? Judith Pickering, Australian Jungian analyst, calls attention to the contributions of St. Augustine along with some contemporary psychoanalytic thinkers who identify a trinity in all loving relationships.[266] For Augustine the nature of God is compassion reflected by the self-giving trinity in God of "the lover, beloved and the mystery of love."[267]

Psychoanalytically, Ronald Britton speaks of "the triangular space" as a quality between partners and friends, which contains and is expansive for those involved.[268] Wilfred Bion envisages an inner transformation in individuals who open to the touch of the Unknown Mover and which he depicts with the sign of "O."[269]

Patricia Fox's theological appreciation of the Trinity accentuates for me the singular beauty of persons becoming themselves through such graced friendship. Building on the view of the Eastern Orthodox theologian, John Zizioulas, she argues that the communion of persons in the divine Trinity "can contribute to humanity's quest for personhood, freedom, community and the world's survival."[270] I hear these four emphases in the following Scripture references.

In the Christian story, the Trinity is present in the overshadowing of Christ at His baptism and in the Incarnation narrative where the Holy Spirit overshadows Mary. In these instances, a woman and a man are drawn into, choose, and are transformed by God's love that still impacts

---

264   C.G. Jung, "The Archetypes and the Collective Unconscious," CW 9i, ¶ 155.
265   Matthew 28:19; 2 Cor. 13:13 in *The New Jerusalem Bible*; Victor White, *God and the Unconscious*, 104.
266   Judith Pickering, *Being in Love*, 63.
267   Gareth B. Mathews, *Augustine: On the Trinity*, Book 9, 26.
268   Ronald Britton, *Belief and Imagination*, 42.
269   Wilfred Bion, *Attention and Interpretation*, 26.
270   Patricia Fox, *God as Communion*, 10.

others. Yet, as the theologian Weinandy emphasizes, the Trinity remains unfathomable.[271] It could be why Louise responds:

> *Lately I have focused…on the mystery of the presence of God, which bears no image and is indefinable.*

Bion's "O" is another metaphor for the God of one thousand and one names.[272] From a feminist critique, Elizabeth Johnson suggests, "Spirit Sophia, Jesus Sophia and Mother Sophia."[273] Dante settled for naming the mystery, "three circles of three colours and one magnitude"[274] while Thomas Aquinas falls back finally into silence. That attitude comes through this woman's response to what helps in her living celibacy:

> *Prayer, especially the depth of prayer experienced in the Thirty day Ignatian Exercises…and the intimacy with the Trinity arising from such prayer.* (Elizabeth)

Taking a clue from another Respondent who referred to Rublev's Trinity, to help my understanding I turn to iconography and to its tradition of contemplation. The 15th century icon attributed to the Russian monk, Andrei Rublev, is a revered depiction of the enigma of the Trinity. In the 16th century, the Russian Church deemed that this icon was "proto-revealed, that is, a symbolic image of God inspired by God."[275]

The icon depicts the three messengers who visited and blessed Sarah and Abraham at Mamre. Muzj links the scene with God's apparition on Mount Sinai where Moses saw the place of God "on what looked like a sapphire pavement pure as the heavens themselves."[276] In Christian spirituality, this place of sapphire was understood as the innermost space of one's soul where God makes a dwelling place. Through contemplating such a sacred image, it was believed that one could go into that inner space and grow in the love of God and love of others—which is where I think the Trinity of Persons invites us.

---

271   Thomas G. Weinandy, *The Father's Spirit of Sonship*, 40-41.
272   Wilfred Bion, *Attention and Interpretation*, 65-89.
273   Elizabeth A. Johnson, *Quest for the Living God*, 221.
274   Dante Alighieri, *Paradiso*, Canto XXXII: 116-117.
275   Maria Giovanna Muzj, *Transfiguration*, 162.
276   Exodus 24:10 in *The New Jerusalem Bible*.

Figure 11: The Trinity, by Andrei Rublev. Source: ARAS Online
Archive. Reprinted with permission.

Muzj conveyed this impression in describing the icon as "a mystery
of total interiority."[277] As one contemplates the image, there is a feeling
of being drawn into the scene. There is a table around which the three

277   Maria Giovanna Muzj, *Transfiguration*, 165.

figures gather. A chalice, which could be an image of the Eucharist and the Grail, sits in the middle of the table.

The beauty of relationship and life shared points to the mystery of the Trinity. It is not about loss of individuality but a relationship of "profound interpenetration."[278] Jackie's prayer reflects this understanding:

> *My prayer is Trinitarian as I move in my prayer from God to Christ to Spirit*

From a Jungian perspective, this number of three-ness suggests the pull of opposites and movement. Out of this tension came a birth of consciousness and possibility of relatedness.[279] Analyst, Victor White, identified this complementarity of opposites as having generative results. It is life flowing from being both singular and in relationship:

> a fundamental role in…the theology of the Trinity…where each in the pair is dependent on the Other in its very singularity…and results wherever processes of birth, physical or symbolic take place.[280]

Appreciation of the Trinity and creative potential are conveyed by Frank. He describes celibacy in terms of genuine relationships that reflect the divine mystery:

> *My theological understanding of celibacy is that the human person is created in the image of God.…God is one and God is three. We are our relations. And I have learned something else, desire is the influence of others…Every desire I have, others also have had…it's the same desire for friendship, for security, for knowledge, for beauty, for travel, to smell roses. Those desires are all over the place. They were first in others and others influenced me. And I think celibacy has this enormous power. Since we are created,*

---

278 Benedict XVI, *Caritas in Veritate*, 5: 54.

279 C.G. Jung, "Symbols of transformation," CW 5, ¶ 500; C.G. Jung, "The Archetypes and the Collective Unconscious," CW 9i, ¶ 426.

280 Ann Conrad-Lammers, *In God's Shadow: The Collaboration of Victor White and C.G. Jung*, 147.

modelled on a God who is 3 persons we can expect that our self
will be in relation, always, always.

Incarnational Theology

Frank's emphasis on relatedness leads me to Incarnational theology and
how this perspective can contribute to an understanding of sexuality,
the body and celibate commitment. The Incarnation speaks of Wisdom
impregnating a young woman called Mary and through the power of
spirit coming to birth.[281] That mystery of Incarnation continues as we
allow grace to become visible in and through our lives. Excerpts like
this one from St. Paul's letter to the Romans convey this transformative
process:

> All of us, though there are so many of us, make up one body
> in Christ, and as different parts we are all joined to one
> another...In brotherly (and sisterly) love let your deep feelings
> of affection for one another come to expression...[282]

In Christianity, the body is a key metaphor and is emphasized with
the image of Christians being temples of the Holy Spirit. The task of
Christians is to bear and give birth to Jesus Sophia in their individual
lives and within the body of the Christian community.[283] As a symbol
and sacrament of unity, the body is critical for appreciating celibacy.
Carthusian monk, David Steindl-Rast, emphasizes the vulnerability of
persons. He suggests that celibate people need to be like Christ and
value the gift of their vulnerability:

> We are rendered vulnerable. But that is a place of possibility
> and opportunity, if it is extended to a place of hospitality...
> How do (celibates) own and publicly admit our vulnerabil-
> ity, not mistaking vulnerability as failure, and invite others to

---

281   Elizabeth A. Johnson, *Quest for the Living God*, 221.
282   Romans 12:5-13 in *The New Jerusalem Bible*.
283   1 Corinthians: 16 in *The New Jerusalem Bible*; Elizabeth A. Johnson, *Quest for*
       the Living God, 221.

help us to learn how to love more freely, more simply, more fully?[284]

The following Respondent reflects this appreciation. She addresses Steindl-Rast's question by taking up Thomas Aquinas' observation of grace requiring and developing who we are as human beings:

> *Grace needs nature, but it cultivates it, makes it a more rich and positive gift of God. Sexual power and desire as genital desire remains both positive and negative within celibate people. Celibate love is called to sublimate the physical desire into spiritual love. This is a life-program and a life-long attempt. Probably in every life—at least in mine—there are moments or phases where this is easy and others where it is difficult...* (Judith)

Judith and Steindl-Rast suggest that recognizing the gift of our sexuality and vulnerability can open us to a deeper relationship with God and others. This view is based on the Christian teaching of the Incarnation where human and divine converge in the person of Jesus Christ. Thomas refers to this realization as taking him from recognition of:

"Christ Son of God" to realizing *'Jesus human like me.'*

The Mystery of the Incarnation was formally proclaimed in 451 AD at the Council of Chalcedon. Liberation theologians like Gutierrez have described history as the revelation of the mystery of God's person.[285] One can see the Incarnation prefigured in the Villa of Mysteries in Pompeii that was once a site for the Dionysiac mysteries. Looking at those frescoes, I become aware of a meeting of humanity and divinity in the company of these figures. The feminine, the body and the spirit have an honoured place with the masculine. The colours and the movement suggest sensuality and intimacy, and the transformation that happens when the initiate (the soul) makes her-self vulnerable and open to the god—the god becomes present to the soul.[286] The Gospel of St. John

---

284   Geoff Orchison, "Priests' Identity Crisis" in *The Catholic Leader*, February 22, 1998: 12.

285   Walter Abbott, *The Documents of Vatican 2*, 247.

286   Nor Hall, *Those Women*.

tells of another twice born, "the Word whom we have heard and seen and touched."[287]

The Eucharist is no Dionysian gathering and dismembering (although from St. Paul's account, it could get quite riotous). Christ calls the Agape meal not a symbol but a remembering of His Body and Blood. This thanksgiving was also known to the early Christians as the Breaking of Bread. The Re-membering celebrated Christ's gift of self to God and to others and what was happening in and to them. During the Agape, those present were urged to offer their lives with Christ to God as one body.

The desire is about becoming more like Christ in one's uniqueness through what Underhill called an impassioned awareness of the real presence it signifies.[288] Judith appreciates this meaning of celibacy:

> *And how have I felt (the call to celibacy)? In Eucharist and at prayer. The sense that God wants me for himself—my whole personality. Somehow I am asked. Not enforced. But I have the choice to answer it.*

The demeaning of sexuality, the body and the feminine distorts what Jesus Christ intended in Eucharist. The next Respondent recognises that her communion with God and others is made flesh in service of God's people. Janice comments:

> *My own growth and understanding of God's presence is—Being with—The Breaking of Bread—the Sermon on the Mount. Personal dream of being called to love God's people.*

In the earlier section on the Trinity, I made a reference to sapphire as marking the dwelling place of God. Another dimension of the incarnation, of virginity and of Eucharist is captured by Piero della Francesca in his *Madonna del Parto*. In this Renaissance painting, Mary is wearing a vibrant blue dress. In full pregnancy, she steps out of a tent whose cur-

---

287   Gertrude Jobes, *Dictionary of Mythology, Folklore and Symbols*, 447; 1 John 1:1 in *The New Jerusalem Bible*.

288   Evelyn Underhill, *The Mystic Way*, 27.

tains are drawn back by two angels. The Virgin has a dignified pose and her right hand points to the child within her.

Figure 12: Madonna del Parto, by Piero della Francesca.
Source: © Art Resource. Reprinted with permission

To understand more of this surprising fresco and its message, I need to take you to the book of Exodus where the writer tells the story of the Ark of the Covenant. Originally, the ark was an acacia box inlaid with gold that contained the stone tablets of the Law given by God to Moses. It was a testimony of God's presence and was carried by the Israelites on their journey through the desert to the land of promise.[289] The most sacred part of the ark was the golden plate of the mercy seal, placed on the top of the ark.[290] Two winged creatures were sculptured on either side of the seal because this was the place of meeting between God and the people.

In the Second Testament, when the Virgin Mary is given the title of "Ark of the New Covenant," instead of a precious box, she becomes the God bearer. When women and men vow celibacy, they too become living reminders that they, like all people, are to carry God's loving mercy. It is a sobering reminder as this Respondent remarks:

> *Love for everyone, (for) God is nothing but mercy and love.*
> (Roger)

Della Francesca's painting was intended to be the backdrop to an altar where Eucharist was celebrated. Originally it was hung in such a strategic position that, at the elevation of the consecrated host in the Mass, the transubstantiated bread that was raised by the priest for the people to see would be right at the place of Mary's open dress. Explicitly and aesthetically, the artist portrayed the feminine as pregnant with the human and divine child. It also reminded the people who gathered for Eucharist that they were like this impressive woman and meant to birth and to generate Christ in their lives. As Karen comments:

> *I still feel my celibacy, the theology and spirituality that is most me, is incarnational. So Christ is significant as much because He is human as He is God.*

In Religious Life

"The consecrated life is at the very heart of the church...and manifests the inner nature of the Christian calling."[291]

---

289 Exodus 25 in *The New Jerusalem Bible*.
290 Exodus 25 in *The New Jerusalem Bible*.
291 John Paul II, *Vita Consecrata*, ¶ 2, http://www.vatican.va/roman_curia/congregations/ccscrlife/documents/hf_jp-ii_exh_25031996_vita consecrata_en.html. Retrieved June 6, 2014.

What is the nature of the Christian calling? The encyclical suggests that everyone is meant to be in the intimate relationship with God that consecrated persons profess in their lives of celibate chastity. Could we actually put the consecrated life in an historical context?

Tracing an historical development of expressions of celibate chastity in the Catholic Church can sound like tracking through a vast genealogy. Sandra Schneiders has done and is doing this work impressively. Go to her books for a description of hermits, anchorites, cenobites, the emergence of Monastic Orders, beguines and beghards, ministerial Religious Orders and ecclesial institutes.[292] In this section, I want to locate some points where the spirit and the law of celibacy came into blossom and also into conflict.

Celibacy gained a firmer standing in Christianity during the 3rd and 4th century after a period of religious persecution in Europe and the Middle East. The place of the martyrs, who were seen as Christianity's heroines and heroes, was taken by ascetic women and men who became hermits or with those who gathered in religious communities in the desert areas around Egypt, Palestine, Syria and Asia Minor.[293]

Stories are told of many characters who either were unable to escape arranged marriages or consciously chose to live a celibate life. Taking Christ as their model and his search for solitude as the priority in their life, they claimed freedom by an anachoresis, or withdrawal into the wilderness.[294] These anchorites linked celibacy with their struggle for holiness. The witness of their lives led to celibacy becoming more sanctioned in the Christian Church.

While it could be argued that those who went to the desert to practice askesis were escapists or individualistic, the religious life of the monos/monachal (the single/alone) became a source of questioning for their society. Their going apart included simplicity, hospitality and spirituality. The writings of John Cassian and Athanasius and the eremitic way of St. Anthony inspired the foundation of communities that led to the emergence of Western monasticism.

---

292 Sandra Schneiders, *Finding the Treasure*, 2000.
293 J. Herrin, *The Formation of Christendom*, 65.
294 Matthew 14:13; John 6:15 in *The New Jerusalem Bible*.

The word *cenobitic* derives from the Greek word *koinonia* which means *a genuine partnership* and was exemplified by the early Christian community.[295] In the 4th century in the Eastern Church, many women and men joined communities of nuns and monks who were attempting to live a similar spiritual life. Pachomius and companion monks were seen as the instigators of a new form of religious life with their first monastery at Thebes. Yet it was Mary, the sister of Pachomius, along with other women who were members of the first known cenobitic community.

Basil of Caesarea (330-370 AD) built on these foundations emphasizing that monasticism was to nurture love of neighbour, an attitude of humility and a love of the common life where each person is considered a vital member of the body of Christ. St. Benedict of Nursia (480-550 AD) and his sister Scholastica further developed this tradition. The resulting Benedictine rule stressed the role of a listening or an obedient love through a Monastic way of life that balanced prayer and work. The vows of Chastity, Poverty, Obedience and Stability became more recognised as a way of conversion of heart to the Gospel.

Problems arose as religious life and priesthood became stepping stones for people seeking economic or political power and where people made a choice for celibate life more for motivations other than a sense of vocation. This attitude fostered by institutional dynamics led to abuses in monastic religious life that are reflected in the sexual abuse crisis in the church today.

In the 6th century, St. Gregory the Great became Pope. He was a Benedictine monk who spread the monastic ideals through the Christian Church. While most of his reforms were positive and ensured security of property and income, Gregory's sanctioning enclosure of nuns restricted their freedom.

Stability became concretized to the detriment of an interior attitude. In the 8th century, Benedict's rule was mandated for all monasteries throughout the Roman Empire. The reforms of St. Bernard of Clairvaux in the 12th century led to the more rigorous reform of the Benedictine rule and the foundation of the Cistercian Order. Judith gives a cameo

---

295   Acts 4:32-34 in *The New Jerusalem Bible.*

of the enclosed way of life that she contrasts with the mobility or itinerancy of the ministerial:

Judith: *We live an enclosed life which means we stay in this one place. We have a vow of Stabilitas, remaining in a place and being faithful to the community. Other Religious Orders live in community but don't have this enclosure and they live for example in the town and go there and there. I think this aspect of enclosure influences the way of our life.*

Interviewer: *In the way of your chastity, your celibacy?*

Judith: *Yes, because I think for a sister in an enclosed abbey it is more a contemplative life. So this life of prayer must have the major place. Whereas somebody who is more in Apostolic Life, it's probably different.*

Fixing the archetype of celibate chastity into the one form of monasticism consequently had to be renegotiated by women and men searching a different expression of living religious life. From the thirteenth to the sixteenth centuries, there were a number of religious communities of women (Beguines) and men (Beghards) that developed in Europe. They were loosely organized and their communities were made up of middle to lower class people who were looking for mutual support in living a religious life. Although their members did not take public vows, they lived the virtues of poverty, chastity and obedience.

The Beguines, and to a lesser extent the Beghards, were known for their spirituality and charitable activities in towns particularly in the Low Countries of Belgium, Holland, northern France and Germany. The survival of these clusters was precarious because of the difficulties of economic survival in Medieval Europe and the attitude of the church hierarchy to women seeking autonomy. Many found enough economic independence to support themselves by needlework, working in bakeries and other crafts. They often expressed their spiritual mothering by taking in orphan children and the wives of those away on crusades. These groups came under the scrutiny of the Inquisition and were later suppressed by a Papal edict.[296] One writer mentions them as 'women's

---

296   Ann Gilroy rsj, Personal Sharing, 2011.

movement' that was not bound by hierarchical control while providing the withdrawal that the desert had given earlier hermits.[297]

There were many individuals and groups that sought to combine the contemplative and apostolic life. Some like the anchoress, Julian of Norwich, had their dwellings attached to a church where people would come for counselling. These uncloistered women and men, though often reclusive in that they did not leave their cells, engaged in charitable works including spiritual advising, education of the poor and herbal dispensaries. The criticism directed at them, particularly by the clergy, forced these groups to look to monastic Orders, like the Cistercians, for protection. This led to more ecclesiastically approved groups. As one of the Respondents suggests, the opposition could have influenced such groups to seek recognition as Religious Orders or Congregations. Frank also attributes their foundation as another expression of celibate love:

> I would say celibate love is expressed in every way that any human love expresses itself with the exception of physical union. And I would add that it must find ways of expressing itself in the physical absence of the beloved, which may be a deep motive for founding a Religious Congregation.

From the 13th century, with the changing demography in Europe, there was a burgeoning of apostolic Religious Orders that were devoted to serving God and meeting social needs. These Religious Orders gave a Gospel perspective to relieving situations of ignorance and poverty. For example, the Franciscans preached the Gospel to new arrivals populating the towns then springing up across Europe. Distinctive charisms still attract people to Religious Congregations as one of the Respondents clarifies:

> I think I made a choice for a way of life in a particular Religious Congregation—not for celibacy itself. There were relevant religious experiences. (Jane)

It would be impossible to list the Religious Orders that have come and gone and continue, in what Sandra Schneiders terms, "this life

---

297   Jo Ann Kay McNamara, *Sisters in Arms*, 239.

form." Instead I want to give an example of these celibate communities through the story of the Franciscans, the Jesuits and Mary Ward's experiment. A new type of Religious Order was inspired by St. Francis and St. Clare. Although Clare wished to follow Francis' freedom of movement, women were forced to remain cloistered. Allowing freedom and independence to women was considered a threat to family and church systems built on gender inequalities. Nevertheless, the Franciscan movement was at the crest of a new expression of a vowed religious life of itinerants—like St. Dominic and his women and men companions. They gave impetus to other itinerant groups throughout the world, including the Australian Congregation of which I am a member.

In the 13th century in Umbria, an exuberant young man named Francis experienced a religious conversion after being wounded in battle. He gave away his inheritance, much to the despair of his wealthy parents, and took to a radical following of Christ. The brothers who joined Francis understood their call was to transform a church corrupted by power and greed and estranged from the lives of people.

Clare was moved by Francis' awareness of God in all creation and his love of the poor. She began a community of women who were devoted to a simple and contemplative religious life. Their celibate choice was lived in enclosure. Nevertheless, the lives of these Franciscans brought a far-reaching renewal. It is interesting that Francis refused ordination and the power that went with the clerical state. His celibacy was chosen for the mission. As an earlier Respondent indicates, the spirituality of Francis left its impact on her vowed life. The message was symbolised in a sculpture, familiarly called 'the hugging' ('amplexus'), which speaks of the sacrifice of love:

> *I like the cross, especially the "amplexus": the Franciscan/Cistercian representation of Christ bending down towards and hugging us.* (Judith)

In 1543, the Society of Jesus was founded by St. Ignatius of Loyola. His desire was to transform the individual and society through the spirituality of the Spiritual Exercises that I describe in more depth later. Simply, they heighten awareness of the individual's freedom, and through a discerning process encourage a capacity to make choices that are focused on bringing God's kingdom into the here and now. The men who became members were bound to an obedient acceptance of their missionary vocation.

The Company of Jesus was formidable in church reforms of the 16th century. This led to conflict with civil and ecclesiastical authorities and in 1773 to the suppression of the Jesuits. This ban was lifted in 1814 and, although the Society suffered stormy periods, it is still a significant Religious Order that is devoted to the spirituality that fires its social justice. For example, in the 19th century, the Jesuits befriended the young Australian Congregation of the Sisters of St. Joseph by helping Mary MacKillop, who needed such brotherly support, to get approval for the Rule of Life.

In the 17th century, Mary Ward found support in Jesuit spirituality and paved a way for an apostolic life form for women. Mary Ward was born in 1585, in Yorkshire, England, into an aristocratic Catholic family. Their adherence to the Catholic faith grew stronger especially after religious persecutions in which Mary's grandmother was imprisoned. As befitted her class, Mary was well educated.

The influence of the Jesuits came through Mary Ward's confessor and she wanted to join an apostolic Religious Order. The existing, more enclosed, Franciscan model of women's religious community was not her way. Mary wanted to offer educational possibilities to girls especially among the poor, and that included religious education. She founded several communities that were independent of the bishops. The Council of Trent, distrustful of women's growing independence, decreed severe enclosure for women and her Institute was disbanded. Mary Ward was observed by the Inquisition and there was always the danger that she would be burnt as a heretic.

After the Institute's dissolution in 1630, there were still little groups of women in Paris, Rome and Munich continuing the work she began. The bishop of Augsburg in 1703 was the first to acknowledge and welcome them into his diocese. Mary's attitude was one of quiet and calm surrender to God and she acted on the intuitions she received as the will of God.

Her influence was profound on women's Religious Orders in and beyond Europe. Her contemporary effect on the human and spiritual role of women is seen in Mother Teresa of Calcutta who founded an Institute to work with the poor in India. Mother Teresa reputedly said, "I am and I remain a Loreto Nun—a daughter of Mary Ward."[298]

The Council of Trent (1542-63) had reacted to the Protestant Reformation and called for unity and doctrinal reform in monasteries and in other institutions. More regulations imposed a model of enclosure and control by the clergy on the lives of women religious. Even though Vatican II instigated the biggest renewal for centuries of religious life, particularly of women's Religious Orders, there are contemporary attempts to stifle the renewal. In what Sandra Schneiders describes of the 2008-2010 Vatican Apostolic Visitation of Institutes of Religious Women in the USA, the message is *get back to the monastery*. There was a similar regressive impact on the priesthood with Trent's requirement of celibacy for the clergy. This was reinforced by the training of priests through seminary structures modelled along monastic lines.

The topic of mandatory celibacy in priesthood is of such significance that its inclusion here would do it a grave disservice and so direct you to the research of people like Richard Sipe. Let me simply make my stance clear and join my voice with Frank and many other Respondents who suggest the Catholic Church should return authority to the church community where it was originally invested:

> It would not trouble me at all if the church were to drop the requirement of celibacy for ordained ministry. I think it should. There can be no theological problem because part of the church has never established this requirement. I would rejoice were it to happen because then the church would be able to go back to the Scriptural practice in choosing whom to ordain.

---

298   Unknown source.

CHAPTER EIGHT

THE FOURTH MOVEMENT
RE-CONTEXTUALIZING THE QUEST OF FIRE

In the Prelude to *Celibacy and Soul*, I questioned the meaning and worth of celibate chastity in what I designated as a quest of fire. By asking others to respond to the clear and grey agenda about celibacy, I have opened up to my own shadowy and seductive aspects. Awareness of how this subject of celibacy can constellate emotional reactions was helpful. I realise it can stir complexes and provoke affect. I want to acknowledge the gift and trust of the Respondents for speaking about their own, and at times intimate, experience. I hope this work respectfully and seriously conveys what they have shared.

Jung emphasizes that each situation is particular. Providing an historical framework is, therefore, important. It tempers generalizations and acknowledges the contributors.[299] Nevertheless, the background details I offer are brief because of my assuring Respondents of both confidentiality and anonymity. Of the twenty-seven people, fifteen Respondents are female, twelve are male and eleven of those men are Catholic priests.

Composition of the 27 Respondents according to
Age, Gender, Nationality:

20s: 1 person: an Asian South-American man living in Italy.

30s: 0

40s: 4 people: a Swiss and an Australian woman, 2 Australian men.

---

299   Elizabeth Kamarck Minnich, *Transforming Knowledge*, 71.

50s: 7 people: 3 Australian women, 3 American women, 1 of whom resides in Italy, 1 South African man.

60s: 9 people: 2 Australian women, 3 Australian men, 2 American men one of whom lives in Italy, 2 English women.

70s: 5 people: 1 German man, 1 American man, 2 Australian women, 1 English woman.

Other: 1 American woman who omitted other biographical details.

Most of the Respondents are in late middle-age and there are no people in their 30s. The reason could be that, no one from this age range was approached by the Co-researchers (or did not complete the questionnaire if they were asked). It could be that this is a delicate time for sorting out issues with celibacy: a time when one may not be comfortable with this choice as Respondents like Catherine substantiated:

I am able to just go where there is a need, or a call, and stay there and give myself without stinginess or regret. I think the freedom to do that is part of celibacy…the love that I experience in my celibate relationships really frees me to do this. I am able to say this now. I could not have said this when I was 30.

While I cannot address the situation of all who choose celibate chastity, I suggest there are significant themes, common ground, shared meaning and anomalies that apply to many who choose this way. In my sorting out and gathering the threads, I note that the myth of Psyche and Eros resonates. Psyche was required to do some sorting and sifting tasks in her search for Eros. In this work, I have also sorted and sifted through a plethora of data.

Thankfully, as in the tale of Psyche and Eros, there were helpers who came to my aid. At the beginning, I had the guidance of Dr. Ian Baker, analyst and mentor. Family, religious community, friends, clients and supervisors inspired and encouraged and continue to do so.

Emerging Themes and Motifs

Choice

While motifs arose and wove from one to another, the theme of choice recurred. It brings in other motifs—like prayer and the developmental process that Elizabeth flags:

> *Some have made a fully aware sacrificial choice; others embarked on celibate life before their sexual drives had fully awakened. These have a hard struggle to faithfully strive after their ideal.*

Georg, a German priest and counsellor, acknowledges the struggle for him and for others to whom he ministers. He notes that choosing consecrated chastity motivated by love of God and love for Christ means suffering through times of loneliness. Georg intimates that the institutionalization and requirement on priesthood are unwarranted:

> *...as a celibate person, I let go of genital sex and marriage because of a strong love for God in Jesus Christ. Celibacy is normally connected with a vow or promise...It's an expression of my affective love for God in Jesus Christ. Sometimes there is a burden of loneliness. But I wished to become a priest and celibacy was a necessary condition for the priesthood.*

In times of loneliness and confusion, some saw an opportunity for the person to deepen her/his relationship with God and with others: that is, where the conflict is faced. Another Respondent wondered, if she could turn back the years, whether she would opt for marriage. Louise identifies a dysfunctional family background influencing her. She articulates how reflection and therapy enabled her to become conscious of her motivations. Becoming aware of this dynamic, Louise says that she became free to choose.

Respondents identified that struggle, including redirecting or sublimating their sexual drive and energy, was critical in coming to self-awareness. Thomas, Frances and Rene acknowledged that initially their focus was religious life. John Terry proposed that people could have a predisposition for celibacy. Along these lines, three women Respondents spoke of their making an early choice of celibate commitment because of desire for God and helping others. In contrast, some acknowledged that the choice could be negative: to escape or withdraw from relating. For Tim and Bernardine it was an option to become generative:

> *Celibacy is a voluntary lifestyle chosen to facilitate generative life…the result of a spiritual call…it is mostly in my awareness in my periods of prayer.* (Tim)

Karen adds that most people are celibate at some time in their lives. As an equal vocation among others, this man underlines it as a distinctive rather than a superior choice:

> *It's not that celibacy or non-celibacy is the way—one is not better than another—some hear a call to celibacy and respond.* (Thomas)

An American Sister working in Pastoral education emphasized the importance of revisiting her decision. Like the next Respondent, she is not afraid to question herself and stays open to engaging with others:

> *I question my choice because I was more of a head person…I do not think others have suffered but may have missed my affectionate and warm ways or desires because, in the past, I protected myself from getting too close and maybe responding to sexual feeling.* (Debra)

Like other Respondents, Juan sees celibacy as a *grace of God*. Similarly Judith a Swiss, and Catherine, an American Sister, spoke of a freedom, independence and availability for prayer and service that they have experienced through their commitment. Some acknowledged a feeling of loss that comes with not having a partner, family or sexual companionship. All Respondents were open about the cost of their choice and its meaning.

> *It's an act of love—gift to God—free for mission.* (Catherine)

Intimacy

I want to gather the second set of threads under intimacy. As Judith and others were keen to clarify, intimacy is relatedness that is not possessive of others:

> *I use the term intimacy in its largest sense, not reduced to genital sexual life. Inner freedom and independence allows me to have deep friendships because celibate love is not a possessive love. Real love can never be possessive, neither in marriage nor in celibacy.*

Frank identified how a contemplative space and knowing and accepting one's limits build relationship with others. He describes feelings of attraction for others as "grace." Jane observed that getting one's need for intimacy in tune with living celibacy is not easy. It follows that making mistakes is a necessary learning. Continuing this narrative, Frank discusses intimacy in terms of friendship which may, but does not necessarily call for sexual intimacy with the one partner in marriage. He shares a vignette of friendship that is about equality and mutual self-giving. The latter can lead to an intimacy that goes beyond physical union even to giving one's life for another:

> *Your question…seems to suggest that marriage intimacy is the fundamental model of human intimacy. I have learned to question that. I believe that the fundamental friendship is that which makes each person whole while building the community or the communion of humankind. In some cases, this friendship entails marriage, and obviously marriage is integral to the continuing community of humankind. But it seems to me that, in the vast majority of cases, friendships which make each person whole while building the community of humankind do not entail marriage.*

Recognizing the importance of space and limits for celibate loving, some Respondents named fear of intimacy and withdrawing as problematic. Desire for sexual intimacy with one other person can be experienced intensely at different stages in life. As childbearing possibilities diminish for women in their 30s and 40s, that makes sense.

From a male perspective, Tim spoke of 35 as a difficult time and found longing for companionship was aggravated by community circumstances. In other responses, women and men spoke of a challenge when prayer is dry and Eros elusive. Midlife awakening and longing for an intimate other came through comments from female and male Respondents. Some noted that when the desire for intimacy is unfulfilled, anger and cynicism can go into 'isms' that include perfectionism, or into substance or other abuses that leave no space for anyone or anything else:

> *It may mean one can work longer hours—receiving praise for work as a substitute for loving.* (Greg)

I would like to say to the previous Respondent that feelings of anger at loneliness or lonesomeness seem natural, even part of a maturational crisis. Hopefully, though not always, it can lead to a deeper understanding of the meaning and choice of celibate chastity, as happens in other relationships.

As for being comfortable with expressions of intimacy, all Respondents indicated that they felt at ease with showing and receiving physical affection. Some people added that their demonstrativeness depended on the level of friendship with the other person to which cultural and personal factors contributed. Elisabeth mentioned that her thirty-two years in South America helped her to feel more comfortable with showing physical signs of affection, like hugs and kisses. Coming out of a reserved English background, she acknowledged this as new learning.

With non-physical expressions of intimacy I noticed gender issues, with one woman and five men having some difficulties. Intimacy needs spontaneity, common sense and self-confidence and I think it is easier for women to be both verbally and physically expressive. From childhood, females are expected and taught to be nurturing. Sexism may have lessened in some contexts, yet in others gender roles and bias are still strong. Compounding this tendency, the sex abuse crisis in the church has made many men more circumspect about expressing feelings, and women more frustrated at their exclusion from decision-making within the church.

Respondents commented that feelings of loneliness, inadequacy and lack of intimacy have prompted people to relinquish their commitment. In my analytic practice, one comment I occasionally hear is that *celibate chastity is no longer life-giving*. At tepid times, Respondents noted that friendships helped them to keep going, to feel accepted and retain a realistic attitude to life. The importance of non-possessive friendship for mirroring God's love came through responses while there were reservations about friendships when they tended towards exclusivity and mutual absorption.

Early in the book, I describe "particular friendships." In my initial experience of religious life, a grey cloud hung around, and was used to inhibit, close relationships with others inside or outside of the community. The inference was that friendship led to some illicit sexual behaviour. Instead of addressing issues of sexual attraction and the effects of exclusivity on relationships, a collective neurotic fear of homo and/or heterosexual relationships grew. That fear sometimes kept individuals isolated, immature or guilt-ridden.

For growing in celibacy and spirituality, Respondents mentioned contemplative prayer such as Eastern meditative practices and the Spiritual Exercises of St. Ignatius. Paradoxically, reflecting on past struggles, many felt a deepening of their acceptance of celibacy after going through arid periods of prayer.

I hear the priority many Respondents place on relationship with Jesus Christ for bringing about transformation. Others, like Karen and David, perceive phases and changes in this relationship which are worthwhile. Respondents shared important symbols and associations. Frank's image of positive fathering is an example of how that God image helps and enriches his living:

> *I remember one a while back: I imagined sitting against a stone fence with Jesus and we were conversing. More recently: I find myself embracing and being embraced by the Father (the image is rooted in an experience with my own father). Once in desolation I heard in myself: 'Wherever you go, I am' and at first thought I was saying it to Christ, but then realised he was saying it to me, and it became mutual.*

In Frank's description of growing in intimacy with Jesus Christ, he points to the initiative coming from the Self rather than ego. As an image of the Self, of God, Christ takes the lead. Likewise, several Respondents affirm that their reason for facing the cost of celibacy is Agape: love of and for Jesus Christ. Juan was able to see this love in an old symbol of self-sacrifice that is identified with Christ.

According to fable, in times of food shortage the pelican pecked her breast to feed her young. Similarly this young priest envisages the nature of unconditional love. Complementing Frank's fathering image of the divine, Juan's description is a tender mothering image:

> *The Pelican. An ancient symbol linked with Christianity. It's important for me, because of that beautiful sense of self-denial that those birds have with their chicks.*

Many Respondents referred to favourite Scripture passages that spoke of desire for union with God and service of others. It substantiates that a spiritual life is vital for living chastely. For some people there were experiences before and after their choice of vocation that were relevant. These experiences included uplifting times and periods of struggle through which God became more present.

I noticed that, in allowing libido to become graced passion, some spoke of growing into intimacy. Yet Frank identifies the conflicting social complex around sex and continence that influences collective attitudes to celibacy. The celibate person can sometimes be left feeling inadequate whereas, in sporting or professional fields, self-denial for a more mundane purpose is legitimated. Frank articulates the conundrum:

> *At a time of self-realization, self-denial is not an easy matter. I guess it never was, but it seems to be complicated now by what we know about the human person. And it is complicated by our cultural attitude toward sex as recreation. I had to struggle like all the rest of us to affirm the importance in my life of continence as I grew mature in a culture, which considers continence a mistake, a big and rather silly mistake.*

Other responses recognised a variety of people in religious life and priesthood, which reflect differences in sexual drive and how people cope. Catherine made another point. Intensity of libido varies depending on one's situation, needs, and the natural attraction that ignites around certain people. As far as I could tell, the Respondents seemed to be aware and consciously facing what they did with sexual energy rather than regressing into neurotic tension.

As to the life-enhancing aspects of consecrated celibacy, all Respondents, except one diocesan priest, wrote that celibacy had contributed to a developing sense of identity, integrity and freedom to be, to do for, and to receive from others:

> At this stage in my life I could say it makes for a sense of wholeness! I really don't know why...Maybe it's because of the opportunities I got as a religious and priest to...confront myself and work through things. (Peter)

Compassionate Service

C.S. Lewis writes that if you selfishly (or could I add, fearfully) bury your heart, it won't break but it will become hard and impermeable for "...to love is to be vulnerable."[300] The quotation leads me to the third theme of compassionate service. I heard Respondents say that vulnerability has contributed to their humanity rather than flooding them with feelings of inadequacy. In wrestling with their own struggles, or seeing others bear their difficulties, many voiced a growing appreciation of this way. Tim saw his struggle as similar to those of married friends and family who also have to work at growing faithfully in their commitment:

> Observing the pains and difficulties of my married brother and sister and my married friends has helped me to put celibacy in the perspective of a radical availability to God (prayer) and to God's people (ministry).

Three Respondents acknowledged their loss of significant experiences as women because of the choice of celibacy: giving birth, raising a family and having one partner for life. They also said that their celibate

---

300   C.S. Lewis, *The Four Loves*, 147.

life enabled them to be lovingly present with and to others. For good and ill, as David mentioned, vowed celibates can take more risks to be with those at the edges. This aspect of going out to those whom society considers insignificant appears intrinsic to celibate chastity:

> *Relationship between living celibacy and relating to the poor and needy? I have found it to be close. I am poor; that is, without one of the great riches of human life. Anyhow it's true to say that I find myself at ease among the poor—among whom I lived for some years.* (Frank)

In a follow-up interview, Judith drew my attention to an aspect she saw missing in my enquiry. She wondered why I had not spoken about the sign value of celibacy. I went back to the responses and noticed that eight people spoke of their celibate commitment as giving them freedom to witness to God's love and serve others. Synchronistically, this prophetic aspect of celibate chastity is taken up by Sandra Schneiders.[301] As I reflect on Judith's criticism, I have to ask myself the key question that Jung posed: *What difficulty in life are you avoiding?* And Judith's comment:

> *I was astonished that you didn't have a question—although it is implied in other questions—but you didn't actually articulate the aspect of celibacy as a sign…it is meant to be understood as a public sign, or a sign in the church. People think, 'Ah, she is not married. Why is she not married?' This sign character, I think is quite important.*

In this next section, with these themes in mind—choice, intimacy and compassionate service, I pick up and highlight what I consider are essential clews for celibate women and men to keep in mind in handling the fire of Eros.

Ethics and Continuing Education

In spite of diversity of attitudes to life, Jung emphasized that Ethos is characteristic of human nature and goes beyond cultural specifics. His

---

301   Sandra Schneiders, *Prophets in their Own Country*, 2011.

view has an Aristotlean ring where ethics is seen as integral to a life of virtue.[302] I am reminded of the 2010 International Congress of Analytical Psychologists in Montreal, when Dr. Bou-Yong Rhi, Korean analyst, referred to ethos as the voice of God and ethical judgement attending to that still, small voice.

Those vowed to celibate love need to be conscious of that ethos in their ministering to others. Then ethical standards have a deeper value than being a set of procedures or rules to which one adheres. Bishop Robinson suggests, *"in building a new sexual ethics there be a return to Christian roots, a Christian ethic [is]...putting the good of the neighbour first and doing all in one's power to help that neighbour."*[303]

The task of ethics is educating persons to attend to the call from the Greater Self. From that base can flow practices for encouraging others on their human journey and protecting the vulnerable from the shadow of abuse. The question becomes: What processes can urge people into more consciousness of why and how we act with integrity and not just generate preventative measures?

I described one of the archetypal expressions of celibacy and the responsibilities of the Virgin as taking care of fire. Handling the fire of sexuality is no easy task and an ethical approach and continuing education are essential. As media reports reveal, when those vowing celibacy seriously cross sexual boundaries, their misconduct wreaks damage on others.

"A 'culture of secrecy' was identified by the Attorney General for Massachusetts...in the case of that diocese...secrecy 'protected the institution' at the expense of children."[304]

Where abuse has occurred, restorative justice needs to happen. Professional Standards Committees have been established in dioceses, and part of their brief is to prescribe mandatory norms for all who minister in the Catholic Church: hence this snippet. In supporting alliances of

---

302   C.G. Jung, "Civilization in Transition," CW 10, ¶ 108.

303   Geoffrey Robinson, *Confronting Power and Sex in the Catholic Church*, 15-19.

304   Kevin Egan, Remaining a Catholic after the Murphy Report, John Jay College of Criminal Justice, http://www.usccb.org/issues-and-action/child-and-youth-protection/upload/The-Causes-and-Context-of-Sexual-Abuse-of-Minors-by-Catholic-Priests-in-the-United-States-1950-2010.pdf. Retrieved June 9, 2014.

survivors of sexual abuse and ministers, a former Vice Chancellor of the Diocese of Milwaukee identified what he called a key question: "What if I had been a victim of sexual abuse by a priest or religious?"[305] Essentially it means putting oneself in the place of the injured persons.

Dr. Monica Applewhite, an American researcher who is involved in the prevention of sexual abuse, brings her expertise to help communities with best practices. I notice a trace of the red thread in Monica's explanation of why she does this work of creating safer environments:

> Through this work with religious, the work with victims of abuse, and the development of response systems, I began to feel close to the church again…I love it like you love your spouse after 40 years of marriage. I love it in its faults and failing (and) its humanness.[306]

It is now protocol to report abuse to civil authorities and to treat victims pastorally while investigating allegations of abuse. An area identified as essential for priests and religious, as for other members of the helping professions, is regular mentoring and supervision. Firstly a comment on psychosexual education programmes that Bishop Robinson recommends for new ministers.[307] Respondent John Terry says that educative opportunities need to be life-long and I think he is right:

> *Sexuality and living a sexual life as a celibate have to be expanded into attitudes that go to the depths of the person and touch every aspect of life. Being a man or woman. Relating. Sexuality can't be reduced to urge or instinct—there's more to it 'than acting out.'*

Sometimes people can get stuck in earlier stages of their development. At the beginning of *Celibacy and Soul*, I gave an introduction to Erik Erikson's Stages of Life. This psychosexual model of maturation

---

305   James Connell, "Critical question leads priest to challenge lax abuse policies," http://ncronline.org/news/accountability/critical-question-leads-priest-challenge-lax-abuse-policies. Retrieved June 9, 2014.

306   Tim Drake, "Change in Vatican Culture." http://www.ncregister.com/daily-news change_in_vatican_culture. Retrieved June 9, 2014.

307   Geoffrey Robinson, *Confronting Power and Sex in the Catholic Church*, 289-292.

happening throughout life suggests markers for a healthy genital and affective sexuality.

In living, everyone experiences difficulties, and these periods can be mildly or seriously traumatizing. An adult fixation at the period of adolescence may show in low self-esteem and a fantasy sex life that leads to compulsive behaviour. For example, Karen reframes masturbation with common sense:

> *I think the prohibition on masturbation is too non-specific and insufficiently acknowledging of its natural occurrence. Of course, when it is habitual, practiced in relation to pornography or the objectification of sex or another it is unacceptable.*

Lack of psychosexual maturation can prevent intimacy. Feeling stuck because of fear and missed opportunities may show in self-centredness or a tendency to be too conforming. In the cycles of sexual awakening, it is important to explore and occasionally to unlearn. Wherever one is on that spiral of human development, wise mentors, friends and family are essential as Patrick recounts:

> *Fostering friendship takes time. For me there can be no real intimate and affectionate relationship without an authentic contemplative prayer life. Each person has to work out their boundaries as each one has their own experiences and formation to deal with. Our basic need for affection and esteem from the womb needs to be addressed for a truly human development and celibacy. For me celibacy is a growing and developing dynamic.*

While I see formal and informal education as important, the question that goes to the heart of being chaste and celibate is this leitmotif, "Do I feel a call to this radical way of loving?" If the answer is "Yes," the person needs to recognise and attend to the human need for intimacy, as Jane clarifies:

> *What to do with sexual attraction? How to appropriately satisfy my needs for intimacy within a celibate commitment?*

In journeying into unconditional love, one has to question what makes for healthy friendships and the many kinds of intimacy. Intimacy with others may grow spontaneously or through a shared interest. The latter may come through nature, art, dedication to social justice, to Someone or Something bigger that encourages meaningful engagement with others in the world.

People also need to be aware of what thwarts intimacy. Out of fear, trauma and lack of self-confidence, addictive behaviours such as substance abuse, cybersex and workaholism can develop. Work can become all-consuming for some religious and priests. The dangers are not only stress and burnout. When one forgets the Other is present and feels alone in carrying a burden or responsibility, the pressure and heaviness of an undertaking can drain and deaden psyche.

Accompaniment and Supervision

Finding a guide for the inner journey is crucial. In the contemporary world, their names and locations have tended to move from the religious into the therapeutic field. You may have noticed that the practice of seeking a soul guide has become more widespread. The roots are ancient as John O'Donohue reminds in the Celtic name, "anam cara."[308] The latter may be spiritual director, analyst, therapist, counsellor or psychologist. Karen gives a sense of their relevance when she reflects on who and what has most helped her to live celibacy:

> *Mostly good relationships with other religious and non-religious friends and the wisdom of a good woman spiritual director. Prayer and contemplation especially during difficult times.*

In early Monasticism, it was a scandal for a young monk or nun not to have a spiritual guide. I hear Respondents recommending this practice. One woman mentioned that she has engaged in spiritual accompaniment for the last twenty years and it has been integral for her growth. While Jung did not suggest that people reconnect to a particular religious tradition or creed, he was adamant that they find some spiritual dimension in their lives that left space for articulating the encounter with the numinous. Consequently, Jung insisted that those training as

---

308 John O'Donohue, *Anam Cara.*

analysts undergo a thorough psychoanalysis with a trained soul guide: this aspect is at the heart of the analytical process.

As I reflect on those people who have journeyed and still journey with me, I know and experience their capacity for celibate loving. A soul guide is a sounding board and encourager. Over the years, different women and men, colleagues, religious sisters, priests and supervisors have handed me the thread when I lost perspective or needed heart. Accompaniment is a favour you do for yourself! What each mentor has in common is his or her personal devotion to the Other and the desire that I would deepen that fire. Dr. Baker would comment about the analytical process in which we engaged, "It is not about you or me; it is about the work."[309] Such comments bring home that something is calling for attention and requires a deliberate response from psyche.

In the choice of soul guide, there is something profoundly changing and synchronistic (more than fortuitous) in the meeting of two people. A spark of connection is essential for the journey of trust that takes persons into sharing their story with another. The Spanish capture this dynamic in the word "flamenco" that describes "a dance of flame and passion."

Thinking of those accompaniers in analysis, in spiritual direction, in my profession, some of whom are religious women and priests, I feel gratitude. They have given and brought out a mellowing, reassurance, a feisty spirit: an "impassioned awareness," as Underhill describes spirituality.[310]

A word about synchronicity, or meaningful coincidence, along with a personal example to clarify this dynamic: What drew me to my training analyst was his English manner which immediately appealed to my need for positive fathering. It didn't require much insight to realise I was projecting on to him the father who had died when I was a teenager. Added to this mix, Dr. Baker's first lecture at the Jung Institute in Zurich was on Mysticism and Individuation. My intuition was that those opposites in my life were coinciding in this guide. For celibate or non-celibate, it is important to trust intuition and desire—or, at the

---

309   Ian Baker, Personal Communication, 2000.
310   Evelyn Underhill, *The Mystic Way*, 27.

very least, to test them out. Incidentally, I have no regrets that I followed this path into analysis!

A Way Through Difficult Emotions

In accompaniment, people can realise how the difficult emotions—anger, sadness, anxiety, guilt, embarrassment, boredom, frustration and shame—can actually be gifts from the Self that call for careful unwrapping. The reassurance of a skilful Other in this process is a blessing. The possibility is that one's vulnerability can transform into grace. I want to describe this place of paradox but first hear how Peter describes the difficult emotions that the celibate and the non-celibate person might face:

> *I know people who experience problems living celibate. The kinds of problems and difficulties are what one might expect: loneliness, a feeling of hollowness, discouragement at a failing in genital activity such as masturbation and petting, and confusion about developing relationship…tremendous difficulties and only compassion helps here. I would say that celibates have problems in about the same proportion as married people.*

In *Owning the Shadow*, Jungian analyst, Dr. Robert Johnson speaks of the Almond or Mandorla Space as potential space. It is where opposites coincide with the birth of a paradoxical "third."[311] An ordinary place of meeting, like the office of one's mentor, can move from what Winnicott called a holding environment to being what Jungian Dr. Henry Abramovitch describes as "sacred space," "a temenos."[312] In their meeting with a spiritual accompanier, analyst or soul guide, people give room for the unknown third, the Self or God to become present. (Of course, any deep encounter with another invites this presence.) With the accompanied, the one accompanying knows to wait, to let go of personal agenda and the need for resolution and to be open to what comes to light. John Terry describes his experience of the graced friendship of accompaniment as:

---

311 Robert A. Johnson, *Owning Your Own Shadow*.
312 Henry Abramovitch, "Temenos Regained: Reflections on the Absence of the Analyst," *Journal of Analytical Psychology*, 47, 2002, 583-598.

Disciplined or self-effacing, that leaves a space or third area...
not possessive, concerned for the other and affectionate—struc-
tured—friendship.

What is this uncanny third area to which John Terry refers? Jung describes the third as a Transcendent symbol of the Self, which cannot be orchestrated. It may be an intuition or a new insight that just walks in, like the saving grace of the unexpected. On a collective level, the Quakers model an opening to this phenomenon in their silent waiting. When they come together, there is firstly silence and then out of that space they discuss the pertinent issue at hand. Henri Nouwen takes up this idea of intentional waiting in his book, *The Wounded Healer*.[313] He suggests that the most important attribute for one who is a soul guide is being prepared to wait with another for a blossoming moment to happen.

The unexpected, the transcendent third, the Self and in some instances, the shadow of the unknown, breaks into life and rearranges our plans. Where have you felt the unexpected coming in and altering your life? Some celibate women and men described their answering a call to religious life or to a new ministry in this way. I found the unexpected third came in the form of a 30-day Retreat at St. Beuno's in Wales, when in 1990 I took a sabbatical opportunity. The discernment experience of the Spiritual Exercises prompted me out of education in Australia and into depth psychology.

It is a good time to describe this discerning process especially as a number of the Respondents referred to its life-changing effects. The Spiritual Exercises of St. Ignatius go back over 450 years. They resulted from the unknown literally knocking the feet from under the feisty Spaniard, Inigo Lopez de Onaz y Loyola (St. Ignatius Loyola). The forced confinement and conversion experience of this first Jesuit set the pattern for the Exercises of Discernment. They consist of a carefully refined four-stage path for contemplating the meaning and direction for one's life by attending to what disturbs and what brings a sense of peace.

The 2013-4 Program for Australian Centres of Ignatian Spirituality describes the Exercises as "a dialogue that becomes prayer through these

---

313 Henri Nouwen, *The Wounded Healer*.

questions: What have I done for Christ? What am I doing for Christ? What ought I do for Christ?"[314] Karen's response gives an idea of this way of discerning:

> *There was a strong experience in prayer of a sense of my woman-*
> *hood and self-worth during the last week of the Ignatian Spiri-*
> *tual Exercises in preparation for my life vows.*

In going deeply into this process, the retreatant traces the call of God in her life. Over 30 days, those on retreat meet individually and regular-ly with their trained director. The latter listens to psyche's experience of the Self-touching the person's ordinary life. The guide suggests Scripture readings and particular meditations into which the retreatant can enter.

Is discernment possible? Does life change? I can say from listening to others and from personal experience: "Yes." With the help of the Exer-cises, I was able to discern a desire to apply for analytical training at the Jung Institute in Zurich. It seemed to be a radically new calling for me and also for the Congregation of the Sisters of St. Joseph. I received the support of the leadership of my religious community (who also risked a costly unknown) to explore my changing from an established ministry. It included my going back to my roots in Africa that meant braving another set of insecurities and trusting this new choice. A change of direction had been set for Zurich—and in between times I was heading to live and work at the edge of the Kalahari in the heart of Africa, an experience which shook my heart and put me in touch again with the Ariadnean thread of my Self.[315]

Recovering Desire

> *God continually creates me including my desiring. My most*
> *authentic desires rise directly out of God's passionately creative*
> *love and they lead to love. But God creates me in and among*
> *humankind, and humankind has fouled our desiring with vio-*

---

314 Australian Centres of Ignatian Spirituality, 2013-4 Program, 16.
315 Irene Claremont de Castillejo. *Knowing Woman*, 137.

*lence, deceit, selfishness and so on. So it becomes a difficult matter
to discover what my most authentic desires are...* (Frank)

Notice how Frank differentiates between authentic desire that is in
tune with love and disordered desire that comes from illusion. Thanks
to the Ignatian Exercises, desire has recovered more respect from where
repressive spirituality had taken it.

To further understand positive and negative desire, I want to take a
clew from Chaucer who tells of *Desire, Woman, Choice and the Loathly
Lady!*[316] In *The Canterbury Tales*, the Wife of Bath takes up these motifs.
King Arthur is confronted with the riddle: *What do women most want?*
In frantically trying to solve the puzzle, Arthur and the readers learn that
what women really desire is the freedom to choose. The deeper message
that the story conveys is that real love is about allowing the Other the
freedom and autonomy to choose.

How does this tale apply to celibate love? I suggest that what char-
acterizes chastity is desiring to love the Other with no strings attached.
While it is a quality of loving to which everyone is called, this Agape is
what celibate chastity professes. In his response, Frank articulates and
affirms the nature of unconditional love and how it is freeing:

> *I have learned from couples (successful, enduring, failing) that a
> man and a woman who are married also have to find their way
> to a love that must be called celibate in some sense. Celibates love
> the whole person as person, and wish to be with the Other in
> loyalty (rather than fidelity, which seems to have to do more with
> consummated human love). Celibate love wishes the Other to
> become and to do all that Other authentically wishes.*

How do the Spiritual Exercises fit with the recovery of desire and the
idea of unconditional love? The Exercises begin with the same questions:
What do you really want? What do you desire? These are not trick questions. They imply that Love desires our freedom. This kind of love goes
past possessiveness and exclusivity to genuine concern for the Other.

---

316 Geoffrey Chaucer, *The Canterbury Tales*, 299-309; Selina Hastings, *Sir Gawain
and the Loathly Lady*.

Frank again offers a clew for putting together desire and unconditional love:

> *My experience of the choice is, first of all, a decision to love God first and all in God. Then to love others for the sake of their complete human fulfilment, without demanding that their fulfilment promote my own.*

I have a picture of how this kind of discerning and celibate love can play out in some Chapters for Religious Congregations. Chapters are special gatherings of prayer and deliberations that involve all members of Religious Orders. These intense meetings usually occur every four to six years. Major issues are raised, discussed and set for the future focus of members. Then leadership changes are made to advance that direction. During the Chapter election, after politicking is addressed, I have observed the occurrence of a generous dynamic where someone nominated for office will, in all freedom and love, indicate that she is free to take or not to accept a new role. It is quite humbling to see what happens to and with others when this freedom is extended to each other. The process renews the group and the individuals.

Linking Back to Eros

In finding the energy for loving unconditionally, we need to link back to the source of Eros. The original meaning of the word "religio" means just that—"a linking back" to the spirit beyond human understanding. It is the deep inner spring of Dadirri which Aboriginal artist, educator and activist, Miriam Rose Therese Ungunmerr-Baumann describes.[317] The importance of connecting with the inner life is true for all people and especially for those who make a profession of loving without expecting anything in return.

All of us are made for love and to respond to love. Ideally at the start of life, the child is immersed in the love of family. Jung chooses the image of an island slowly rising out of the sea to describe the ego growing into consciousness. As we develop, "the true self," to which Don-

---

317   Eileen Farrelly, *Dadirri: The Spring Within*, vii-viii.

ald Winnicott originally alluded, gains more visible ground.[318] Then as human development verifies, children who are secure can take risks to move away from the mothering figure because they are confident and know that they will not be abandoned. Strong family and social networks also help individuals to step out of their comfort zone, and many Respondents referred to the gift of families in nurturing their commitment to celibate chastity.

Where attachment does not happen, there is the danger of a falseness (the false Self) taking over in defence of a fragile psyche. An individual can become too responsible too soon and become mother or father to parents or to family. Strangely while this dynamic can lead to a dissociating effect in a personality, the defence can also protect the delicate ego. Sometimes, the only way for psyche to survive is to split-off into a fantasy world or to have problems with responsibility and control. So are those who have a strong sense of their commitment to God escaping off into fantasy or repeating a lost childhood? It could be so, if their imaginal life is not concretized into actually living in a caring and concerned way for themselves and for others.

Perhaps a delayed attachment might happen through a grandparent, a teacher or some positive caring figure where psyche can be reassured. I have the impression that many Respondents seem to provide such a link for others. For example, Thomas said that celibacy gave him a freedom,

> *to be for those who are poor.*

In some situations, celibate people have had to make this journey themselves out of early experiences of rejection. In one response, a person clearly shows how she worked through a difficult bonding with her mother who suffered postnatal depression and now her Self was flourishing.

In the therapeutic setting, as research confirms, this dynamic of attachment often grows. That relationship is called "the transference" and it is central to the healing process.[319] I have learned as a therapist, or accompanier, not to be anxious about clients developing a positive or

---

318   Erik Erikson, *Identity and the Life Cycle*, 140-152.
319   Jan Wiener, *The Therapeutic Relationship*, 78 ff.

negative attachment. It is not about me personally but what the psyche of the client needs to experience of both reliability and trust in order to counter early dissociating patterns. Where restorative linking back occurs and when the time is right, I see dependence lifting and freedom growing: "Deo concedente."[320]

On the other hand, it is a mistake made too often in relationships that people look to some person, group or cause or even some thing to fill what is lacking. While "philia," "the love between friends," teaches us about trust, generosity and companionship, I have come to realise it is unfair to ask anyone or any community to fill one's needs. Other Respondents also commented how the gift of friendship has helped them to mature.

Clearly, friendship and the capacity to be a friend are to be treasured. There is great comfort in being able to tell a friend what frustrates, worries or delights. Emotion is less likely to spill over inappropriately. So too when faith is shared with a friend, there is the possibility for the friendship to go even deeper and take on a spiritual quality. Dr. Baker's words come back to me: "for those who trust in Christ, there is no death."[321] Frank amplifies this sense:

> *The majority of my close friends have not only helped my spiritual life but have been integral parts of it. The ones who hinder me draw me to activities and coax me to accept feelings and adopt attitudes which occasion failure for me. I once had some drinking buddies, which was a mistake, and some friends who could handle explicit sexual material better than I could. Of my good friends who led me to God: they helped my prayer. They shared ideas and convictions…they have held me when I wept in grief. They have helped me play in wonderful ways.*

Eros' darts can hit without warning and be all-consuming. The disarming look of love can come through a glance. Projections and infatuation just happen and bring a headiness and exuberance to life. Some Respondents acknowledged falling in love after taking vows or being ordained to the priesthood, and their resulting anxiety and uncertainty:

---

320 C.G. Jung, "Psychology of the Transference," CW 16, ¶ 385.
321 Ian Baker, Personal Communication, 2000.

I've doubted myself and felt stressed and confused at times...
where I've gone beyond the boundaries of what would have been
accepted/permitted of someone who professes to be celibate. I guess
they were sexual experiences though I (we) managed to put some
limits on our behaviours. That was during my 30s and 40s and
I think it was quite difficult for me during those years of my life.
(Rose)

Such times bring home to vowed celibates that one primary relationship with one special man or woman who will love and be totally available for them and vice versa are what celibacy forgoes. As Karen comments, while vowing chastity does not prevent the celibate (or married person) from subsequently falling in love, celibacy has the difficulty that other chaste commitments assuage. The chaste celibate does not have a partner who is exclusively for him or her:

Falling in love again and again, and then feeling depressed about
not falling in love with anyone when I was most lonely.

Is celibate chastity about being loveless and alone? On the contrary, vowing to love tenderly, consecrated celibates are impelled to link back to what St. Paul describes as "Agape": connecting with "the love of Christ and the love for Christ." This they can share with others. This "fuerza del amor" ("force of love") motivated John of the Cross[322] which I hear in this man's desire:

At the moment I experience celibacy as an unquenchable desire
or hunger for an intimate relationship with God (who dwells
alas away). And so celibacy becomes my prayer. It means trying
to become a celibate-lover and trying to make my body more and
more expressive of my personal relationship to others. (Peter)

Agape is different from family ties and the spontaneous feelings of affection that just happen in relating with certain people. It is not the friendship of "philia" that grows with a few others where I share my intimate thoughts, feelings, attitudes and interests. It is not the desire aroused by a sexual, aesthetic or spiritual passion and attraction. Agape

---

322 Andres Rafael Luevano, *Endless Transforming Love*, 11.

involves loving all others without conditions and without being servile. Thomas says it well:

> *That which (as in all true love) promotes the well-being of the Other. This means mutual respect, recognition and articulation of boundaries. It's a love which expresses itself in ways other than genital.*

In the Second Testament, Christ shows *agape* as a *caritas* of service.[323] A similar understanding is communicated by Debra:

> *As I get older I am convinced that the only thing that really matters to me is that I have loved and been loved...*

Agape is the antithesis of fear, manipulation and selfishness and goes to the core of Christian identity. Love of and for Christ is at the heart of Christian baptism. It is the love that the chaste celibate professes. "Love now becomes concern and care for the Other. No longer is it self-seeking."[324]

For those living into celibate chastity, choice of the love of and for Christ is the primary relationship and affects how they see others. I recall a visit to one of the Respondents when a dishevelled man called at his door. The priest assisted the visitor and quietly remarked after the person had left. *Why does Jesus have to look so dirty?* While Agape is celibate love, it is clearly not reserved for those who vow celibacy. Those who promise to live unconditional love need to be conscious of and grow in expressing this love to others. Tim's comment reminds me that growing into celibate love is similar to Psyche's journey in which she seeks to link back to Eros:

> *Most definitely celibacy has contributed to my human and religious wholeness. It is a developmental journey marked by ups and downs. The reward is gradual but worthy.*

---

323   Elizabeth Kamarck Minnich, *Transforming Knowledge*, 16; Matthew 23:11 in *The New Jerusalem Bible*.

324   Benedict XV1, *Deus Caritas Est*, ¶ 6.

CHAPTER NINE

EMERGENCE: TRACES OF BEAUTY

The Unfillable Space

Many Respondents identified loneliness as their biggest difficulty in living celibacy. It belongs to the dilemma of the human condition which psychoanalyst, Erich Fromm, describes as the prison from which people seek to escape. It is the gaping unease about which Toni Morrison writes and the dread that Wilfred Bion names.[325] There are levels and degrees of loneliness. One Respondent takes us on a developmental journey, through privation, struggle and contradiction to a sense of complementarity and a kind of synthesis of this dilemma. I want to quote the whole text because Frank's description is clear and comprehensive as he unlocks the anguish of loneliness:

> Loneliness? At times when I was much younger I felt the aloneness
> of one who is not relating. I had to learn that the experience is
> not tightly related to celibacy, and is rather more tightly related to
> self-centredness and narcissism. But these last two are difficulties
> that are magnified by celibacy, and I had to go through consider-
> able pain on the way to growing out of them. Fortunately, my life
> has been blessed with good and trustworthy friends. One mani-
> festation of this is the difficult struggle against letting sexuality
> become a solitary, interior reality instead of the social reality it
> really is…I muffed a lot of situations and caused hurt feelings
> before I grasped that every human person will very likely attract
> some other persons sexually. I mentioned lonesomeness: What I

---

325   Erich Fromm, *The Art of Loving*, 8; Toni Morrison, *Beloved*, 174; W.R. Bion, *The
Long Week-End 1897-1919: Part of a Life.*

heard…was to avoid friendship. Lots of mistakes there. With dif-
ficulty, I accepted friendship and in time made friends. Now, I
know what lonesomeness is—a great difficulty in celibacy. I miss
my friends, who make up who I am, and are scattered all over the
globe. This is not unique to celibacy, but it is endemic to living
in a Religious Congregation which sends its women and men all
over the place as almost all Congregations do now.

Frank's comments do more than differentiate between loneliness, aloneness and lonesomeness and the kinds of obstacles to friendship for celibate religious. He tackles the question of how one deals with loneliness and desire, and shares how he deals with their shadow. Frank's insight comes through facing rather than avoiding intimacy. That courage takes him and us to the place of all-oneness: what Ignatian spirituality might describe as the grace of consolation, and what psychoanalyst, James Grotstein, calls the "transcendent position."[326]

A slight pause on Frank's story, while I make mention of the delightful quality of humour that is essential for psychic health: In the course of conversations and reflections, I came across different people who show that wit can defuse, not only mask, a complex. For a positive defusing, I like this example that Timothy Radcliffe provides. He wrote of how an old monk put the neurotic fear of friendship into perspective by simply remarking, "I have nothing against particular friendships; it's particular enmities to which I object!"[327]

A trust in the Self enables such expansiveness. Frank has a solid trust in God and Self. Otherwise he would not have noted his motivation for facing the shadow of loneliness…namely: *It is for God's sake.* In that remark too we get an inkling of what Jung meant when he suggested that healing happens as one connects with the religious factor. Frank shares how his experience of going through personal emptiness and misunderstanding brought him to another realization.

---

326   James S. Grotstein, *Bion's Transformation in O & the Concept of the Transcendent Position,* http://www.sicap.it/~merciai/bion/papers/grots.htm. Retrieved June 9, 2014.

327   Timothy Radcliffe, *The Promise of Life* http:/dominicans.ca/Documents/masters/Radcliffe/promise_life.html. Retrieved June 8, 2014.

You need to know of a special woman in Frank's story. She is like an anima figure leading Frank to an observation that he breaks open. In their conversation, we hear that while friendship could not take away Frank's loneliness or the woman's emptiness, they allow each other to become aware of and receptive to what I like to call the unfillable space.

> *The important matter is an openness of my whole Self...Catherine of Siena says that 'there is a little room inside of myself which only God and I go into and no else ever goes.' I read that decades ago and it stuck in my mind. And then I began reading all this material on masculine spirituality who...say that the problem is a hollowness in the middle of males because of the failure of fathering. I begin to think it is not a failure at all. That is a misidentification. There really is a room inside of everyone, where only that person, and God if the person knows God, go.*
>
> *Now one of the women whom I knew some years ago went through an experience when she was perhaps, maybe forty-five, where she felt she was nothing but an empty womb. At first, I didn't know what that meant and I said, 'I don't know if I can help you with this because I don't have that experience.' But we kept talking and the more she described what she was going through, the more it became clear to me that that was her image for an experience I recognised. There is a space in the middle of each of us where only I and God can go. And I think celibacy promotes that experience. Indeed, it demands it.*

In meeting with the Unknown, Frank indicates that a crucial stage can come when tension is not short-circuited and, together with one's limitations, one travels into "the darksome night."[328] What I find strong in Frank's narrative is his pinpointing of how vulnerability can bring one to the threshold of a new recognition as I become, in the language of object-relations psychology, my own object.[329] James Grotstein describes "the transcendent position" as one where persons look within and catch

---

328   St. John of the Cross, *The Spiritual Canticle and Poems*, stanza 1, 5.
329   W.R.D. Fairburn, *Psychoanalytic Studies of the Personality*, 109 ff.

a glimpse of their real Self beyond projections. Seeing one's self in this way is an experience of both "solitude and serenity."[330]

I consider this is the compelling insight that Frank receives in his conversation with the woman religious. It is an awareness that their emptiness was not primarily about self-centredness or sexuality. Through her mediation and their sharing, Frank became aware of the inner room, which he recognised as the space of the Other within the human soul.

The image of the empty womb that the Sister experienced and Frank's feeling of hollowness could be attributed to midlife crisis and left at that juncture. Note the critical age of the woman and remember Frank was reading John Bly on the midlife dilemma in males. While it may be true at one level that this is about a midlife crisis, in really listening to his friend, Frank is taken to an archetypal level. The imagery points him, and us, to a Scriptural conversation between Christ and Nicodemus and to Tertullian's description of chastity. By amplifying those associations, we are led to see celibate love as one way to a deeper humanity, "to the second birth."[331] The woman's experience of the empty womb faces her with denial of the Incarnation, and Frank's experience of hollowness confronts him with the empty tomb after Christ's resurrection.

Such dilemmas lead one to a vivid space of feeling wide open and to a potentially transforming experience of what Bion calls the "O" of infinite.[332] They are crises of life and faith that also connect with my initial question about celibate chastity: how emptiness can become pregnant space. In my search into celibate love, a turning point came for me in this conversation with Frank as he pointed not to an empty space but to the unfillable space. Later I remembered that at the centre of the labyrinth is the unfillable space...the temenos...sacred space.

---

330   James S. Grotstein, *Bion's Transformation in O & the Concept of the Transcendent Position*, http://www.sicap.it/~merciai/bion/papers/grots.htm. Retrieved June 9, 2014.

331   John 3:3-8 in *The New Jerusalem Bible*.

332   James S. Grotstein, *Bion's Transformation in O & the Concept of the Transcendent Position*, http://www.sicap.it/~merciai/bion/papers/grots.htm. Retrieved June 9, 2014.

Consenting

Touched by the breath of Spring
My heart shoots tender quivering leaves
Still remembering
Past pruning.

God's birth in the human soul demands something. In literature, Mary Renault conveys this sense and yet shifts the accent from sacrifice to one of opening oneself to God and to life: "Listen, and do not forget…It is not the sacrifice, whether it comes in youth or age…It is the consenting. The readiness is all."[333]

Mary Renault adds that the consenting makes one free. My own journey into celibate love has been one of desiring and wanting to consent wholeheartedly. I have been unsure of just how to get to that place of holding nothing back. There are women and men who seem to get there more definitely, with less struggle.

It is heartening when Renault asserts that the readiness is what counts. Her reply brings together the paradoxical desire to let go of and to hold on. These are sometimes critical questions to ask someone in the analytical process: "What do you need to hold on to?" and "What do you need to let go of?" It points to a process of becoming. In her inimitable style, Simone de Beauvoir quips: "…you become woman."[334] Listening to some male friends and clients, I think the becoming holds true for men too…to which I add there seems to be a process of becoming chastely celibate.

Why so gradual a consenting? As well as personality, more shadowy reasons come into play such as an attitude of wanting it all. I can identify with those Respondents who had hoped to escape a sense of vocation to this way of life. Analysis in Zurich gave me another freedom and space for growing in to a freer consent. For, as Renault observed, renewing consent at different stages of life takes one progressively deeper into the mystery of what one holds on to and lets go of.

---

333 Mary Renault, *The King Must Die*, 18.
334 Simone De Beauvoir, *The Second Sex*, 301.

The *consenting that is everything* on which I am focusing here is accepting the vocation to chaste celibacy. I see it as part of that deep ongoing pattern that applies to other paths in life. Individual differences mean that the age of consent can be early for some, while for others, consenting may take a lifetime. At a recent vocational discernment meeting, the coordinator remarked, "It takes as long as it takes."[335]

In this maturing, the person may experience a tension of opposites as the holding on and letting go play out. Moments of grace occur, and take psyche to a new moment. One may still lack certainties yet the renewing or choosing differently is transforming.

The consenting phenomenon cuts across all stages of human development. As children and adults, we take decisive steps into the unknown. In ageing, perhaps the most painful consenting happens. The body that is so integral to oneself reminds that I am not as in control as I once thought. To accept this reality and to trust the Self in this vulnerability is an act of faith and conscious choice. Many elders, unable to keep hold of memory and mobility, accept what is the greatest Unknown and let go into their dying.

Alongside daily scenarios of holding on and letting go, there are celibate women and men who, in love, give up a sexual partnership with one other to be sister and brother to all others. I am remembering a priest who had a deteriorating medical condition that meant regular hospitalization. Allan's compassion for other people whom he met on his hospital visits instilled courage in many to face their suffering: as he was doing.

To illustrate the embodying of celibate love in the life of a well-known woman religious, I quote Helen Prejean. You might be familiar with her life through the book and/or film, *Dead Man Walking*.[336] During an interview in 1997, and a more recent communication in 2012, Helen spoke of celibate chastity as her way of consenting to be a sister to others and particularly with people on the margins of society. She made it clear that the choice was not all hers, and intimates that grace and love are at work:

---

335 Katrina Brill rsj, Personal communication, 2010.
336 Helen Prejean, *Dead Man Walking*.

The sister thing—they (those in prison) know I am there in another dimension for them. There is real love involved. I am an affectionate person, a woman: and I can really do this work…The sister thing has been liberating. Not to mention the time and energy I have. Celibacy is a way of giving my love in a wider way. You choose but it chooses you…Celibacy is a choice of love that is dangerous and very tricky. If it is not for a person, you shrivel up inside, or you get desperate inside or you're unconscious of your own loneliness in a way that you get involved with things that are not healthy or not good…

The spiritual life is a way of being present; it has to do with a personal relationship with Christ and with others. It has to do with presence, listening, conversation, a moving into intimacy…being a co-creator with God."[337]

Helen and Allan show what a contemporary virginal consent could look like. For an archetypal image of the Virgin's consenting, take another look at Figure 4, Simone Martini and Lippo Memmi's *Annunciation*, where the artists give visual clews for holding on and letting go. Mary who is invited by the angel to be "theotokos" or "birther of God" is depicted as visibly pulling back from what is before her. She discerns and tentatively opens psyche's box.

If you go to the Scriptural account, the narrative reveals that Mary asked one big question before saying "I am God's servant. Let it happen."[338] The power of God waits on one young woman's consenting. This girl, from a Middle Eastern culture, knew that her "Yes" could lead to her being disowned by her family or rejected by Joseph or even being stoned to death by the community. After her discerning, Mary gives a "Yes" to becoming mother of Christ that is conscious and unconditional. In her consent to the incarnation of Jesus Christ, Mary asks for no other assurances. Accepting the call of celibacy is about consenting to bear God's life through one's life. It is not about repressing sexuality. This attitude of responding to grace, generating life for others and allowing the emergence of new life is put into words by Tim:

---

337   Helen Prejean, Personal Communication, 1997/2012.
338   Luke 1:38 in *The New Jerusalem Bible*.

Celibacy has become linked to freedom especially in the sense that it expresses a goal of generativity and generosity that I have clearly chosen by God's grace. I still struggle with times of selfishness and times of emptiness, but more and more I am confident that I have entered the mystery of God's love in a clear and permanent way.

A Cosmic Song

In *Caritas in Veritate*, Benedict XVI speaks about the book of nature as a self-disclosure of God's love and specifically mentions sexuality.[339] Evolutionary cosmology develops the picture of the divine presence in the uniqueness, the variety and fecundity of all creation. Irish spirituality understood this cosmic song and conveys it in the lilting Celtic prayer known as "The Deer's Cry," the Lorica of St. Patrick.[340]

Living with that kind of sensibility, Brianne Swimme and Thomas Berry can name celebration as most expressive of the universe and of what is human. Similarly, Scripture scholar, Richard Bauckham, emphasizes that creation's theme song praises the source of all being.[341] *Nature's book* then is a labyrinth sited inconspicuously everywhere, which invites people in their ordinary situations to accept, receive and enjoy their singular beauty.

Looking at the universe from this perspective, Teilhard de Chardin saw there the real symbol of the body of Christ. Contemporary theologians like Janette Gray and Denis Edwards take up the song of creation in their descriptions of theology as an earthy concern calling for humanity's compassionate awareness. Against such a canvas, the Grail question: "Whom do I serve and Whom does celibate chastity serve?" has to reach out to and include the way we relate with the whole cosmos. Elizabeth Johnson articulates this cosmic view echoed by Sally McFague:

> If nature is the new poor, then our passion to establish justice for the poor and oppressed now must extend to include

---

339   Benedict XVI, *Caritas in Veritate*, 4: 51.
340   St. Patrick, Traditional Celtic prayer.
341   Richard Bauckham, *Bible and the Ecology*, 82-83.

suffering human beings AND life systems and other species under threat.[342]

Celibate love, or loving with no strings attached, involves an impassioned caring for the wounded body of the cosmos. "The vow of virginity, which tradition has always understood as an anticipation (of resurrection)…already at work."[343] Examples of the enormity of the eco crisis range from human trafficking, floating debris littering the oceans, deforestation in the Amazon and mining impacts on the Great Artesian Basin in Australia. Inhuman domination and greed dumps collective shadow on a vulnerable world. I am not optimistic but I am hopeful about a change in world consciousness and collective action. Many fronts cry out for love's pragmatic response.[344] How does that look in a celibate life? I quote Patrick:

> *I experience myself as always growing, changing and being made new. My relationship with Jesus from a man to man, to whole person with a whole person—ever unfolding, ever new. I see this with everyone I relate to, deeper meaning, richer life, day by day.*

Rose, another of the Respondents, articulates that celibate love finds expression outwardly from *an intimacy within my-self that is at such depth that it reaches into God within and around me.* A generative theology of the body recognises the imago Dei: divine beauty embodied in everywoman and everyman, in the body of the People of God, in the body of the cosmos stretching across time and space.

This kind of consciousness takes a broader picture of church as the body of Christ in all of creation—rich, generous and vulnerable. This awareness recognises the unfolding potential in the individual psyche and in universal psyche. In *Memories, Dreams, Reflections* Jung ponders the meaning of a sense of kinship with creation, an "objective psyche"

---

342 Elizabeth A. Johnson, *An Ecological Theology of the Holy Spirit*, http://www.duq.edu/events/holy-spirit-lecture-and-colloquium/2008. Retrieved June 7, 2014.

343 John Paul II, *Vita Consecrata*, ¶ 26, http://www.vatican.va/roman_curia/congregations/ccscrlife/documents/hf_jp-ii_exh_25031996_vita-consecrata_en.html. Retrieved June 6, 2014.

344 Congregation for Institutes of Consecrated Life and Societies of Apostolic Life. *Starting Afresh from Christ*, Part 1, ¶ 8.

that spans all dimensions.[345] Such an ecological perspective can generate both wonder and loving service of the Creator in whose image woman and man are reflected—and in a universe that unconsciously reflects that presence. How do we do this? Jung's clue:

> (we) have not served God rightly unless (we) have served God in beauty.[346]

Taking positive action implies a strong connection to the Self, which brings me to an icon that Georg treasures.

Figure 13: Christ and St. Menas, by unknown artist.
Source: ARAS Online Archive. Reprinted with permission.

---

345   C.G. Jung, *Memories, Dreams, Reflections*, 392.
346   C.G. Jung, "Psychology and Religion," CW 11, ¶ 378.

In contemplating this sacred image, which the French familiarly call "Christ and his Friend," Georg reconnects personally with a cosmic dimension of Christ. This Presence who reaches back in time, walks with us in the present and into an unknown future. To this Omega point with its eschatological dimension, developing theologies and psychology point.[347] No wonder this ancient Egyptian icon gives Georg encouragement.

In the 6th century image, Christ has his arm around Menas' shoulder. As in most icons, the eyes are prominent features. One of Christ's eyes seems trained on his friend and the other looks out at the world. This expression conveys *not only is my gaze outward, I have a protective eye on you.* The ears of Menas are painted large as if to emphasize the listening quality that this friendship requires of the disciple.

Strangely Christ has no feet. Is Menas to take him to others? Christ carries what looks like the book of Scripture while his friend holds a scroll, intimating that Menas has part of the bigger story that Christ holds. In contemplating this icon, Georg was reminded that he is not alone but has a companion in reaching out to others in the pilgrimage of life. I am reminded of Mary of Guadalupe who met me at the beginning of my path into *Celibacy and Soul: Exploring the Depths of Chastity.* The Dark Virgin often realigns my focus: inward to Christ and outward to others in whom and where the Word is becoming flesh. For American theologian, John Haught, the transformative drama of life is the cosmic Eucharist in which everyone and everything have their part to play and where the universe itself is being transformed "… into the bodily abode of God."[348]

---

347   Ursula King, *Teilhard de Chardin and Eastern Religions*, p 219: King; Colossians 1:18 in *The New Jerusalem Bible*; *Vita Consecrata*, ¶ 16. http://www.vatican.va/roman_curia/congregations/ccscrlife/documents/hf_jp-ii_exh_25031996_vita-consecrata_en.html. Retrieved June 6, 2014.
348   John Haught, *Making Sense of Evolution*, 53.

Sum of the Understandings: Emergence

> ...the doors of perception open slightly and the other time
> appears, the real one we are searching for without knowing it:
> the present, the presence.[349]

Octavio Paz leads me in to the *present, the presence* of the One who stands behind any creative work and every journey.[350] I have seen *Celibacy and Soul* as a dialogue offering a thread for going further into an understanding of celibate chastity. As passion prompted Ariadne to give Theseus the clew he needed, I found desire and unrest urging and drawing me further into the heart of my search.

Initially, I acknowledge that motivation came out of a sense of absence more than Presence: Is celibate chastity worth the struggle? In one sense that dilemma remains because celibacy continues to invite an ongoing acceptance and consent to "the present, the Presence" who draws us all into an Unknown.[351] In this process of sorting, gathering, sifting and writing, I have found my trust deepening in the generative potential of celibate chastity.

Although I have a way to go in resolving this paradox of celibate love about which mystics, analysts and theologians speak, I have listened to Respondents who are relatively comfortable and happy with their choice of celibacy. They embody something prophetic. Rather than denying sex, they want to allow the flame of Love to become visible in their lives.[352]

You have heard these Respondents affirm that intimacy is essential for celibate women and men to blossom. The thread of Eros, as well as courage, is a lifeline for people going into celibacy which brings to mind

---

349 Octavio Paz, *In Search of the Present*, http://www.nobelprize.org/nobel_prizes/literature/laureates/1990/paz-lecture.html. Retrieved June 9, 2014.

350 Octavio Paz, *In Search of the Present*, http://www.nobelprize.org/nobel_prizes/literature/laureates/1990/paz-lecture.html. Retrieved June 9, 2014.

351 Octavio Paz, *In Search of the Present*, http://www.nobelprize.org/nobel_prizes/literature/laureates/1990/paz-lecture.html. Retrieved June 9, 2014.

352 Andres Rafael Luevano, *Endless Transforming Love*, 11.

Jung's description of Eros as "relatedness."[353] Celibate chastity could well be renamed "a vow of and for relatedness."[354]

This perception grows as I listen to women and men who see, face, and have dared to share the hard times. Going through the shadow of un-relatedness, loneliness and immaturity, some mentioned a new appreciation of celibate chastity and of themselves. Its refrain ran that non-possessive and non-controlling love is grounded in a deep trust in God's love and is learned by those who are open and vulnerable to others. It seems that celibacy moves into celibate chastity as individuals come to accept this is *who I am* and make an ongoing choice for this graced way as their path.

Symbolic and clinical material, the Respondents' comments and my own experience have contributed to the bigger picture of celibate chastity. These interlacing sources have kept me listening and trying to understand and describe the archetypal phenomenon of the virgin that has informed and profoundly affected the lives of so many women and men, including my own. On the last turn of the spiral and still in the company of the Dark Virgin, I want to gather up other traces of silk.

I have become aware of the importance of an aesthetic dimension in celibate chastity and the need to open to the source of beauty. Inner and outer guides challenged me to articulate this aspect and I am grateful for this and other promptings. Through their graced friendship, I have seen that the space of emptiness can shift to an awareness of inner space where there is a consciousness of another *Presence* at work. That awareness of the unfillable space was a defining point for me.

In looking at the beliefs and experiences of those who find celibate chastity worthwhile, I have also come to more awareness of what can come from doubt, questioning and uncertainty. As I explained in the Dynamic View of Jungian psychology, the analytic framework invites the hard questions. I want to mention again the Dominican priest, Victor White, who speaks of the necessity of going through an unravelling process if one is to come to consciousness. He had learned from his analysis with Carl Jung that holding the tension of opposites somehow

---

353   C.G. Jung, *Dream Analysis: Notes of Seminars Given in 1928-1930*, 172.
354   Diarmuid O'Murchu, *Poverty, Celibacy and Obedience*, 41-63.

touches the soul and urges her on the way. This insight can be reassuring to someone exploring the complexities of celibate chastity.

To that more convoluted question that I asked in the Prelude about celibate chastity maximising one's capacity to receive and give life, I heard Respondents say that celibacy can deepen one's self-giving. The question and choice evolve into a reflection on what primary relationship will enable people to give all of themselves to all other relationships. Tim clarifies:

> *Celibate love is essentially generativity; it includes kindness, faithfulness, hospitality, patience, joy and caring for others...It is an education in generativity—a lifelong learning that leads eventually to profound meaning and spiritual joy.*

Yet, there are still knots in this complex of celibate chastity that need disentangling by those who choose this path. As the word "complex" implies, the process of un-knotting aspects is complicated. Earlier I had asked *if celibate women and men are bundles of neurotic tension*. It is a difficult and dangerous question. Who can generalize? A lot depends on whether individuals are prepared to stand with and to live at the fine point of this dilemma going deeper into its meaning and maybe never completely resolving the struggle. It is like writing this book, to which I have been adding and refining continually, as I ponder my lived experience and what others tell. I have found the process calls for a kind of fortitude and acceptance of the beauty of limitation, incompleteness and mystery.

Human development is individual but happens in and through our relationships. Various religious traditions have much wisdom to contribute to living celibate love. Sex abuse scandals in and outside the churches have their strange gift and substantiate that hierarchical structures can foster a power shadow. For example, the institutional Catholic Church has failed to help people grow in chaste celibacy by imposing celibacy as a superior way of life and requirement for priesthood. In spite of this disconnection, many women and men committed to celibate chastity belong to holding environments of mutual care and support.

A way forward through the "power over" to "power with" others was suggested by Benedict XV1 in the encyclical, *Caritas in Veritate:* and hopefully becomes embodied and encouraged more by his successor, Pope Francis. Enacting the principle of subsidiarity recognises the dignity of others by acknowledging that all have something valuable to contribute to their situation.[355] There is a companion who shows a way of relating based on friendship rather than domination, and walks with us in the pilgrimage of life. In Frank's words:

> *The great image for me has been walking with Jesus of Nazareth as his friend, and he as mine.*

I am convinced that celibate chastity is an evolutionary process. It fits with current understandings of human and cosmic development that consciously anticipates love's breakthroughs in ordinary ways. Many of the Respondents confirmed that kind of consciousness and point to a Trinitarian and Incarnational theology which "acknowledges the one God to be transcendent, incarnate, and immanent in the world."[356]

As I consider these findings, I am able to respond more clearly to an earlier question about unlived aspects of sexuality and the danger it holds for others. I consider that celibate people need to be conscious of the positive and negative shadow of celibacy. When celibacy is made the goal of virginity instead of an ongoing intimacy with God and with others, the celibate becomes neurotic.

A theology and psychology of generativity invites a re-visioning of sexuality, celibacy and spirituality that simply continue to unfold through real conversation. It brings me to a second defining point for which John Layard's words are helpful: "True celibacy far from being an affair of sexual repression, if rightly understood, is the most complete expression of the transformed sex instinct."[357] The virgin archetype is alive and visible psychologically if not physically, in those who choose to stand in mercy and love with those at the edges of society. Such women and men point to a transformation of heart that comes from union

---

355   Benedict XVI, *Caritas in Veritate.*
356   Elizabeth A. Johnson, "An Ecological Theology of the Holy Spirit." http://www. duq.edu/events/holy-spirit-lecture-and-colloquium/2008. Retrieved June 7, 2014.
357   John Layard, "The Incest Taboo and the Virgin Archetype," 286.

with God, leads to connection with one Self and generous self-giving to others.[358]

The Respondents have been open and trusting. Their preparedness to participate in the project indicates a degree of maturity and comfortableness in their own skin and a certain power of articulation, which distinguishes them from many of their colleagues and perhaps affects my capacity to draw generalizations. With these difficulties in mind, the data emphasizes that becoming chastely celibate is a long, ongoing heart change. Respondents were candid in facing the question of how to *satisfy the human need for intimacy*. They called attention to the importance of relatedness that is learned in warm and inclusive friendships where the person dares to risk vulnerability with others. As Catherine and others indicated, the gift of non-possessive friendship with others was and is changing them:

> **Catherine:** *My heart has been stretched, moulded and shaped and I became celibate. It has been a process of becoming celibate over the years. It is a process in which something happened to me.*
>
> **Interviewer:** *What's that something?*
>
> **Catherine:** *I guess it is a freedom to love.*

This woman's response speaks of a freedom to love that is more concerned with loving than being loved, and addresses an important question asked earlier: *Can the yearning to love and be loved be met in religious life?* Respondent Tim also picked up this element when he admitted to difficult moments of loneliness and longing for sexual expression and companionship. Yet almost in the same breath he adds, *that is an inescapable part of honest living.* It is important, and can be sometimes forgotten by celibate women and men. I found Respondents pointing to a critical problem where an absence of a caring community makes celibacy more painful. That gap can become insidious. For when men and women are not deliberately giving room for and growing in intimacy with God and in relatedness with others, it seems that celibate chastity is virtually impossible.

---

358   St. Teresa of Avila, *Interior Castle*, 209-210.

I needed to ask if people's decision to live chaste celibacy rests on their having a strong ego or relationship to the Self. From what Respondents have said and what my own experience indicates, the answer is "Yes." A deepening self-knowledge and trust in the Greater Self are essential for positively choosing celibate chastity. It includes grace as well as awareness and acceptance of one's own fragility and vulnerability. I have also come to see that there is a psychological propensity for celibacy that is not only dependent on ego strength and decision but on whether it is one's vocation that is freely accepted and daily chosen.[359]

As I gather the clew, I see with delight and surprise that *Celibacy and Soul: Exploring the Depths of Chastity* has gradually emerged. It contains traces of silk and fragrance willingly shared and entrusted by very real women and men whose voices you have heard in these pages. Their gift and their beautiful lives of celibate chastity speak volumes. As you know, on this pilgrimage into the heart space of celibate chastity, the Dark Virgin and the multi-coloured cross synchronistically came across my path: and their light has constantly kept me focused and anticipating.

At this last turn of the spiral, I wonder if you have realised this trace of "good news." The journey into unconditional love is one that each person and all the cosmos share. Loving with no strings attached, or celibate love, is calling you, whoever you are, to recognise the gift of your singular beauty and inviting you into graced friendship to make that blessing available to others…and as for celibate chastity?

> *it is not easy and may be rare. Like anything, it is a lifelong project.* (Brendan)

> *Celibacy is not for everyone. It frees you for love, for vulnerability, for surprise, for unanticipated friendships. It's not an end in itself.* (Jane)

While my exploration of the transforming potential of celibate love concludes here, I trust that unconditional love may continue to grow, blossom and bear fruit in your life, in mine and in all creation—like "fire in earthen vessels."

---

359   C.G. Jung, "The Structure and Dynamics of the Psyche," CW 8, ¶ 771.

BIBLIOGRAPHY

Abbott, Walter M. (Ed.). *The Documents of Vatican II*, (J. Gallagher, Trans.). London: Geoffrey Chapman Limited, 1967.

Abramovitch, Henry. "Brothers and Sisters: Archetypal and Personal Dynamics." Lecture presented at the C.G. Jung Institute, Kusnacht, Zurich, June, 1999.

_____. "Temenos Regained: Reflections on the Absence of the Analyst," *Journal of Analytical Psychology*, 47, 2002.

_____. "Stimulating Ethical Awareness During Training," *Journal of Analytical Psychology*, 52, 2007.

Alighieri, Dante. *The Divine Comedy, Inferno* (Vol. 1). (Charles S. Singleton, Trans.). London: Routledge & Kegan Paul, 1971.

_____. *The Divine Comedy, Purgatorio* (Vols. 2 & 3). (Charles S. Singleton, Trans.). New Jersey: Princeton University Press, 1977.

American Psychiatric Association, *Diagnostic & Statistical Manual of Mental Disorders*, Fourth Edition. Washington: American Psychiatric Press, 2000.

Australian Centres of Ignatian Spirituality, *Program 2013-2014*. www.cis.jesuit.org.au/program.html. Retrieved January 23, 2014

Bauckham, Richard. *Bible and the Ecology*. East Kilbride: Darton, Longman, Todd, 2010.

Beal, John; Conden, James; Green, Thomas. *New Commentary on the Code of Canon Law*. Mahwah: Paulist Press, 2000.

Beauvois, Xavier. (Dir). *Of Gods and Men*. France: DVD, 2010.

Benedict XVI. *Deus Caritas Est*. Boston: Pauline Books and Media, 2006.

_____. *Caritas Veritate*. Boston: Pauline Books and Media, 2009.

Berry, Thomas. *The Christian Future and Fate of the Earth*. Maryknoll: Orbis Books, 2009.

Bion, Wilfred. *Attention and Interpretation*. London: Tavistock, 1970.

Bransfield, J. Brian. *The Human Person According to John Paul II*. Boston: Pauline Books and Media, 2010.

Britton, Ronald. *Belief and Imagination*. London: Routledge, 1998.

Brother Roger of Taize. *Essential Writings*. Compiled by Marcello Fidarco. Maryknoll: Orbis Books, 2006.

Brown, Peter. *The Body and Society: Men and Women and Sexual Renunciation in Early Christianity*. New York: Columbia University Press, 1988.

Brutsche, Diane Cousineau. *Le Paradoxe de l'âme* [*The Paradox of the Soul*]. Geneva: Georg, 1993.

Buchanan, Scott, (Ed.). *The Portable Plato*, Third Edition. (Benjamin Jowett, Trans.). New York: Viking Press, 1955.

Chaucer, Geoffrey. *The Canterbury Tales*. (Nevill Coghill, Trans.). Middlesex: Penguin Classics, 1951.

Chittister, Joan. *The Fire in These Ashes: A Spirituality of Contemporary Religious Life*. Kansas City: Sheed and Ward, 1996.

Cochini, Christian. *Apostolic Origins of Priestly Celibacy*. San Francisco: Ignatius Press, 1990.

Cohen, Leonard. *More Best of Leonard Cohen*. Nashville: CD, Sony Music Entertainment Inc., 1993.

Commission of Investigation 2009. *Report Into the Catholic Archdiocese of Dublin*. http://www.justice.ie/en/JELR/Pages/PB09000504. Retrieved January 11, 2012.

Congregation for Institutes of Consecrated Life and Societies of Apostolic Life. *Starting Afresh from Christ*. London: Catholic Truth Society, 2002.

Connell, James. "Critical Question Leads Priest to Challenge Lax Abuse Policies." http://ncronline.org/news/accountability/critical-question-leads-priest-challenge-lax-abuse-policies. Retrieved June 9, 2014.

Conrad-Lammers, Ann. *In God's Shadow: The Collaboration of Victor White and C.G. Jung*. Mahwah: Paulist Press, 1994.

Crosby, Michael H. *Celibacy*. Indiana: Ave Maria Press, 1996.

Dalrymple, William. *City of Djinns*. London: HarperCollins, 1993.

De Beauvoir, Simone. *The Second Sex*. New York: Vintage Books, 1973.

De Castillejo, Irene Claremont. *Knowing Woman*. New York: Harper and Row, 1973.

De Chardin, Pierre Teilhard. "The Evolution of Chastity," in *Toward the Future*. (René Hague, Trans.). London, England: Collins, 1975.

De Vries, A. *Dictionary of Symbols and Imagery*. Amsterdam: Elsevier Science Publishers, 1984.

Di Bernardino, Angelo. *Encyclopedia of the Early Church*, (Vol. 1). Cambridge: James Clarke and Co., 1992.

Dowrick, Stephanie. *Creative Journal Writing*. Sydney: Allen and Unwin, 2007.

Drake, Tim. "Change in Vatican Culture." http://www.ncregister.com/daily-news/change_in_vatican_culture/. Retrieved June 9, 2014.

Drewermann, Eugen. *Heil und Heilung: Theologie und Psychoanalyse Lecture Notes*. Basel, Switzerland: Conference of Therapists, May 21, 1997.

Driot, Marcel. *Fathers of the Desert* (Vol. 2). Guernsey: St. Paul Publications, 1992.

Edwards, Denis. *The God of Evolution*. New York, NY: Paulist Press, 1999.

Egan, Kevin. *Remaining a Catholic After the Murphy Report*. Dublin: Columba Press, 2011.

Eliade, M. *The Myth of the Eternal Return*. Princeton: Princeton University Press, 1971.

_____. *The Encyclopedia of Religion* (Vol.3). London: MacMillan Publishing Com, 1987.

Eliot, T.S. *Collected Poems, 1909-1962*. London: Faber and Faber, 1963.

Ellenberger, Henri F. *The Discovery of the Unconscious*. New York, NY: Basic Books, 1970.

Erikson, Erik H. *Childhood and Society*, Second Edition. New York, NY: W.W. Norton and Company Inc., 1963.

_____. *Identity and the Life Cycle*. New York, NY: W.W. Norton and Company Inc., 1980.

Estes, C.P. *Women Who Run With the Wolves: Myths and Stories of the Wild Woman Archetype*. New York, NY: Ballantine Books, 1992.

Fairburn, W.R.D. *Psychoanalytic Studies of the Personality*. London: Routledge and Kegan, 1952.

Farrelly, Eileen. *Dadirri: The Spring Within*. Darwin: Terry Knight and Associates, 2003.

Feehan, John. *The Singing Heart of the World*. Blackrock: Columba Press, 2010.

Flack, Roberta. *The Best of Roberta Flack*. New York, NY: Atlantic Recording Corporation, CD, 1981.

Fox, Patricia A. *God as Communion*. Collegeville: The Liturgical Press, 2001.

Freud, S. *The Interpretation of Dreams*. (James Strachey, Ed. and Trans.). New York, NY: Basic Books, 1955.

_____. *Moses and Monotheism: An Outline of Psycho-analysis and Other Works*. Standard Edition of the Complete Psychological Works of Sigmund Freud, Vol. XXIII. London: The Hogarth Press and Institute of Psycho-Analysis, 1964.

Fromm, Erich. *The Art of Loving*. New York, NY: Harper, 1956.

Gimbutas, Marija. *The Goddesses and Gods of Old Europe*. Hampshire: BAS Printers, (original work printed in 1974), 1996.

Goergen, D. *The Sexual Celibate*. New York, NY: Image Books, 1979.

Goethe, Johann Wolfgang. *Selected Poems*. (John Whaley, Trans.). Evanston, Illinois: Northwestern University Press, 1998.

Gordimer, Nadine. Writing and Being. (Nobel Lecture, December 7, 1991).http://www.nobelprize.org/nobel_prizes/literature/laureates/1991/gordimer- lecture.html. Retrieved October 21, 2011.

Graves, Robert. The Greek Myths (2 Vols.). Harmondswoth: Penguin Books, 1995.

Gray, Janette. *Neither Escaping nor Exploiting Sex: Women's Celibacy. Homebush*: St. Pauls, 1995.

Greek Myth & Characters. http: www.greekmythology.com. Retrieved June 7, 2014.

Greene, Graham. *Journey Without Maps*. USA: Penguin, 1992.

Grotstein, James S. *A Beam of Intense Darkness: Wilfred Bion's Legacy to Psychoanalysis*. London: Karnac Books, 2007.

_____. *Bion's Transformation in O & the Concept of the Transcendent Position*. http://www.sicap.it/mGerciai/bion/papers/grots.htm. Retrieved June 9, 2014.

Hall, Nor. *Those Women*. Dallas: Spring Publications, 1990.

Hastings, Selina. *Sir Gawain and the Loathly Lady*. New York, NY: Lothrop, Lee & Shepard Books, 1985.

Haught, John F. *Making Sense of Evolution*. Louisville: Westminster John Knox Press, 2010.

Hawking, S. and Mlodinov, L. *The Grand Design*. New York, NY: Bantam Press, 2010.

Herrin, J. *The Formation of Christendom*. Princeton: Princeton University Press, 1987.

Hilu, Virginia. (Ed.). *Beloved Prophet*. London: Barrie and Jenkins, 1972.

His Holiness the Dalai Lama and Cutler, Howard C. *The Art of Happiness: A Handbook for Living*. Sydney: Hodder, 1998.

Hoffman, Kent. "Thirst." http://www.thirsthome.org/#resources. Retrieved January 6, 2012.

Jacq, Christian. *Ramses: The Son of Light*. (Mary Feeney, Trans.). London: Pocket Books, 1998.

James, William. *The Varieties of Religious Experience: A Study in Human Nature*. London: Longmans, Green and Co., 1929.

Jobes, Gertrude. *Dictionary of Mythology: Folklore and Symbols Parts 1 & 2*. New York, NY: Scarecrow Press, 1962.

John Paul II. *Veritatis Splendor*. Boston: Pauline Books and Media, 1993.

_____. *Man and Woman He Created Them: A Theology of the Body*. Boston: Pauline Books and Media, 2006.

_____. "Vita Consecrata." http://www.vatican.va/roman_curia/congregations/ccscrlife/documents/hf_jp-ii_exh_25031996_vita-consecrata_en.html. Retrieved June 6, 2014.

Johnson, Elizabeth A. *The Church Women Want*. New York, NY: The Crossroad Publishing Company, 2002.

_____. *Quest for the Living God*. New York, NY: Continuum, 2007.

_____. "An Ecological Theology of the Holy Spirit." http://www.duq.edu/events/holy-spirit-lecture-and-colloquium/2008. Retrieved June 7, 2014.

Johnson, Robert A. *Owning Your Own Shadow*. New York, NY: HarperCollins, 1993.

Jones, Alexander, (Ed.). *The New Jerusalem Bible*. London: Darton, Longman and Todd, 1985.

Jones, Ernest. *The Life and Work of Sigmund Freud*. London: Hogarth Press, 1953.

Jung, C.G. *The Collected Works, Second Edition*. (Bollingen Series XX; H. Read, M. Fordham & G. Adler, Eds.; R.F.C. Hull, Trans.). Princeton, NJ: Princeton University Press, 1953-1979.

_____. *Aion: Researches into the Phenomenology of the Self, The Collected Works Vol. 9ii, Second Edition*. (Bollingen Series XX). Princeton, NJ: Princeton University Press, 1969.

_____. *Alchemical Studies, The Collected Works Vol. 13, Second Edition*. (Bollingen Series XX). Princeton, NJ: Princeton University Press, 1968.

_____. *Mysterium Coniunctionis, The Collected Works Vol. 14, Second Edition*. (Bollingen Series XX). Princeton, NJ: Princeton University Press, 1970.

_____. *Psychological Types, The Collected Works Vol. 6, Second Edition*. (Bollingen Series XX). Princeton, NJ: Princeton University Press, 1971.

_____. *Psychology and Alchemy, The Collected Works Vol. 12, Second Edition*. (Bollingen Series XX). Princeton, NJ: Princeton University Press, 1968.

_____. *Psychology and Religion, The Collected Works Vol. 11, Second Edition*. (Bollingen Series XX). Princeton, NJ: Princeton University Press, 1970.

_____. *Symbols of Transformation, The Collected Works Vol. 5, Second Edition*, (Bollingen Series XX). Princeton NJ: Princeton University Press, 1967.

_____. *The Archetypes and the Collective Unconscious, The Collected Works Vol. 9i, Second Edition*. (Bollingen Series XX). Princeton, NJ: Princeton University Press, 1969.

_____. *The Practice of Psychotherapy, The Collected Works Vol. 16, Second Edition*. (Bollingen Series XX). Princeton, NJ: Princeton University Press, 1966.

_____. *Development of Personality, The Collected Works Vol. 17, Second Edition*. (Bollingen Series XX). Princeton, NJ: Princeton University Press, 1954.

_____. *Freud and Psychoanalysis, The Collected Works Vol. 4, Second Edition*. (Bollingen Series XX). Princeton, NJ: Princeton University Press, 1970.

_____. *The Structure and Dynamics of the Psyche, The Collected Works Vol. 8, Second Edition.* (Bollingen Series XX). Princeton, NJ: Princeton University Press, 1969.

_____. *Civilization in Transition, The Collected Works Vol. 10, Second Edition.* (Bollingen Series XX). Princeton, NJ: Princeton University Press, 1970.

_____. *The Symbolic Life: Miscellaneous Writings, The Collected Works Vol. 18, Second Edition.* (Bollingen Series XX). Princeton, NJ: Princeton University Press, 1970.

_____. *Letters.* (Gerhard Adler & A. Jaffe, Eds.) Princeton, NJ: Princeton University Press, 1973.

_____. *Memories, Dreams, Reflections.* (A. Jaffe, Ed.; R. & C. Winston, Trans.). London, England: Collins & Routledge & Kegan Paul, 1983.

_____. *Dream Analysis: Notes of Seminars Given in 1928-1930 by C.G. Jung,* Princeton, NJ:

Princeton University Press, 1984.

_____. *Visions: Notes of Seminars Given in 1930-1934 by C.G. Jung,* Vols.1 & 2, (Claire Douglas, Ed.). Princeton, NJ: Princeton University Press, 1984.

_____. *The Red Book: Liber Novus.* (S. Shamdasani, Ed.; M. Kyburz, J. Peck, S. Shamdasani, Trans.). New York, NY: W.W. Norton Pty. Ltd., 2009.

Jung, Emma & von Franz, M-L. *The Grail Legend.* New York, NY: C.G. Jung Foundation, 1970.

Kalsched, Donald. "Narcissism and the Search for Interiority," *Quadrant*, Vol. 13, No. 2, 46-74, 1980.

_____. *The Inner World of Trauma.* London, England: Routledge, 1996.

Kamarck, Minnich Elizabeth. *Transforming Knowledge.* Philadelphia: Temple University Press, 1980.

Kannengiesser, Charles & Petersen, William L. *Origen of Alexandria: His World and His Legacy.* Notre Dame: University of Notre Dame, 1988.

Keating, Thomas. *Open Mind Open Heart.* New York, NY: Continuum Publishing Company, 1997.

Kerenyi, Karl. *Athene*, Third Edition. Woodstock: Spring Publications, 1996.

King, Ursula. *Teilhard de Chardin and Eastern Religions: Spirituality and Mysticism in an Evolutionary World*. New York, NY: Paulist Press, 2011.

Lapierre, Dominique. *City of Joy*. New York, NY: Warner Books, 1985.

Lawson, Anthea. "Four of These People are Depressed," *The Times*, p.18, May 8, 1999.

Layard, John. "The Incest Taboo and the Virgin Archetype," *Eranos* 12 (1945): 253-307.

Lewis, C.S. *Till We have Faces*. New York, NY: Harvest, 1956.

_____. *The Four Loves*. Hammersmith: HarperCollins Publishers, 1960.

Luevano, Andres Rafael. *Endless Transforming Love*. Rome: Institutum Carmelitanum, 1990.

Mathews, Gareth B. (Ed.). *Augustine: On the Trinity. Books 8-15*. Cambridge: Cambridge University Press, 2002.

McClone, Kevin. "Sexual Health: A Christian Perspective," *Human Development*, 32:1, (2011): 3-9.

McNamara, Joann Kay. *Sisters in Arms*. Cambridge: Harvard University Press, 1996.

Meade, Catherine M. csj. *My Nature is Fire*. New York, NY: Alba House, 1991.

Merkle, Judith. *A Different Touch*. Collegeville, MN: The Liturgical Press, 1998.

Merton, Thomas. *The Wisdom of the Desert*. New York: A New Directions Book, 1970.

Micklem, Niel. "The Psychology of the Vow," *The Guild of Pastoral Liturgy*, 218 (1985): 7-17.

"More depressed," *The Times*, April 12, 1999, 13.

Morrison, Toni. *Beloved*. New York, NY: A Plume Book, 1988.

Muzj, Maria Giovanna. *Transfiguration*. (Kenneth D. Whitehead, Trans.). Boston: St. Paul Books and Media, 1945.

Murray, C.J. & Lopez, A.D. *The Global Burden of Disease: A Comprehensive Assessment of Mortality and Disability from Diseases, Injuries and Risk Factors in 1990 and Projected to the Year 2020*. Boston: Harvard School of Public Health, 1996.

Nouwen, H. *The Wounded Healer*. New York, NY: Bantam Doubleday, 1979.

O'Brien, Lewis. "Tjulbruke the Ibis Man," *Dreaming Trails and Culture Contact*. Adelaide: Education Department of South Australia, 1988.

O'Donohue, John. *Anam Cara*. New York, NY: HarperCollins, 1998.

O'Murchu, Diarmuid. *Poverty, Celibacy and Obedience*. New York, NY: A Crossroad Book, 1999.

Orchison, Geoff. "Priests' Identity Crisis," *The Catholic Leader*, 22 February1998: 12.

Otto, Rudolf, *The Idea of the Holy*. New York, NY: Oxford University Press.

Ovid's Metamorphoses, (C. Boer, Trans.). Dallas: Spring Publications, 1989.

Panzer, Wolfgang. (Dir.). *Broken Silence*. Switzerland: Camera Obscura Inc., DVD, 1996.

Paul VI. *Sacerdotalis Caelibatus*. Boston: Pauline Books and Media, 1967.

Paz, Octavio. *In Search of the Present*. (Anthony Stanton, Trans.). http://www.nobelprize.org/nobel_prizes/literature/laureates/1990/paz-lecture.html. Retrieved June 9, 2014.

Pease, A. & Pease, B. *Why Men Want Sex and Women Need Love*. Australia: Griffen Press, 2009.

Pedraza Lopes, Rafael. *Hermes and His Children*. Einsiedeln: Daimon Verlag (original work published in 1977), 1989.

Pessoa, Fernando. *Poems of Fernando Pessoa*. (Edwin Honig and Susan M. Brown, Trans.). San Francisco: City Lights Books, 1998.

Pickering, Judith. *Being in Love*. London, England: Routledge, 2008.

Prejean, Helen. *Dead Man Walking*. New York, NY: Vintage Books, 1993

Proust, Marcel. *In Search of Lost Time: Swann's Way, Vol. 1*. (D.J. Enright, Trans.). New York: Random House, 1992.

Qualls-Corbett, Nancy. *The Sacred Prostitute*. Toronto: Inner City Books, 1988.

Radcliffe, Timothy. *I Call You Friends*. New York, NY: Continuum, 2003.

_____. "The Promise of Life." February, 1998. http:/dominicans.ca/Documents/masters/Radcliffe/promise_life.html. Retrieved June 8, 2014.

_____. Lecture for the CMSM, Timothy Radcliffe. http://www.marianist.com/articles/radcliffe.pdf. Retrieved June 10, 2014.

Rahner, Karl. *Encounters with Silence*. South Bend: St. Augustine's Press, 1999.

Ranke-Heinemann, Uta. *Eunuchs for the Kingdom of Heaven*. New York, NY: Penguin Books, 1990.

Reinhardt, Kurt F. *The Dark Night of the Soul*. New York, NY: Frederick Ungar Publishing Co, 1957.

Renault, Mary. *The King Must Die*. New York, NY: Pantheon, 1958.

Robbins, Tim. (Dir.). *Dead Man Walking*. Universal City, CA: Polygram Pictures, DVD, 1995.

Robinson, Geoffery. *Confronting Power and Sex in the Catholic Church*. Sydney, Australia: John Garratt Publishing, 2008.

Ronnberg, A. & Martin, K. (Eds.). *The Book of Symbols*. Cologne, Germany: Taschen, 2010.

Salzgeber, J. *Einsiedeln*. Einsiedeln: Beat Eberle, 1998.

Sammon, Sean. *An Undivided Heart: Making Sense of Celibate Chastity*. New York, NY: Alba House, 1993.

Sayre, Kenneth M. *Plato's Literary Garden*. Notre Dame: University of Notre Dame Press, 1995.

Schillebeeckx, E. *Celibacy*. New York, NY: Sheed and Ward, 1968.

Schneiders, Sandra M. *Finding the Treasure*. Mahwah: Paulist Press, 2000.

_____. *Prophets in their Own Country*. New York, NY: Orbis Books, 2011.

Schottroff, Luise; Schroer, Silvia & Wacker, Marie-Therese. *Feminist Interpretation: The Bible in Women's Perspective*. (Martin & Barbara Rumscheidt, Trans.). Augsburg: Fortress Press, 1998.

Scott, Alan. *Origin and the Life of the Stars*. Oxford, England: Clarendon Press, 1991.

Shakespeare, William. *The Complete Works of William Shakespeare*. (Denis Allen, Trans.). London: Hightext Ltd., 1983.

Shearer, Ann. *Athene: Image and Energy*. Suffolk: Viking Arkana, 1996.

Sheehy, Gail. *New Passages*. New York, NY: Ballantine Books, 1996.

Shorter, Aylward. *Celibacy and African Culture*. Kenya: Pauline Publications, 1998.

Simpson, J.A. & Weiner, E.S.C. *The Oxford English Dictionary* (Vols. 1-20, 2nd Ed.). Oxford: Clarendon Press, 1989.

Sipe, Richard A.W. *Sex, Priests and Power*. New York, NY: Bruner/Mazel, 1995.

_____. *Celibacy*. Liguori: Triumph Books, 1996.

Soelle, Dorothee. *The Silent Cry: Mysticism & Resistance*. (Barbara & Martin Rusmcheidt, Trans.). Minneapolis: Augsburg Fortress, 2001.

"Spirit of the age." *The Economist* 349, (December 19, 1998): 115-123.

St. Jerome. "Letter XXII To Eustochium." http://www.ccel.org/ccel/schaff/npnf206.v.XXII.html. Retrieved June 8, 2014.

St. John of the Cross. *The Spiritual Canticle and Poems*. (E. Allison Peers, Trans.). Guildford: Burns and Oates, 1978.

St. Teresa of Avila. *Interior Castle*. (E. Allison Peers, Trans.). New York, NY: Image Book, 1961.

_____. *The Collected Works of St. Teresa of Avila*. (Kieran Kavanaugh and Otilio Rodriguez Trans.).Washington, DC: ICS Publications, 1991.

Stein, Edith. *The Hidden Life*. (Dr. L. Gelber and Michael Linssen, Eds.; Waltraut Stein, Trans.). Washington: ICS Publications, 1992.

Steinbeck, John. *The Pearl*. London: Pan Books, 1983.

Storr, Anthony. *Solitude*. Hammersmith: Flamingo, 1989.

Stroud, Joanne & Thomas, Gail (Eds.). *Images of the Untouched*. Dallas: Spring Publications, 1982.

Swimme, Brian & Berry, Thomas. *The Universe Story*. San Francisco: Harper, 1992.

Swimme, Brian Thomas. *Comprehensive Compassion*. Interview with Brian Swimme by Susan Bridle, http://thegreatstory.org/SwimmeWIE.pdf. Retrieved June 8,2014.

Taylor, Joan E. *Jewish Women Philosophers: Philo's Therapeutae Re-examined*. New York, NY: Oxford University Press, 2003.

The Bhagavad Gita. (Juan Mascaro, Trans.). London: Penguin Books, 1962.

The Confessions of St. Augustine. (F.J. Sheed, Trans.). New York, NY: Sheed & Ward, 1943.

The Roman Missal, (3rd Edition.). 2011.

The Way of a Pilgrim, (Helen Bacovcin, Trans.). New York, NY: Image Books, 1978.

Thich Nhat Hanh. *Living Buddha, Living Christ.* New York, NY: Riverhead Books, 1995.

Thompson, Della. (Ed.). *The Concise Oxford Dictionary of Current English,* 9th Edition. Oxford: Clarendon Press, 1995.

Turner, Victor & Edith. *Image and Pilgrimage in Christian Culture.* New York: Columbia University Press, 1978.

Ulanov, Ann & Barry. *Transforming Sexuality.* Boston: Shambhala, 1994.

Underhill, Evelyn. *The Mystic Way.* Alpharetta: Ariel Press, 1992.

van der Post, Laurens. *The Heart of the Hunter.* Hammondsmith: Penguin Books, 1961.

van Gennep, Arnold. *The Rites of Passage.* London, England: Routledge and Kegan Paul, 1960.

Vermes, Geza & Goodman, Martin D. (Eds.). *The Essenes: According to the Classical Sources.* Sheffield: JSOT Press, 1989.

von Eschenbach, Wolfram. *Parzival.* (A.T. Hatto, Trans.). Middlesex: Penguin Books, 1980.

von Franz, M-L. *A Psychological Interpretation of the Golden Ass of Apulius.* New York, NY: Spring Publications, 1970.

Weinandy, Thomas G. *The Father's Spirit of Sonship.* Edinburgh: T and T Clark, 1995.

Wheelwright, Jane Hollister. *The Death of a Woman.* New York, NY: St. Martin's Press, 1981.

White, Victor. *God and the Unconscious.* Chicago: Henry Regnery Company, 1953.

White, Victor. "Kinds of opposites," *Studien zu Analytischen Psychologie: Beitrage aus Theorie_und Praxis.* Verlag, (1955): 140-150.

Whitehead, E. & L. *A Sense of Sexuality: Christian Love and Intimacy.* New York, NY: Doubleday, 1989.

_____. *Wisdom of the Body: Making Sense of our Sexuality*. New York, NY: Crossroad, 2001.

Wiener, Jan. *The Therapeutic Relationship*. College Station, Texas: A & M University Press, 2009.

Winnicott, D.W. *The Maturational Processes and the Facilitating Environment*. Connecticut: International Universities Press, 1980.

_____. *Playing and Reality*. London: Routledge and Kegan, 1982.

Zaehner, R.C. *Hinduism*. Oxford: Oxford University Press, 1962.

PERMISSIONS

Many thanks to all who have directly or indirectly provided permission to quote their works, including the following individuals and organizations:

Verse

Fernando Pessoa, Angelus Silesius, Dante Alighieri, Meister Eckhart, C.S. Lewis, St. John of the Cross, St. Teresa of Avila, Roberta Flack, Leonard Cohen, T.S. Eliot, Johann Wolfgang Goethe, William Shakespeare, The Bhagavad Gita, St. Augustine, Geoffrey Chaucer, Octavio Paz.

The New Jerusalem Bible

Scripture quotations contained in this book are from The New Jerusalem Bible, copyright 1985, by Darton, Longman and Todd Ltd., and Doubleday. Used with permission. All rights reserved.

Images

Andrei Rublev, "The Trinity" - 5Fa.009. c. 1411, icon, by Andrei Rublev, Cathedral of the Trinity of St. Sergius, Tretiakov Gallery, Moscow. ARAS Online Archive. New York: The Archive for Research in Archetypal Symbolism: available from www.aras.org: 5/1/14.

"Christian Labyrinth" - 5Df068. c. 1220-1230, pavement labyrinth, Cathedral of Notre Dame, Chartres. ARAS Online Archive. New York: The Archive for Research in Archetypal Symbolism; available from www.aras.org: 5/1/14.

Dorothy Grills, Story of the Wolves Within. 2007, © Dorothy Grills CSJ.

Fra Beato Angelico, "The Annunciation." Fresco in the former dormitory of the Dominican monastery San Marco, Florence. See 40-07-09/59-62 (Around 1450), 230 x 297 cm. Museo di S. Marco, Florence, Italy. Photo Credit : Erich Lessing / Art Resource, NY.

Gian Lorenzo Bernini, "Ecstasy of St. Teresa" - 5Gc 29. c. 1600, marble sculpture in Chiesa di Santa Maria della Vittoria, Rome. ARAS Online Archive. New York: The Archive for Research in Archetypal Symbolism: available from www.aras.org: 5/1/14.

Jan Williamson, painting, "Mary of the Southern Cross." 2009, © Jan Williamson.

Michelangelo Buonarroti, "Creation of Adam" (and Eve) - 5Ga.070. c. 1500, ceiling fresco, Sistine Chapel, Rome. ARAS Online Archive. New York: The Archive for Research in Archetypal Symbolism: available from www.aras.org: 5/1/14.

Piero della Francesca (1410/20-92). "Madonna del Parto" (Madonna of the birth) fresco, cemetery chapel, Monterchi, Italy. Photo Credit: Gianni Dagli Orti/The Art Archive at Art Resource, NY.

Rembrandt van Rijn, "Heimkehr des Verlorenen Sohnes" (The Homecoming of the Prodigal Son) - 5Ga.102. c. 1668, painting, Museum of St. Petersburg. ARAS Online Archive. New York: The Archive for Research in Archetypal Symbolism: available from www.aras.org: 5/1/14.

Simone Martini, "The Annunciation with St. Ansano and St. Giulitta," painting - Ea.026. c. 1333, Uffizi Gallery, Florence. ARAS Online Archive. New York: The Archive for Research in Archetypal Symbolism: available from www. aras.org: 5/1/14.

Southard, Mary, "Meditation" cover image, www.MarySouthardArt.Org.

Unknown Artist, "Christ and St. Menas" - 5Ba.004. c. 500, Coptic icon, Louvre, Paris. ARAS Online Archive. New York: The Archive for Research in Archetypal Symbolism: available from www.aras.org: 5/1/14.

Unknown Artist, "Our Lady of Guadalupe" - 5Ga231. c. 1531, Tilma, Basilica of Guadalupe, Mexico City. ARAS Online Archive. New York: The Archive for Research in Archetypal Symbolism: available from www.aras.org: 5/1/14.

Unknown Artist, "The Yellow Badge." Photo Credit HIP / Art Archive at Art Resource, NY.

ACKNOWLEDGEMENTS

Sincere Thanks to:

The Editing Team of Mary Reardon rsj, Marie Frances, Marie White rsj, Patty Cabanas and patient and creative publisher, Mel Mathews.

The Community of the Sisters of St. Joseph of the Sacred Heart for their loving and practical generosity.

While I acknowledge the Sisters of St. Joseph, I am particularly grateful for assistance and encouragement received from: Mary Cresp, Anne Derwin, Anne-Marie Gallagher, Ann Gilroy, Sheila McCreanor, Marion Gambin, Margaret McKenna, Margaret Cleary, Catherine Clark, Josephine Huppatz, Anna Spaccatore, Joan Healy, Catherine Shelton, Katrina Brill, Monica Cavanagh, Kerry Keenan, Louise Reeves, Christine Rowan, Therese Carroll, Caroline Duggan.

My loving parents, Madge and Victor, and my family—Ann, Bob, Beatrice, Tony, Malcolm, Helene ,Verity, Bob, and my nieces and nephews—and their great children.

Among close friends: Madeleine, Maria Teresa, Anne-Marie, Mary, Judy, Margaret, Peter, Liz, Anna, Alex Liz, Kathryn, Pilawuk, Nicky and Franklin, and deceased friends, John, Justin, and Ian.

I am grateful to the Respondents and Clients, who though anonymous, have shared their experience of living celibate love.

Perceptive insights came from authors and from colleagues: Henry Abramovitch, Ian Baker, Helen Prejean, Diane Cousineau Brutsche, Timothy Radcliffe, Richard Rohr, Richard Sipe, Joan Chittister, Patricia Fox, Sandra Schneiders, Denis Edwards, Stephanie Dowrick, Veronica Lawson, Geoffery Robinson, Alitja Rigney, Lewis Yerloburka O'Brien, Kent Hoffman, Louis Gendron, Anthony Smith, Janette Gray, James Johnston, Elizabeth Johnson, Sonya Marjasch, Marge Denis, Judith Pickering, Eva Solomon, Mechtilde O'Mara, Paul Bishop, John Haught, Elizabeth Kamarck Minnich, Bou-Yong Rhi.

In searching for Images: Allison Tuzo, Esther Gyorki, Kay Menick, Kenise Neill, Sandy Leutiea, Tracy Dall, Liz Kurtulik Mercuri, Nici Cumpston, Lachlan Warner, Margaret Broadbent, Nick and Liz Thompson offered their assistance.

Permission to include paintings and other illustrations is gratefully acknowledged to ARAS The Archive for Research in Archetypal Symbolism www.aras.org; www.artres.com; Artists Jan Williamson, Dorothy Grills; feathers drawn by Ian Roberts; Mary Southard csj for cover image, *Meditation*.

While every effort has been made to be accurate, I am responsible and apologise for any errors of fact or judgement or omissions.

Thank you to so many well-wishers along the way and you who are taking time to read this work. And deep gratitude to…

The One whose love holds us all.

ABOUT THE AUTHOR

Susan Pollard, Ph.D, is a Diplomate Jungian Analyst (Zurich) and member of the Association of Graduate Analytical Psychologists. She is a member and training analyst with the Australian and New Zealand Jungian Analysts and a member of the Sisters of St. Joseph of the Sacred Heart. She has lectured both nationally and internationally on subjects related to analytical psychology and religion and has a full time analytical practice in South Australia.

INDEX

You might also enjoy reading:

Marked By Fire: Stories of the Jungian Way edited by Patricia Damery & Naomi Ruth Lowinsky, 1ˢᵗ Ed., Trade Paperback, 180pp, Biblio., 2012 — ISBN 978-1-926715-68-1

The Dream and Its Amplification edited by Erel Shalit & Nancy Swift Furlotti, 1ˢᵗ Ed., Trade Paperback, 180pp, Biblio., 2013 — ISBN 978-1-926715-89-6

Shared Realities: Participation Mystique and Beyond edited by Mark Windborn, 1ˢᵗ Ed., Trade Paperback, 270pp, Index, Biblio., 2014 — ISBN 978-1-77169-009-6

Pierre Teilhard de Chardin and C.G. Jung: Side by Side edited by Fred Gustafson, 1ˢᵗ Ed., Trade Paperback, 270pp, Index, Biblio., 2014 — ISBN 978-1-77169-014-0

Re-Imagining Mary: A Journey Through Art to the Feminine Self by Mariann Burke, 1ˢᵗ Ed., Trade Paperback, 180pp, Index, Biblio., 2009 — ISBN 978-0-9810344-1-6

Sea Glass: A Jungian Analyst's Exploration of Suffering and Individuation by Gilda Frantz, 1ˢᵗ Ed., Trade Paperback, 250pp, 2014 — ISBN 978-1-77169-020-1

Transforming Body and Soul by Steven Galipeau, Rev. Ed., Trade Paperback, 180pp, Index, Biblio., 2011 — ISBN 978-1-926715-62-9

Lifting the Veil: Revealing the Other Side by Fred Gustafson & Jane Kamerling, 1ˢᵗ Ed, Paperback, 170pp, Biblio., 2012 — ISBN 978-1-926715-75-9

Resurrecting the Unicorn: Masculinity in the 21ˢᵗ Century by Bud Harris, Rev. Ed., Trade Paperback, 300pp, Index, Biblio., 2009 — ISBN 978-0-9810344-0-9

The Father Quest: Rediscovering an Elemental Force by Bud Harris, Reprint, Trade Paperback, 180pp, Index, Biblio., 2009 — ISBN 978-0-9810344-9-2

Like Gold Through Fire: The Transforming Power of Suffering by Massimilla & Bud Harris, Reprint, Trade Paperback, 150pp, Index, Biblio., 2009 — ISBN 978-0-9810344-5-4

The Art of Love: The Craft of Relationship by Massimilla and Bud Harris, 1st Ed. Trade Paperback, 150pp, 2010 — ISBN 978-1-926715-02-5

Divine Madness: Archetypes of Romantic Love by John R. Haule, Rev. Ed., Trade Paperback, 282pp, Index, Biblio., 2010 — ISBN 978-1-926715-04-9

Tantra and Erotic Trance in 2 volumes by John R. Haule

   Volume 1 - Outer Work, 1st Ed. Trade Paperback, 215pp, Index, Bibliograpy, 2012 — ISBN 978-0-9776076-8-6

   Volume 2 - Inner Work, 1st Ed. Trade Paperback, 215pp, Index, Bibliograpy, 2012 — ISBN 978-0-9776076-9-3

Eros and the Shattering Gaze: Transcending Narcissism
by Ken Kimmel, 1st Ed., Trade Paperback, 310pp, Index, Biblio., 2011 — ISBN 978-1-926715-49-0

The Sister From Below: When the Muse Gets Her Way
by Naomi Ruth Lowinsky, 1st Ed., Trade Paperback, 248pp, Index, Biblio., 2009 — ISBN 978-0-9810344-2-3

The Motherline: Every Woman's Journey to find her Female Roots
by Naomi Ruth Lowinsky, Reprint, Trade Paperback, 252pp, Index, Biblio., 2009 — ISBN 978-0-9810344-6-1

The Dairy Farmer's Guide to the Universe in 4 volumes
by Dennis L. Merritt:

   Volume 1 - Jung and Ecopsychology, 1st Ed., Trade Paperback, 242pp, Index, Biblio., 2011 — ISBN 978-1-926715-42-1

   Volume 2 - The Cry of Merlin: Jung the Prototypical Ecopsychologist, 1st Ed., Trade Paperback, 204pp, Index, Biblio., 2012 — ISBN 978-1-926715-43-8

   Volume 3 - Hermes, Ecopsychology, and Complexity Theory, 1st Ed., Trade Paperback, 228pp, Index, Biblio., 2012 — ISBN 978-1-926715-44-5

   Volume 4 - Land, Weather, Seasons, Insects: An Archetypal View, 1st Ed., Trade Paperback, 134pp, Index, Biblio., 2012 — ISBN 978-1-926715-45-2

Four Eternal Women: Toni Wolff Revisited—A Study In Opposites
by Mary Dian Molton & Lucy Anne Sikes, 1st Ed., 320pp, Index, Biblio., 2011 — ISBN 978-1-926715-31-5

Becoming: An Introduction to Jung's Concept of Individuation
by Deldon Anne McNeely, 1st Ed., Trade Paperback, 230pp, Index, Biblio., 2010 — ISBN 978-1-926715-12-4

Animus Aeternus: Exploring the Inner Masculine by Deldon Anne McNeely, Reprint, Trade Paperback, 196pp, Index, Biblio., 2011 — ISBN 978-1-926715-37-7

Mercury Rising: Women, Evil, and the Trickster Gods
by Deldon Anne McNeely, Revised, Trade Paperback, 200pp, Index, Biblio., 2011 — ISBN 978-1-926715-54-4

Gathering the Light: A Jungian View of Meditation
by V. Walter Odajnyk, Revised Ed., Trade Paperback, 264pp, Index, Biblio., 2011 — ISBN 978-1-926715-55-1

The Promiscuity Papers
by Matjaz Regovec, 1st Ed., Trade Paperback, 86pp, Index, Biblio., 2011 — ISBN 978-1-926715-38-4

Enemy, Cripple, Beggar: Shadows in the Hero's Path
by Erel Shalit, 1st Ed., Trade Paperback, 248pp, Index, Biblio., 2008 — ISBN 978-0-9776076-7-9

The Cycle of Life: Themes and Tales of the Journey
by Erel Shalit, 1st Ed., Trade Paperback, 210pp, Index, Biblio., 2011 — ISBN 978-1-926715-50-6

The Hero and His Shadow
by Erel Shalit, Revised Ed., Trade Paperback, 208pp, Index, Biblio., 2012 — ISBN 978-1-926715-69-8

Riting Myth, Mythic Writing: Plotting Your Personal Story
by Dennis Patrick Slattery, Trade Paperback, 220 pp. Biblio., 2012 — ISBN 978-1-926715-77-3

The Guilt Cure
by Nancy Carter Pennington & Lawrence H. Staples, 1st Ed., Trade Paperback, 200pp, Index, Biblio., 2011 — ISBN 978-1-926715-53-7

Guilt with a Twist: The Promethean Way
by Lawrence Staples,1st Ed., Trade Paperback, 256pp, Index, Biblio., 2008 — ISBN 978-0-9776076-4-8

The Creative Soul: Art and the Quest for Wholeness
by Lawrence Staples, 1st Ed., Trade Paperback, 100pp, Index, Biblio., 2009 — ISBN 978-0-9810344-4-7

Deep Blues: Human Soundscapes for the Archetypal Journey
by Mark Winborn, 1st Ed., Trade Paperback, 130pp, Index, Biblio., 2011 — ISBN 978-1-926715-52-0

Phone Orders Welcomed
Credit Cards Accepted
In Canada & the U.S. call 1-800-228-9316
International call +1-831-238-7799
www.fisherkingpress.com